PCs FOR DUMMIES®
12TH EDITION

by Dan Gookin

WILEY

John Wiley & Sons, Inc.

PCs For Dummies®, 12th Edition

Published by
John Wiley & Sons, Inc.
111 River Street
Hoboken, NJ 07030-5774
www.wiley.com

WILEY

About the Author

Dan Gookin has been writing about technology for over 25 years. He combines his love of writing with his gizmo fascination to create books that are informative, entertaining, and not boring. Having written more than 130 titles with millions of copies in print translated into over 30 languages, Dan can attest that his method of crafting computer tomes seems to work.

Perhaps his most famous title is the original *DOS For Dummies,* published in 1991. It became the world's fastest-selling computer book, at one time moving more copies per week than the New York Times #1 bestseller (though as a reference book, it could not be listed on the NYT bestseller list). From that book spawned the entire line of *For Dummies* books, which remains a publishing phenomenon to this day.

Dan's most popular titles include *Android Phones For Dummies, Word For Dummies,* and *Laptops For Dummies.* He also maintains the vast and helpful website, www.wambooli.com.

Dan holds a degree in Communications/Visual Arts from the University of California, San Diego. Presently, he lives in the Pacific Northwest, where he serves as Councilman for the City of Coeur d'Alene. Dan enjoys spending time with his sons playing video games inside while they watch the gentle woods of Idaho.

Publisher's Acknowledgments

We're proud of this book; please send us your comments at http://dummies.custhelp.com. For other comments, please contact our Customer Care Department within the U.S. at 877-762-2974, outside the U.S. at 317-572-3993, or fax 317-572-4002.

Some of the people who helped bring this book to market include the following:

Acquisitions and Editorial

Project Editor: Susan Pink

Acquisitions Editor: Katie Mohr

Copy Editor: Susan Pink
   (Previous Edition: Rebecca Whitney)

Technical Editor: James Kelly

Editorial Manager: Jodi Jensen

Editorial Assistant: Annie Sullivan

Sr. Editorial Assistant: Cherie Case

Cover Photo: © Tommy Ingberg/iStockphoto

Cartoons: Rich Tennant (www.the5thwave.com)

Composition Services

Project Coordinator: Patrick Redmond

Layout and Graphics: Carrie A. Cesavice, Melanee Habig, Amy Hassos, Joyce Haughey

Proofreaders: John Greenough, Nancy Rapoport

Indexer: BIM Indexing & Proofreading Services

Publishing and Editorial for Technology Dummies

   Richard Swadley, Vice President and Executive Group Publisher

   Andy Cummings, Vice President and Publisher

   Mary Bednarek, Executive Acquisitions Director

   Mary C. Corder, Editorial Director

Publishing for Consumer Dummies

   Kathleen Nebenhaus, Vice President and Executive Publisher

Composition Services

   Debbie Stailey, Director of Composition Services

Table of Contents

Introduction 1

What's New in This Edition? 1
Where to Start 2
Conventions Used in This Book 3
What You Don't Need to Read 4
Foolish Assumptions 4
Icons Used in This Book 4
Getting in Touch with the Author 5
Where to Go from Here 5

Part 1: Hello, PC! 7

Chapter 1: What Is This Thing, This PC? 9

Some Quick Questions to Get Out of the Way 9
"What is a PC?" 10
"Why not just use a tablet or smartphone instead of a PC?" 11
"Should I buy a Dell?" 11
"Will my computer explode?" 11
Basic Computer Concepts in Easily Digestible Chunks 12
What a computer does 12
Hardware and software 13
Buy Yourself a PC! 14
Step 1. What do you want the PC to do? 14
Step 2. Find software 14
Step 3. Match hardware to the software 15
Step 4. Locate your service and support 15
Step 5. Buy it! 15
A Final Thing to Remember 16

Chapter 2: The PC Knobs, Buttons, and Doodads Tour 17

The Big Picture 17
All Around the Console 19
There is no typical console 19
Major points of interest on the console, front 21
Stuff found on the console's rump 23
The I/O panel 25
Helpful hints, hieroglyphics, and hues 27

Chapter 3: PC Setup **29**

Computer Assembly...29
Unpacking the boxes 29
Setting up the console...30
Plugging in and connecting..31
The Plugging-Things-In Guide 31
Attaching the keyboard and mouse 31
Setting up the monitor 33
Connecting to the network 33
Adding a printer 34
Hooking up other random peripherals 34
It Must Have Power 35
Plugging everything into a power strip............................35
Taking advantage of a UPS..38
Using the UPS (a short play) 39

Chapter 4: On and Off **41**

Turn On Your PC 41
Windows, Ahoy! 43
Turn Off the Computer 44
Finding the shutdown options 44
Turning the darn thing off 46
Reviewing other shutdown options.................................47
Should You Leave the Computer On All the Time?...................50
"I want to leave my computer off all the time" 50
"I want to leave my computer on all the time"................50

Part II: The Nerd's-Eye View **51**

Chapter 5: Deep Inside the Console **53**

Console Guts 53
Looking under the hood...54
Going inside the console (not recommended) 55
The Mother of All Boards 57
The Processor Rules 57
Understanding the processor's role.................................58
Naming PC processors 58
Measuring processor speed 58
Discovering your PC's processor 59
Your Computer Is Also a Timepiece 60
Viewing the date and time 60
Setting the clock...60
Using the Internet to set the clock 61
About the PC's Battery 62
The Chipset 62
The Source of PC Power 63

Chapter 6: PC Memory **65**

What Is Computer Memory? 65
Tasty Chocolate Memory Chips 66
Memory One Byte at a Time.. 68
Memory Q&A.. 70
"How much memory is in my PC right now?"........................ 70
"Do I have enough memory?".. 70
"Does my PC have enough memory?" 70
"Can I test whether my PC has enough memory?" 71
"Can I add memory to my PC?"... 71
"Will the computer ever run out of memory?"........................ 72
"What is virtual memory?".. 72
"What is video memory?" 72
"What about shared video memory?" 73

Chapter 7: Mass Storage **75**

What Is Mass Storage? 75
Surveying the storage media landscape 76
Reviewing mass storage technical terms................................ 77
Your PCs Primary Storage Media 78
Understanding the Hard Drive 78
Introducing the SSD 79
Removable Storage.. 79
Exploring removable storage 79
Identifying removable storage drives 81
Inserting removable media.. 83
Ejecting removable media 84
External Storage... 84
Adding external storage.. 85
Exploring the cloud (Internet storage) 85
Permanent Storage ABCs 86
Identifying mass storage devices.. 87
Assigning drive letters 87

Chapter 8: Merry Monitor Mayhem **89**

The PC's Graphics System... 89
Understanding PC graphics 90
Minding the monitor.. 91
Discovering the display adapter 92
Descriptive Display Data 93
Measuring a monitor 93
Connecting to the PC... 95
Reading monitor messages 95
Adjusting the display.. 96
Windows Controls What You See 96
Adding a second monitor.. 97
Setting display size (resolution) 99
Saving the screen.. 100

Chapter 9: Input This! 101

Meet Mr. Keyboard...101
    Attaching a keyboard 102
    Examining the typical PC keyboard.............................102
    Using modifier keys 103
    Changing keyboard behavior keys 105
    Touring the most useful keys 106
    Understanding strange keys...................................107
    Understanding keys for math 107
    Controlling the keyboard in Windows 108
Say "Eeek!" to the Mouse 109
    Connecting the mouse...109
    Reviewing basic mouse parts 110
    Exploring mouse species 111
    Moving the mouse 112
    Controlling the mouse in Windows 113
Touchscreen Input 114

Chapter 10: System Expansion 117

It's a Port...117
USB, a Most Versatile Port 118
    Understanding USB cables.....................................118
    Connecting a USB device 120
    Using USB-powered gizmos 120
    Removing a USB device..121
    Expanding the USB universe with hubs 121
Legacy Ports..123
Expansion Slots...124

Chapter 11: P Is for Printer 125

The Printer, the Paper, the Document Maker..........................125
    Surveying the printer landscape..............................125
    Touring the typical printer 126
    Using the printer's control panel............................128
    Drinking ink...128
    Eating paper...129
    Choosing the proper paper 130
Where the Printer Meets the PC 131
    Connecting the printer.......................................131
    Finding the printer in Windows 132
    Setting the default printer..................................133
Basic Printer Operation 134
    Printing something 134
    Printing in reverse order....................................135
    Stopping a printer run amok 136

Chapter 12: PC Audio Abilities.............................137

The Noisy PC 137
Speakers hither and thither....................................138
In your own world with headphones 140
Microphone options 140
Sound Control in Windows...141
Configuring the speakers 142
Configuring the microphone 142
Adjusting the volume 142
Windows Goes Bleep..143
It Listens 145
Recording your own sounds.....................................145
Dictating to the PC 146

Chapter 13: Delicious Hardware Leftovers 149

Manage the PC's Power 149
Choosing a power management plan 150
Adding a hibernation option 151
Setting options for battery-powered PCs....................152
Merry Modems..153
Adding a dial-up modem 153
Measuring modem speed...154
Configuring a dial-up Internet connection....................154

Part III: Basic Computing 157

Chapter 14: The Windows Tour 159

What's an Operating System? 160
Windows and Its Gooey, Glorious Graphical Interface.........160
Exploring the Start screen 161
Summoning the charms bar 162
Working at the desktop...163
Using the taskbar 164
Accessing the Start menu 165
Looking at the notification area 166
The Control Panel...167

Chapter 15: It's the Software Chapter.........................169

Software Cavalcade 169
Programs on Your PC..170
Hunting down programs in Windows...........................170
Running a program from the desktop 171
Running a program manually....................................172

More Software, Less Software 172
   Installing a program from an optical disc 173
   Finding programs on the Internet 174
   Uninstalling a program 175
The Latest Version 176
   Updating and upgrading 176
   Updating Windows 177
   Upgrading to the latest version of Windows 178

Chapter 16: Fun with Files and Folders 179

Behold the File! 179
   Describing a file 180
   Creating a new file 181
   Naming files 183
   Understanding the filename extension 184
Folder Folderol 185
   Understanding subfolders and parent folders 185
   Reviewing famous folders 186
   Finding a place for your stuff 187
   Making a new folder 189
   Working with libraries 190
   Using folders in the Open dialog box 191

Chapter 17: The Grim Topic of File Management 193

Organized File Torture 193
   Managing files because they can't manage themselves 194
   Selecting files for torment 194
   Releasing files from selection 197
The Actual File Torture Itself 197
   Copying a file 197
   Moving a file 198
   Creating a shortcut 198
   Renaming files 199
   Deleting files 200
   Bringing dead files back to life 200
Find Escaped Files 201

Chapter 18: Save Your Butt When You Really Screw Up 203

The File You Had Yesterday...203
   Recovering with File History 204
   Restoring previous versions...206
The OMG Safety Copy 207
Zip-a-dee-do Folders...208
   Compressing files..208
   Examining a compressed folder archive.....................................209
   Installing software from a compressed folder 211

Chapter 19: The Optical Disc Factory 213
  Disc Creation Overview 213
  Birth of a Disc..215
    Burning a disc...215
    Working with a USB flash drive or live file format disc..............217
    Working with a CD/DVD player or mastered disc 218
    Using the Burn button..219
    Erasing an RW disc 219
    Labeling the disc 220
    Disposing of a disc...221

Part 1V: Networking Nonsense **223**

Chapter 20: The Non-TV Kind of Network 225
  The Whole Network Enchilada 225
    Understanding the network...225
    Going wired or wireless 226
  The Wired Network 227
    Connecting to Saint NIC 229
    Wiring the network hoses..229
    Putting the gateway, which isn't really a router, at
      the center of your network 230
  The Wireless Life 230
    Getting used to the 802.11 thing 232
    Hooking up the wireless NIC 232
    Obtaining a wireless gateway...233
  The Broadband Modem 233

Chapter 21: Network Abuse 235
  "Am I On the Network?"...235
    Connecting to a wired network..235
    Connecting to a wireless network 236
    Connecting to an unknown wireless network 238
    Confirming the network connection...................................239
    Disconnecting from a network 239
  Windows Network Central...239
  Network Sharing 241
    Demanding that Windows share resources............................241
    Sharing your PC's mass storage......................................243
    Accessing a network folder 244
    Adding a network printer..245
    Sharing your PC's printer 245

Chapter 22: Why Does This Book Have a Bluetooth Chapter? 247
  That Bluetooth Thing..247
    Understanding Bluetooth...248
    Checking for Bluetooth 248

Adding a Bluetooth adapter 249
Controlling Bluetooth in Windows 249
Bluetooth Pairing...250
Walking through the pairing operation..250
Pairing with a device 251
Reviewing paired devices 252
Un-pairing a Bluetooth device..253

Chapter 23: As Little of the Internet as Possible...................**255**

What Is the Internet?..255
How to Access the Internet 256
Choosing an ISP 256
Configuring Windows for the Internet..257
Connecting to the Internet...257
It's a World Wide Web We Weave 258
Browsing tips...258
Printing web pages 259
Searching-the-web tips 259
Get Stuff from a Web Page 260
Saving an image from a web page..260
Grabbing text from a web page...261
Sharing a web page...261

Chapter 24: PC Nightmares......................................**263**

Fight the Bad Guys 263
The Action Center 265
Setting up the Windows Firewall 266
Protecting the PC with Windows Defender 268
Using antivirus protection...268
Paying attention to the UAC warnings 269

Part V: Your Digital Life *271*

Chapter 25: The Whole Digital Photography Thing **273**

The Digital Camera...274
Connecting a digital camera 274
Importing images 275
The Scanner 276
Introducing the scanner...276
Scanning an image 277
Picture Files...279
Storing pictures in Windows 280
Viewing pictures in Windows 282
Changing picture file formats 282
Image Resolution 283
Setting resolution...283
Choosing the best resolution 284

Chapter 26: Electronic Entertainment.........................**285**

PC Movies 285
    Getting video into your PC 286
    Storing video in Windows 287
    Viewing a video 288
    Editing video...288
Your PC Is a TV 289
    Getting a TV tuner..290
    Watching Internet TV 290
Your TV Is a PC 291
Your PC Is Your Stereo 292
    Running Windows Media Player 293
    Ripping music from a CD 293
    Copying music to a portable gizmo........................294
    Listening to Internet radio 295

Chapter 27: Sharing Your Life Online **297**

The Scourge of Social Networking..............................297
    Sharing your life on Facebook.............................298
    Tweeting your thoughts 299
Share Your Photos Online 300
    Signing up for the site...300
    Uploading images..301
    Sharing your images 303
Your Video Life 304
    Creating a YouTube account.................................304
    Uploading a video to YouTube..............................304
    Sharing your videos 305
Network Media Sharing...305
    Setting up for media sharing 306
    Rifling through a device's shared media.................306

Chapter 28: Kid-Safe Computing **309**

An Account for Junior...309
    Setting up your own account 310
    Limiting Junior's account 311
Parental Controls...312
    Filtering websites 313
    Setting time limits 313
    Controlling access to games.................................313
    Blocking programs 314
    Reviewing the activity log....................................314
PC Parenting..315
    Spying on your kids 315
    Dealing with a cyberbully 316

Part VI: The Part of Tens 317

Chapter 29: Ten PC Commandments 319
I. Thou Shalt Not Fear Thy PC... 319
II. Thou Shalt Save Thy Work.. 320
III. Thou Shalt Back Up Thy Files 320
IV. That Shalt Not Open or Delete Things Unknownst........................... 320
V. Thou Shalt Not Be a Sucker 321
VI. Thou Shalt Use Antivirus Software, Yea Verily,
    and Keepeth It Up-to-Date... 321
VII. Thou Shalt Upgrade Wisely 321
VIII. Thou Shalt Compute at a Proper Posture................................... 322
IX. Thou Shalt Keepeth Windows Up-to-Date...................................... 322
X. Thou Shalt Properly Shut Down Windows....................................... 322

Chapter 30: Ten Tips from a PC Guru 323
Remember That You're in Charge... 323
Mind Who "Helps" You 324
Give Yourself Time to Learn 324
Create Separate Accounts 324
Use a UPS.. 325
Consider Some Hardware Upgrades 325
Don't Reinstall Windows.. 326
Shun the Hype.. 326
Keep on Going!... 327
Remember Not to Take This Computer Stuff Too Seriously......................... 327

Index 329

Introduction

t's been ten years and 60 lbs. since I wrote the original *PCs For Dummies.* My, how the time and fat has flown. In all those years, the prospect of owning and using a PC just hasn't gotten simpler. It's a conspiracy, of course. The marketing wizards tell you that the PC is easy to use, but the engineers — most of whom are evil robots from the planet Neptune — design the computer to frustrate you endlessly.

This book's job is to convince you that you're not a dummy. You may feel that way, but your feelings are misplaced. Computers are intimidating only when you believe them to be. Peel back that sleek case and you find a timid, scared beast that wants only to help you. This book takes you on a journey that makes that task easy, fun, and enjoyable.

Oh, and don't peel back the skin on your computer. It doesn't hurt the computer if you do so, but you can get in touch with your PC's emotional core in better ways than resorting to a surgical procedure.

What's New in This Edition?

Hey! Thanks for continuing to read this Introduction. Most people don't bother, so you're special! I mean, why read all this blather when you could jump to Chapter 1, or open the book at a random spot, stroke your chin, and say, "Wow! This is really appealing." Anyone watching would be impressed. But no, you're reading the very front of the book. The best you can hope for is that any onlooker believes you can't find the price or are trying to look up a relative on the details page. Sorry about that.

This is the 12th edition of *PCs For Dummies,* freshly updated and approved for the latest assault of computer technology in the 21st century. This book was written just weeks before the end of the Maya calendar, on December 21, 2012. Consider yourself lucky that humanity has survived.

Beyond updating many of this book's less-important parts to reflect the Windows 8 operating system, I've invigorated the text with all the new whiz-bang technology introduced since the last edition did basically the same thing. When technology sits still, this book won't have a new edition. Well, either that or the whole Mayan thing turned out to be true.

Here are some topics new to the 12th edition:

- Information on how to buy the best computer to meet your needs today
- Updates on the USB 3.0 standard, the latest in PC processors, mass storage choices, and computer monitors
- Updates covering some of the new things Windows 8 does
- Ridicule for some of the new things Windows 8 does poorly
- Details on keeping your data safe, including Internet backups
- The latest on computer networking and cloud storage
- A whole chapter on the Bluetooth wireless peripheral standard
- Information on Internet-ready HDTV and how to share media on a local network
- Refreshing and honest information about Facebook and online sharing
- Lots of other things that add incredible value to the book but that I cannot remember well enough to include in this list
- A new, sassy attitude that didn't involve heavy drinking

As in years past, I present all the information in this book in a sane, soothing, and gentle tone that calms even the most panicked computerphobe.

Where to Start

This book is a reference. You can start reading at any point. Use the index or table of contents to see what interests you. After you read the information, feel free to close the book and perform whatever task you need; there's no need to read any further. Well, unless you just enjoy my pithy writing style.

Each of this book's 30 chapters covers a specific aspect of the computer — turning it on, using a printer, using software, or heaving the computer out a window without incurring back injury, for example. Each chapter is divided into self-contained nuggets of knowledge — sections — all relating to the major theme of the chapter. Sample sections you may find include

- Turning the darn computer off
- Using the Internet to set the clock
- Ejecting removable media
- Stopping a printer run amok
- Finding programs on the Internet
- Connecting to a wireless network
- Uploading a video to YouTube

You don't have to memorize anything in this book. Nothing about a computer is memorable. Each section is designed so that you can read the information quickly, digest what you have read, and then put down the book and get on with using the computer. If anything technical crops up, you're alerted to its presence so that you can cleanly avoid it.

Conventions Used in This Book

Menu items, links, and other controls on the screen are written using initial cap text. So if the option is named "Turn off the computer," you see Turn Off the Computer (without quotes or commas) shown in this book, whether it appears that way onscreen or not.

Whenever I describe a message or information on the screen, it looks like this:

```
This is a message onscreen.
```

If you have to type something, it looks like this:

Type me

You type the text *Type me* as shown. You're told when and whether to press the Enter key. You're also told whether to type a period; periods end sentences written in English, but not always when you type text on a computer.

Windows menu commands are shown like this:

Choose File➪Exit.

This line directs you to choose the File menu and then choose the Exit command.

Key combinations you may have to press are shown like this:

Ctrl+S

This line says to press and hold down the Ctrl (Control) key, type an *S*, and then release the Ctrl key. It works the same as pressing Shift+S on the keyboard to produce an uppercase *S*. Same deal, different shift key.

What You Don't Need to Read

It's a given that computers are technical, but you can avoid reading the technical stuff. To assist you, I've put some of the more obnoxious technical stuff into sidebars clearly marked as technical information. Read that information at your own peril. Often, it's just a complex explanation of stuff already discussed in the chapter. Reading that information only tells you something substantial about your computer, which is not my goal here.

Foolish Assumptions

I make some admittedly foolish assumptions about you: You have a computer, and you use it somehow to do something. You use Windows as that computer's operating system. That last point brings up a vital issue:

This book was updated to coincide with the release of Windows 8, but it's not specifically a book about Windows 8. Up front, I'll confess that I despise Windows 8. I shower you with pity if you've been subjected to it against your will. Like Microsoft, my publisher assumes that Planet Earth will upgrade to Windows 8 *en masse.* Humanoid robots from the future have told me otherwise, so I approach Windows 8 with cautious derision throughout the text.

Despite the Windows 8 update, this book amply covers previous Windows releases, specifically Windows 7 and Windows Vista. I even tossed in a modicum of material friendly to good ol' Windows XP. I don't want anyone to feel left out. Well, except for those people who think Windows 8 is like 24 hours of sunshine.

When this book refers to Windows without a specific edition or version, the information applies generically to all releases of Windows.

Icons Used in This Book

This icon alerts you to needless technical information — drivel I added because even though I can't help but unleash the nerd in me, I can successfully flag that type of material. Feel free to skip over anything tagged with this little picture.

This icon usually indicates helpful advice or an insight that makes using the computer interesting. For example, when you're dunking the computer into liquid nitrogen, be sure to wear protective goggles.

This icon indicates something to remember, like turning off the iron before you leave the house or not trimming your nose hairs with a butane lighter.

This icon indicates that you need to be careful with the information that's presented; usually, it's a reminder for you not to do something, like trying to balance a cup of coffee atop the computer monitor.

Getting in Touch with the Author

My e-mail address is listed here in case you want to send me a note: dgookin@wambooli.com.

Yes, that's my address, and I respond to every e-mail message. Note that I reply to short, to-the-point messages quickly. Long messages may take more time for me to reply to. Plus, I cannot troubleshoot or fix your PC. Remember that you paid others for their technical support, and you should use their services.

You can also visit my website, which is chock-full of helpful support pages, bonus information, games, and fun. Go to www.wambooli.com/.

The specific *PCs For Dummies* support page is found at www.wambooli.com/help/pcs/.

Where to Go from Here

With this book in hand, you're now ready to go out and conquer your PC. Start by looking through the table of contents or the index. Find a topic and turn to the page indicated, and you're ready to go. Also, feel free to write in this book, fill in the blanks, dog-ear the pages, and do anything that would make a librarian blanch. Enjoy.

Part I
Hello, PC!

In this part . . .

It's been called a fast idiot, the ultimate solution for which there was no problem, a toy, Satan's spawn, a godsend, *Time* magazine's Machine of the Year 1982, and perhaps the most miraculous gadget ever invented. I'm speaking, of course, about the personal computer, the PC.

Loathe it or love it, the PC is now a part of everyday life, as common as a desk lamp and with more uses than a Swiss Army knife. Whether you're looking to get a PC or find yourself already saddled with one, use this part of the book to bone up on basic, good-to-know computer stuff.

Chapter 1

What Is This Thing, This PC?

. . . .

In This Chapter

▶ Answering some common PC questions

▶ Understanding basic computer concepts

▶ Knowing about hardware and software

▶ Buying a computer

▶ Realizing that your PC is quite dumb

. . . .

I wish that computers were evil. It would be easier to understand the computer if it were evil and out to get you. Instead, you end up operating the thing under a constant suspicion. But because the cold, calculating collection of capacitors isn't malevolently disposed against you, your better course of action is to get to know more about the computer.

So relax! The key to building a productive, long-term relationship with your high-tech electronics investment is to understand this thing, this PC. You don't need to have Einstein's IQ to do that. You just need to read and enjoy the easy, helpful information in this chapter.

Some Quick Questions to Get Out of the Way

Doubtless, your mind is abuzz with various questions about computers. I ask myself computer questions often, so don't think that your curiosity is unusual. Trust me, few people are comfortable when first encountering anything high-tech.

"What is a PC?"

A *PC* is a computer, specifically an acronym for *personal computer.*

Historically, the beast was known as a *microcomputer.* That's because back in the 1970s computers were huge, room-sized things that required legions of bespectacled scientists to operate. Individuals didn't own such computers — well, unless you were eccentric or enjoyed printing your own phone bill. So mere mortals were sold a smaller version, which the Computer Professionals Union insisted be called a *micro*computer.

Micro means teensy. The term is preferred by computer scientists because you can't wear a white lab coat and be taken seriously when you use the word "teensy."

Actually, the term *micro* came from *microprocessor,* the main computer chip inside the device.

When IBM unveiled its first business microcomputer back in 1982, they called it the IBM Personal Computer, or PC for short. All of today's computers are descended from that original model, so they've inherited the term PC. Figure 1-1 displays a timeline of the PC's history, in case you're curious.

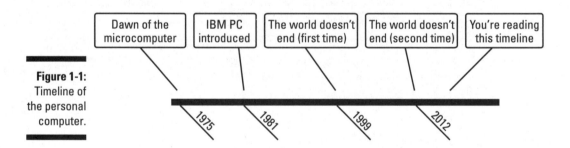

Figure 1-1: Timeline of the personal computer.

The only PC that's not called "PC" is Apple's Macintosh computer. Mac users refer to their computers as *Macs.* That's based on an old IBM–Apple rivalry that no one cares about anymore. Still, many Mac users get all verklempt when you call their computers PCs. So it's fine by me to tease those crybabies by referring to their expensive toys as "PCs."

✔ The term *PC* now generally refers to any computer that can run the Windows operating system.

✔ Although your car, sewing machine, or the machine that goes *boop* at the hospital may contain computer electronics, those devices are not PCs.

✔ Curiously, IBM got out of the PC manufacturing business in the early 2000s.

✔ The success of the PC is based on its use of off-the-shelf parts that are easily replaced. The PC can also be configured and upgraded with ease, which is another reason it's so popular.

"Why not just use a tablet or smartphone instead of a PC?"

Sure, you can get by in today's well-connected, digital world by getting your-self a tablet or smartphone. To hell with computers!

Smartphones and tablets can send and receive e-mail, browse the web, play games, and do all sorts of interesting things. But they lack the expandability of a PC. They also lack the capability to easily create things. The PC is used to create; it's a productivity tool. As such, it has power and potential far beyond a cheesy-ass tablet or smartphone.

Now if you've changed your mind about getting a PC, remember that you cannot return this book once you've started reading this material.

"Should I buy a Dell?"

I get this question all the time, though "Dell" might be replaced by some other brand name. See the later section, "Buy Yourself a PC!"

"Will my computer explode?"

This question is important, so please skip all the other questions I put before this question and read this question first!

If you're a fan of science fiction television or film, you're probably familiar with the concept of the exploding computer. Sparks, smoke, flying debris — it all appears to be a common function of computers in the future. Sure, they could just beep and display error messages when they die, but where's the fun in that?

The answer is: No, your computer will not explode. At least, not spontane-ously. If you pour fruit punch into the computer, or lightning strikes, or the power supply unexplainably fails, the most you may see is a puff of blue smoke. But no explosions.

Basic Computer Concepts in Easily Digestible Chunks

You either use or are about to purchase one of the most advanced pieces of technology ever made available to humans. Why not be a sport about it and take a few moments to not avoid some of the more technical mumbo jumbo surrounding that technology? Don't fret: I'll be gentle.

What a computer does

Computers can do anything and try to do just about everything. At their core, however, computers are simple gizmos with oodles of potential.

A computer takes input, processes it, and then generates output. That's kind of how a baby works, though to keep you from being utterly befuddled, you can refer to Figure 1-2, which completely illustrates that basic computer concept.

Figure 1-2: What a computer does at its simplest level.

The "input goes into the computer and produces output" equation is the foundation of these three primary computer concepts:

- ✔ I/O
- ✔ Processing
- ✔ Storage

I/O: IO stands for input and output. It's pronounced "I owe," like *Io*, the third-largest moon of Jupiter. I/O is pretty much the *only* thing a computer does: It receives input from devices — the keyboard, mouse, Internet. It generates output, displayed on the screen, printed, or sent back to the Internet. That's I/O.

Processing: What the computer does between input and output is *processing*. It's what happens to the input to make the output significant. Otherwise, the computer would simply be a tube and computer science would be the same as plumbing.

Processing is handled inside the computer by a gizmo known as (logically enough) a processor. See Chapter 5 for more information on the processor.

Storage: The final part of the basic computer equation is storage, which is where the processing takes place. Two types of storage are used, temporary and long-term. Temporary storage is the computer *memory,* or *RAM.* Long-term storage is provided by the computer's storage media.

RAM is covered in Chapter 6. Long-term storage is covered in Chapter 7.

Hardware and software

The computer universe is divided into two parts. There is hardware. There is software.

Hardware is the physical part of a computer: anything you can touch and anything you can see — or anything that smells like burning plastic. The computer console, the monitor, the keyboard, the mouse — that physical stuff is hardware.

Software is the brain of the computer. Software tells the hardware what to do.

In a way, it helps to think of hardware and software as a symphony orchestra. For hardware, you have the musicians and their instruments. Their software is the music. As with a computer, the music (software) tells the musicians and their instruments (hardware) what to do.

Without software, hardware just sits around and looks pretty. It can't do anything because it has no instructions and nothing telling it what to do next. And, like a symphony orchestra without music, that can be an expensive waste of time, especially at union scale.

To make the computer system work, software must be in charge. In fact, software determines your computer's personality and potential.

- ✔ If you can throw it out a window, it's hardware.
- ✔ If you can throw it out a window and it comes back, it's a cat.
- ✔ Computer software includes all the programs you use on the PC.
- ✔ The most important piece of software is the computer's *operating system.* That's the main program in charge of everything. Chapter 14 covers Windows, which is the PC's least popular yet most common operating system.

Buy Yourself a PC!

If you don't yet have a PC, you can rush out and buy one. My advice is not to rush, despite having just directed you do to so.

A computer is a complex piece of electronics. Buying one isn't like purchasing a riding lawnmower or nose-hair trimmer. To make your purchase a successful one, consider my friendly, five-step method for buying a PC.

1. **Know what it is you want the computer to do.**
2. **Find software to accomplish that task.**
3. **Find hardware to match the software.**
4. **Locate service and support.**
5. **Buy the computer!**

Yes, it's really that easy. If you obey these steps and pay attention, you'll be a lot more satisfied with your computer purchase.

Step 1. What do you want the PC to do?

Believe it or not, most people don't know why they want a computer. If that's you, consider what you're getting into. Computers aren't for everyone, especially with advanced cell phones and tablets available at far less cost.

If you do really need a computer, figure out what you want to do. Do you just want to do some word processing, e-mail, and social networking? Perhaps you want a machine that plays the latest games? Or maybe you need some graphics horsepower to create illustrations or animation? Limitless possibilities exist with a computer, but the more you know about what you want, the better you can get the PC perfect for your needs.

Step 2. Find software

Software makes the computer go, so before you discuss brand names or stores, you need to look at the programs you plan on buying. That's because some software — games, video production, graphics — requires specific computer hardware. Knowing about that hardware ahead of time means you'll be happier with your purchase.

By recognizing which software you need first, you can easily move on to the next step.

Step 3. Match hardware to the software

How can you match hardware to the software you need? Simple: Read the side of the software box. It tells you exactly what kind of hardware you need: specifically, what kind of processor is required, how much memory is preferred, and how much storage the software demands. You might also learn of other requirements, such as a high-end graphics card or a specialized interface.

- ✔ For general computer uses, any PC that can run the Windows operating system will probably work just fine for you. But when you have specific software you plan on running, you should make sure that the computer you get has the hardware you need.

- ✔ All that hardware nonsense is covered later in this book. Don't worry about trying to understand everything on the side of the software box when you're just starting out. Use this book's index to help you learn about different PC hardware thingies.

Step 4. Locate your service and support

Most people assume that Step 4 would have to do with brand names or big-box stores. Nope! What's more important is ensuring that you get proper service and support for your new computer purchase — especially when you're just starting out and you blanch at the thought of fixing your own computer.

Service means one thing: Who fixes the computer? That's one reason I recommend buying a PC at a local, "Mom-and-Pop" type of store. You develop a personal relationship with the people who service your computer. Otherwise, discover who really fixes your computer and where it gets fixed by asking.

Support is about getting help for your computer system. Some people need lots of help. If that's you, buy from a place that offers free classes or has a toll-free support number. That support may add to the purchase price, but it's worth every penny if it saves you aggravation in the future.

Step 5. Buy it!

The final step to getting a new computer — or your first computer — is to buy it. Do it!

The hesitation many people have about buying a new computer is that some newer, better, faster model is coming down the pike. That's always true! So rather than wait forever, just get up and buy the computer! 'Nuff said.

A Final Thing to Remember

 Computers aren't evil. They harbor no sinister intelligence. In fact, when you get to know them, you see that they're rather dumb.

Chapter 2

The PC Knobs, Buttons, and Doodads Tour

....

In This Chapter
▶ Looking at the basic PC hardware
▶ Recognizing different types of PCs
▶ Perusing items on the console
▶ Locating PC connectors, holes, and jacks
▶ Using helpful symbols and colors

....

1f I were to use one word to describe the typical PC design, that word would be *uninspired.* Face it: The PC is a box. It's not aerodynamic or sleek or award-winning. No one will confuse a PC sitting on your desk with modern art. People in the year 2045 won't hang posters of early 21st-century PCs on their walls. Sad, but true.

This chapter explores perhaps the dullest aspect of a PC: The PC itself. Forgiving its utilitarian look, it's important to identify some of the basic parts of a computer system, as well as know the purpose behind the many buttons, holes, nooks, and crannies that festoon the plain, dull, tin can known as a PC.

The Big Picture

Figure 2-1 shows a typical personal computer system. Try to avoid the urge to barf.

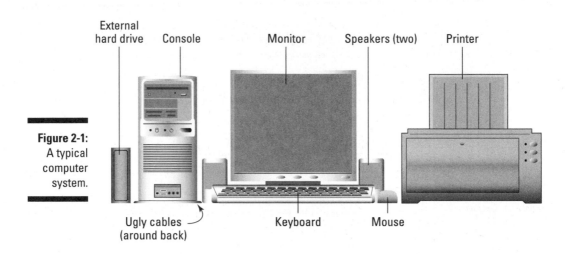

Figure 2-1:
A typical
computer
system.

The big, important pieces have been labeled in Figure 2-1 for your enjoyment. You should know which piece is which and what the proper terms are:

Console: The main computer box, and centerpiece of the computer system, is the console. It is *not* the CPU, though plenty of dorks out there refer to it as such. The console contains the computer's electronic guts. It's also home to various buttons, lights, and holes into which you plug the rest of the computer system.

Monitor: The monitor is the device where the computer displays information — its output. A common mistake made by new computer users is to assume that the monitor is the computer. Nope. The console is the computer. The monitor merely displays stuff.

Keyboard: The keyboard is the thing you type on and is the primary way you communicate with the computer.

Mouse: No rodent or pest, the computer mouse is a helpful device that lets you work with graphical objects displayed on the monitor.

Speakers: PCs bleep and squawk through a set of stereo speakers, which can be external jobbies you set up (refer to Figure 2-1), speakers built into the console or monitor, or perhaps even headphones. Pay more money and you can even get a subwoofer to sit under your desk. Now, *that* will rattle the neighborhood's windows.

External hard drive: You may or may not have one (yet), but an external hard drive is used to *back up,* or create a safety copy of, the important stuff you store on your computer.

Printer: The printer is where you get the computer's printed output, also called *hard copy.*

You may find, in addition to these basic items, other gizmos clustered around your computer, such as a scanner, a digital camera, a gamepad, a high-speed modem, or many, many other toys — er, vital computer components.

One thing definitely not shown in Figure 2-1 is the ganglion of cable that dwells behind each and every computer. What a mess! These cables are required to plug things into the wall and into each other. No shampoo or conditioner on Earth can clean up those tangles.

✔ Ensure that you know where the console, keyboard, mouse, speakers, monitor, and printer are in your own system. If the printer isn't present, it's probably a network printer lurking elsewhere.

✔ Chapters in Part II go into more detail on the computer components just introduced and illustrated in Figure 2-1.

✔ Some computer types combine the console and monitor. Refer to the later section, "There is no typical console."

✔ CPU stands for *central processing unit*. It's another term for the computer's processor. See Chapter 5.

All Around the Console

The pride and joy of any computer system is the console, the main box into which all the other pieces plug. Because of the console's importance, and its surplus of interesting buttons and such, consider reviewing this section to better familiarize yourself with the typical computer console.

There is no typical console

Thanks to major conspiracies and a wicked sense of humor in the computer industry, not all PC consoles look the same. To keep you confused, manufacturers like to shake it up a bit when it comes to PC design. So while all the consoles do feature the same basic components and connections, no single prototype or base model exists for me to show you. Instead, I offer Figure 2-2, which illustrates six common PC console configurations.

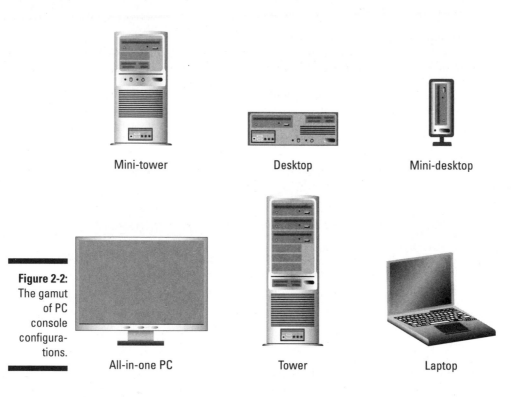

Mini-tower   Desktop   Mini-desktop

Figure 2-2:
The gamut
of PC
console
configura-
tions.

All-in-one PC   Tower   Laptop

Mini-tower: The mini-tower is the most popular console type. It can sit on top of a desk, right next to the monitor (refer to Figure 2-1). It can also be tucked away out of sight, below the desk.

Desktop: Once the most popular type of console, the desktop sits flat on the desk. The monitor usually squats on top of the console in the traditional PC configuration.

Mini-desktop: The mini-desktop console is just too cute and tiny, about the size of a college dictionary. That makes it ideal for places where space — and money — is tight. The downside is that these consoles lack internal expansion options.

All-in-one desktop: A popular and trendy computer design combines the console and monitor into a single unit. From the front, the console looks like a monitor, though it's thicker. On the sides, you find an optical drive plus the myriad of connectors and other computer doodads.

Tower: The tower console is essentially a taller version of the mini-tower. The bonus with the tower is internal expansion options, making this type of console ideal for power-mad users. A tower typically sits on the floor, often propping up one end of the table.

Laptop: A specialty type of computer that folds into a handy, lightweight package, ideal for slowing down the security checkpoints in airports. Laptop PCs work just like their desktop brethren; any exceptions are noted throughout this book.

Choosing the proper PC configuration depends on your needs. Power users love the expandability of the tower. Those on a budget may go for a mini-desktop. Folks on the go love laptops.

- ✔ Gookin's axiom: No matter how big your computer, the amount of clutter you have always expands to fill the available desk space.

- ✔ Another type of laptop is the *tablet PC,* which lets you enter information by writing on the screen using a special tool called a *stylus.*

- ✔ More laptop (and tablet) information is in my book *Laptops For Dummies,* 5th Edition (Wiley), available at fine bookstores wherever fine bookstores still exist.

- ✔ The amount of space a PC console occupies is often referred to as its *footprint.* Smaller consoles are *small footprint* PCs.

Major points of interest on the console, front

After many years, PC manufacturers discovered that it works best to put those items designed for you, the human, on the *front* part of the console. I'm not joking: Nearly everything you needed on an early PC was located on the console's back side. So consider yourself blessed and use Figure 2-3 as your reference as you go hunting for the following items:

Optical drive: The computer's primary removable storage media is the optical disc. The optical drive reads optical discs, CDs, and DVDs. Read more about this topic in Chapter 7.

Future expansion: Most consoles feature blank spots. They may look interesting or useful, but they're not! They simply cover holes used for adding new features to your PC.

Media card slots: These slots are used for reading common media cards, such as those used by digital cameras and other portable electronics. See Chapter 7 for more information about media cards.

Air vents: Air vents aren't impressive, but they're necessary. They keep the console cool by helping air circulate inside.

I/O panel: Your PC most likely features a clutch of various connectors somewhere on its front, covered by a door or not. Nestled in that area, you find places to connect joysticks, microphones, headphones, digital video, or other handy gizmos you may need to plug and unplug from time to time.

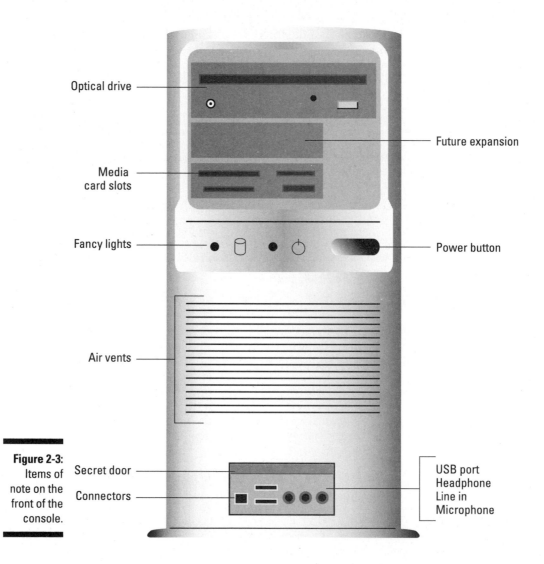

Optical drive

Future expansion

Media
card slots

Fancy lights

Power button

Air vents

Figure 2-3:
Items of
note on the
front of the
console.

Secret door

Connectors

USB port
Headphone
Line in
Microphone

Buttons and lights: Most computer buttons are on the keyboard. A few of the more important buttons are on the console. And on fancier PCs, the buttons are accompanied by many impressive, tiny lights. These buttons and lights include

- ✔ **Power button:** No longer a plain on–off button, the *power button* can do more than just turn the computer on or off. See Chapter 4 for the details.

- ✔ **Reset button:** Rare but still found on some consoles is a button that forces the computer into a restart during times of woe.

- ✔ **Hard drive light:** This wee light flashes when the PC's primary storage media, the hard drive, is being accessed. A light that's sometimes on the optical drive does the same thing.

You might be lucky and find other fun and unusual items living on the front of your PC's console. They're probably particular to a certain computer brand or model. Consider them a bonus.

- ✔ The front of the console may also boast a brand label or manufacturer's tattoo.

- ✔ Some newer computers have stickers that show the secret Windows installation number or proclaim such nonsense as "I was built to run Windows Optimus Prime" or "An Intel Hoohah lurks inside this box."

- ✔ For more specific information on the connectors lurking behind a secret panel, see the section "The I/O panel," later in this chapter.

- ✔ Don't block the air vents on the front of the console. If you do, the computer may suffocate. (It gets too hot.)

- ✔ The all-in-one type of PC features all its holes, switches, and slots on its sides or back.

- ✔ A hard drive light can be red or green or yellow, and it flickers when the hard drive is in use. The flickering is not an alarm, so don't let it freak you out! The hard drive is just doing its job.

Stuff found on the console's rump

Just like an exotic dancer, the console's backside is its busy side. That's where you find various connectors for the many devices in your computer system: a place to plug in the monitor, keyboard, mouse, speakers, and just about anything else that you want to have in your computer system.

Use Figure 2-4 as a guide for finding important items on the back of the PC's console. Note that some things may look different and some may be missing; not every console is the same.

Power: The console needs power, and the power connector is where you plug in the power cord. The other end of the power cord plugs into the wall.

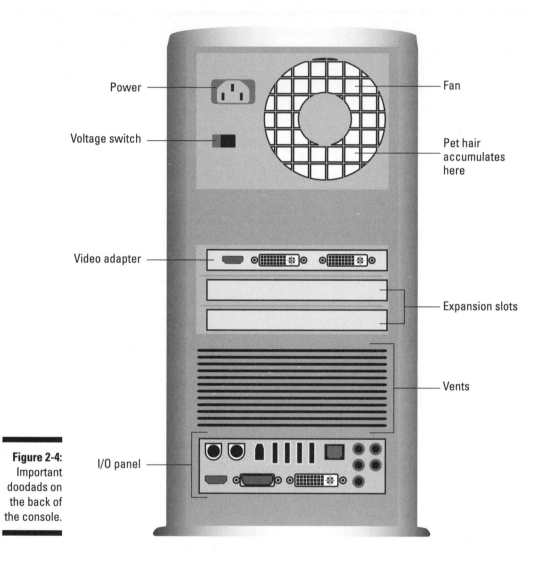

Power — Fan

Voltage switch — Pet hair accumulates here

Video adapter —

Expansion slots

Vents

Figure 2-4:
Important
doodads on
the back of
the console.

I/O panel —

Fan: Air gets sucked in here. Or it might be blown out. I forget which.

Voltage switch: Use this switch to change power frequencies to match the specifications for your country, region, or planet.

Expansion slots: These slots are available for adding new components on expansion cards to the console and expanding your PC's hardware. Any connectors on the expansion cards appear in this area, such as the video connectors on a graphics adapter (refer to Figure 2-4).

Vents: The breathing thing again.

I/O panel: Aside from the power cord, and anything attached to an expansion card, the rest of your PC's expansion options and plug-in-type things are located in a central area that I call the I/O panel. Details of what you can find there are covered in the next section.

The I/O panel

To either help keep all connectors in one spot or just create an intensely cable-crammed location, your PC's console features an I/O panel on its rear. That location is where you add various expansion options to the PC as well as plug in the standard devices shown way back in Figure 2-1.

Use Figure 2-5 as your guide for what's what. The items you find on your PC's I/O panel may be labeled with text or may include the symbols listed later, in Table 2-1. Also keep in mind that Figure 2-5 is only a guide; your PC console may have a different layout and sport more or fewer items on the I/O panel.

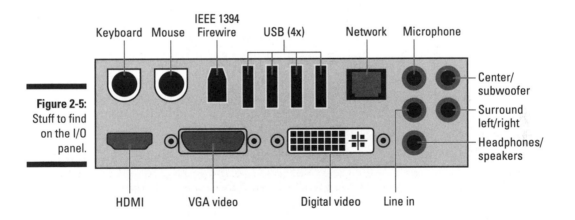

Figure 2-5: Stuff to find on the I/O panel.

Here are some of the things you may find on the I/O panel:

Center/subwoofer: For a surround sound audio system, you plug the center speaker, or subwoofer, or both into this jack.

Headphones/speakers: Into this hole, you plug in your PC's external speakers or headphones or hook up the PC to a sound system. (Also check the "secret panel" on the front of the console for a headphone connector.)

IEEE 1394 (FireWire): This type of versatile connector is similar to USB, although not as common.

Keyboard: Older keyboards plug into this little hole.

Line in: You use this jack to plug a traditional audio-producing device (stereo, phonograph, or VCR, for example) into the PC for capturing sound.

Microphone: The computer's microphone plugs into this jack. A similar jack might also appear on the front side of the console.

Mini 1394: This special version of the IEEE 1394 connector is designed specifically for digital video.

Mouse: Older mice plug into this hole.

Network: Plug in a local area network (LAN) connector or attach a broadband modem to the PC.

SPDIF in, SPDIF out: These connectors are used for digital audio. Special fiber-optic cable is required: Audio coming into the computer plugs into the in hole; the sound the computer generates goes out the out hole.

Surround left/right: Also for surround sound, this jack is the one into which you plug the rear left and right speakers.

USB: Plug snazzy devices into these Certs-size Universal Serial Bus (USB) slots. See Chapter 10 for more information about USB.

Video: Your PC's monitor can plug into one of the video adapters on the I/O panel. You may find a traditional VGA adapter, a digital video adapter, an HDMI adapter, or a combination of all three. See Chapter 8 for more information on computer video.

The good news? You connect all this stuff only once. Then your PC's butt faces the wall for the rest of its life and you never have to look at it again — well, unless you add something in the future or you just enjoy looking at PC butts.

  ✔ The old keyboard and mouse connectors *are* different! Be certain that you plug the proper device into the proper hole, lest the keyboard and mouse don't work!

  ✔ For those of you who must use a dial-up modem, see Chapter 13 for information on connecting it to yet another hole on your PC's rump.

  ✔ Older PCs may sport ports not shown in Figure 2-5. These ports include the serial or COM port, the printer port, and the joystick port. The functions of these ports have been replaced with USB ports, which are plentiful on modern PCs.

Helpful hints, hieroglyphics, and hues

Even though most PC connectors are different, manufacturers have relented and agreed upon a set of common colors and symbols used to label the various holes, connectors, and ports on the console's hindquarters. They're listed in Table 2-1 to help you find things, in case the need arises.

Table 2-1	Shapes, Connections, Symbols, and Colors		
Name	*Connector*	*Symbol*	*Color*
Center/subwoofer			Brown
Digital video			White
eSATA		eSATA	Raspberry
HDMI		HDMI	Black
IEEE 1394			None
IEEE 1394 mini			None
Infrared			None
Joystick			Mustard
Keyboard			Purple
Line in (audio)			Gray
Microphone			Pink
Modem			None

(continued)

Table 2-1 *(continued)*

Name	Connector	Symbol	Color
Mouse			Green
Network			None
Power			Yellow
Speakers/ headphones			Lime
S-video			Yellow
Surround left/right			Black
USB			Black/ Blue
VGA video			Blue

Chapter 3

PC Setup

In This Chapter

▶ Putting together your PC

▶ Understanding computer cables

▶ Plugging things into the console

▶ Using a power strip

▶ Managing with a UPS

I could lie to you and say that setting up a PC is so simple that a child could do it. A Vulcan child, perhaps. Even so, setting up a computer isn't as difficult as assembling backyard play equipment or programming 1980s VCRs. The process does, however, involve a lot of cable plugging, which must be done properly if you want the computer system to work. Therefore, I present to you this chapter, which should help you get your PC assembled.

Computer Assembly

Consider yourself lucky if your new PC pops right out of the box, ready to run. Many all-in-one PCs work that way — or close to it. Laptops come out of the box ready to go (well, perhaps needing a battery charge). For the rest of the lot, peruse this section on how to get your PC out of the box and assembled.

Unpacking the boxes

Your computer runs faster when you take it out of the box.

I don't need to describe how to open a box, but often the question looms: Which box to open first? If you're lucky, one of the boxes says Open Me First. Open that one first. Otherwise, attempt to locate the box containing the console. Open that one first.

As you open boxes, check to ensure that you have all the pieces necessary for your computer system. Look through all the packing materials inside the box. Sometimes, manufacturers stick important items inside boxes inside boxes, or nestled in the Styrofoam. Refer to the packing slip or invoice for the list of pieces. If you're missing anything, call someone!

✔ Keep the packing slip, warranty, sales receipt, and other important pieces of paper together.

✔ Don't fill out the warranty card until after the computer is set up and running fine. If you have to return the computer, the store prefers that the warranty card *not* be filled in.

✔ Keep all boxes and packing materials. You need them if you have to return the computer. Also, the boxes are the best way to ship the computer if you ever have to move. Some movers don't insure a computer unless it's packed in its original box.

Setting up the console

The *console* is the main computer box, the locus of all PC activities, so you should set it up first. Put the console in the location where you've always dreamed it would be. If you plan to put the console beneath your desk, put it there now.

Don't back the console up against the wall just yet because you need to plug things into the console's back. Not until everything is connected to the console do you want to push it up against the wall. (Even then, leave some room so that you don't crimp the cables.)

✔ The console needs to breathe. Don't set up the computer in a confined space or inside a cabinet where there's no air circulation.

✔ Avoid setting the console by a window where the sun will heat it up. Computers don't like to operate in extreme heat — or extreme cold, for that matter. A PC is happiest when it operates at temperatures between 40 and 80 degrees Fahrenheit or, for the world outside the United States, between 4 and 27 degrees Celsius.

✔ Also avoid humidity, which can gum up a computer. Readers in tropical climes have reported mold growing inside their PCs — the humidity was that bad! If you compute where it's humid, do so in an air-conditioned room.

✔ Don't put the console in a cabinet unless the cabinet is well-ventilated. Shoot some bullet holes in the cabinet if it requires more ventilation.

✔ A computer by a window makes a tempting target for a smash-and-grab thief.

Plugging in and connecting

After setting up the console, your next job is to obtain the various other devices — the *peripherals* — and attach them to the console. You'll also need to plug things in to a power supply.

I recommend setting up a peripheral, connecting it to the console, and moving on to the next peripheral. So you set up the monitor, and then plug it into the console. Set up the keyboard, and then plug it into the console. For specific directions on connecting individual items, refer to the next section.

Some computer peripherals get their power directly from the wall socket. I recommend that you plug in their power cords last. Helpful tips on connecting your PC and its components to a power source are covered in the later section, "It Must Have Power."

The Plugging-Things-In Guide

This section covers the basics of connecting many popular items to a standard computer console. Use this information instead of glue and adhesive tape when you first set up the computer, as well as later when you expand or add to your computer system.

- ✔ All major parts of a computer system plug directly into the console, which is why I recommend unpacking and setting up the console first.

- ✔ If this is the first time you're setting up the computer, don't plug in the console yet. You can turn on the console after connecting all the pieces.

- ✔ Plug things into the console before you plug them into the wall. Review the information in the section "It Must Have Power" for details.

- ✔ It's generally okay to plug something into the console while the computer is on. Exceptions exist to this rule, so read this section carefully!

- ✔ Also see Chapter 22 for information on wirelessly connecting peripherals to your PC.

Attaching the keyboard and mouse

Set up the keyboard right in front of where you sit when you use the computer, between you and the monitor. The mouse lives to the right or left of the keyboard, depending on whether you're right- or left-handed.

Know your computer cables

A computer cable is known by which hole, or *port,* it plugs into. For example, USB cables plug into USB ports.

The ends of a computer cable are configured so that you cannot plug the cable in backward: The connector for the console is one shape, and the connector for the gizmo is another shape. When the connectors are the same shape, it doesn't matter which end plugs in where.

All cables fasten snugly. Network cables have little tabs on them that snap when the cable is properly inserted. You must squeeze the tab to remove the cable. Some video connectors have

tiny thumbscrews on the side, which help cinch the cable to the connector.

Some cables are permanently attached to their devices: The mouse and keyboard have this type of cable, for example. Other cables are separate; remember to plug in both ends.

Extra cables, if you need them, can be purchased at any computer or office supply store. As a suggestion, measure the distance for which you need a cable and then double it to get a cable of the proper length. For example, if it's 2 feet between your console and where you want a microphone, get a 4-foot microphone cable.

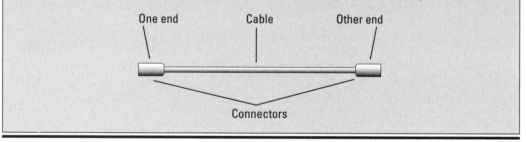

The PC keyboard plugs into a USB port. The mouse plugs into a USB port. Older model keyboards and mice plug into specific keyboard and mouse ports. How can you tell which is which? Look at the end of the cable.

✔ The older mouse and keyboard ports look identical, but they're not. Yes, they're different colors, but more importantly, they're different *electronics.* Don't plug the keyboard or mouse into the wrong port or else neither device works.

✔ You can attach or remove a USB keyboard or mouse at any time, but don't plug a keyboard or mouse into the keyboard or mouse port unless the PC is turned off.

Setting up the monitor

Set the monitor atop your desk, generally away from where you sit, to accommodate room for the keyboard. For best results, the monitor should face you.

The monitor's cable may be attached or separate. If separate, attach the cable to the monitor. Plug the monitor's cable into the console's graphics adapter jack. Several jack types are available, so choose the cable that matches the jack.

The monitor also requires power. See the later section "It Must Have Power."

- ✔ If the monitor comes with several cable options, use the digital or HDMI connector. Shun the older VGA (blue) connector unless it's the only jack available on the console.

- ✔ If the console has two sets of connectors, use the one on an expansion card rather than the one found on the console's I/O panel. That expansion card jack indicates a high-end graphics adapter, which offers better features.

- ✔ You can use digital-to-VGA adapters when you have a VGA monitor and a digital graphics adapter. Such an adapter should have come with the monitor.

- ✔ It's possible to use a large-screen TV as your computer monitor. What's better is showing that setup to your computer friends to make them jealous.

- ✔ HDMI stands for High-Definition Multimedia Interface.

- ✔ See Chapter 8 for more information about PC monitors and graphics.

Connecting to the network

Plug the network cable into the network jack on the back of the console. This is how you connect your PC to a network, a router, a broadband modem, or any of a number of oddly named networking things. Well, unless you have a Wi-Fi (wireless) connection.

For more info, refer to Part IV, which covers computer networking.

Adding a printer

You can add a printer to the computer system at any time. Try to position the printer where it's within arm's reach of the console so you can reach over and pluck out whatever it is you're printing.

The printer connects directly to the PC with a USB cable. However, you might need to install the printer's software before you make the connection. See Chapter 11.

You can also access printers on the network, in which case connecting the network also connects the printers. Job finished! See Chapter 21 for networking printing info.

The printer requires power, so you need to plug it into a wall socket. See the section "It Must Have Power," later in this chapter.

Hooking up other random peripherals

With the advent of the USB port, adding things to a PC console is easy. (See Chapter 10 for more details on the USB connection.) However, two common items that might not have a USB connector are audio devices and a dial-up modem.

The audio connection

Computer audio involves both output and input — the famous I/O you probably sang songs about when you went to computer camp as a teen.

All computer audio uses the standard *mini-DIN* connector, which looks like a tiny pointy thing. Audio input is supplied by a microphone that connects to the computer's microphone jack. Audio output is supplied by headphones, left–right speakers, or full-on, wake- the-neighbors surround sound, also using the mini-DIN connector and the appropriate jacks on the console.

✔ Refer to Chapter 12 for more information on PC audio, including some speaker layout instructions.

✔ Both headphones and speakers use the line out, headphone, or speakers jack. Furthermore, speakers may need to be plugged into the wall for more power; see the section "It Must Have Power," later in this chapter.

✔ Be sure to check the front of the console for another spot to plug in the headphones or microphone. This location is much handier than using the connector on the back.

✔ The line in connector is used to connect any nonamplified sound source, such as your stereo, TV, Victrola, or other antique audio devices.

✔ The difference between the line in and microphone jacks is that line in devices aren't amplified.

✔ If your audio equipment lacks a mini-DIN connector, you can buy an adapter at any audio store or Radio Shack.

✔ Some PCs have special audio hardware, which you can determine by looking at the console's rear for audio connectors on an expansion slot cover. If your PC is configured this way, be sure to plug the speakers into the audio card's output jacks, not into the standard audio output jacks on the I/O panel.

The dial-up modem

Many people out there — several in fact — still use dial-up modems. If you're one of them, you connect the modem as follows. First, the modem connects to the phone company's wall jack by using a standard telephone cord. You plug in the modem just like you plug in a telephone, and you leave the cord connected all the time, just like a telephone.

Second, use the modem's second phone jack, if available, to connect a real telephone so that you can use the phone when the computer isn't on the line. The second phone jack is labeled *Phone* and may have a telephone symbol by it. (The first jack is labeled *Line.*)

✔ Broadband modems — either cable, DSL, or satellite — don't plug directly into a PC. See Chapter 20.

✔ Be careful not to confuse the modem's jack with the network jack. They look similar, but the network jack is slightly wider.

It Must Have Power

Computer devices crave power like an armband-wearing, short-haired, high school hall monitor. The last thing you need to do, after plugging your computer components into the console, is to plug all those gizmos into the wall.

Plugging everything into a power strip

You may have noticed that the computer system has far more devices that need to be plugged in than the number of available wall sockets. No problem! That's why Thomas Edison invented power strips. The idea is to plug everything into a power strip and then plug that single power strip into the wall, as illustrated in Figure 3-1.

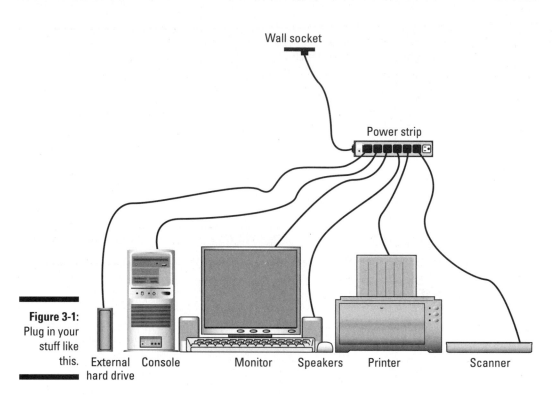

Figure 3-1:
Plug in your
stuff like
this.

Wall socket

Power strip

External
hard drive Console Monitor Speakers Printer Scanner

Follow these steps:

1. **Ensure that all your gizmos with on–off switches are in the Off position.**

2. **Ensure that the power strip is in the Off position.**

3. **Plug everything into the power strip.**

4. **Turn your gizmos to the On position.**

Now you're ready to turn on the computer system, by turning on the power strip. But not yet! The official on–off information is in Chapter 4. See that chapter for more information.

✔ Yes, sometimes it's difficult to tell whether an electronic gizmo's power button is "in the Off position." Just plug it into the power strip anyway.

✔ Try to find a power strip with line noise filtering. Even better, pay more to buy a power strip that has line conditioning! That's super nice for your electronic goodies.

- I recommend the Kensington SmartSockets-brand power strips. Unlike cheaper power strips, the SmartSockets brand lines up its sockets in an arrangement that makes it easier to plug in bulky transformers.

- Most power strips have six sockets, which is plenty for a typical computer system. If not, buy a second power strip, plug it into its own wall socket, and use it for the rest of your computer devices. But:

- Don't plug one power strip into another power strip; it's electrically unsafe!

- Don't plug a laser printer into a power strip. The laser printer draws too much juice. Instead, you must plug the laser printer directly into the wall socket. (It says so in your laser printer's manual — if you ever get around to reading it.)

Surges, spikes, and lightning strikes

The power that comes from the wall socket into your computer isn't as pure as the wind-driven snow. Occasionally, it may be corrupted by some of the various electrical nasties that, every now and then, come uninvited into your home or office. Here's the lowdown:

Line noise: Electrical interference on the power line, most commonly caused by some electric motor on the same circuit. For example, the TV image turns fuzzy when you use the blender. That's line noise.

Surge: A gradual increase in power.

Serge: Some guy from Europe.

Spike: A sudden increase in the power, such as what happens when lightning strikes nearby.

Dip: The opposite of a surge; a decrease in power. Some electrical motors don't work, and room lights are dimmer than normal. A dip is also known as a *brownout*.

Power outage: An absence of power coming through the line. People in the 1960s called it a *blackout*.

A power strip with surge protection helps keep your electronics happy during a surge. If the power strip has noise filtering or line conditioning, it works even better.

The most expensive form of protection is spike protection, in which the power strip lays down its life by taking the full brunt of the spike and saving your computer equipment.

Spikes, because they're particularly nasty, come through not only the power lines but also the phone and cable TV lines. So, if lightning strikes are a common occurrence in your area, use a power strip with phone line, cable, and maybe even network protection.

Taking advantage of a UPS

UPS stands for *uninterruptible power supply,* and it's the best thing to have for hooking up your computer system to the wall socket. Basically, a *UPS* is a power strip combined with a battery to keep your computer running when the power goes out.

Figure 3-2 illustrates the proper way to set up your computer system with a UPS and power strip. Not shown is a USB cable, which is used on some UPS systems to alert the computer about a power outage. Refer to Chapter 13 for information on how a USB cable works.

The idea behind a UPS isn't to keep computing while the power is out. Instead, the UPS is designed to keep your basic computer components — the console and monitor — up and running just long enough for you to save your work and properly shut down the computer. That way, you never lose anything from an unexpected power outage.

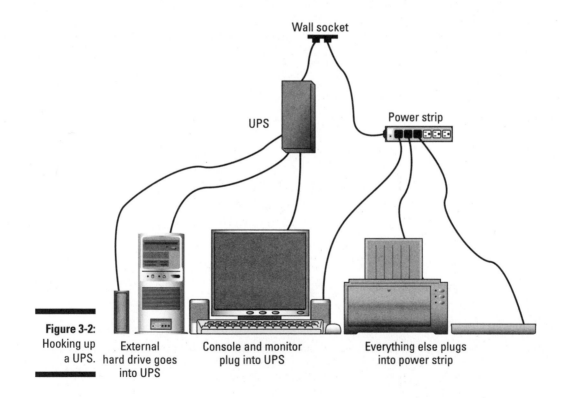

Figure 3-2: Hooking up a UPS.

External hard drive goes into UPS

Console and monitor plug into UPS

Everything else plugs into power strip

✔ Ignore what it says on the box: A UPS gives you *maybe* five minutes of computer power. Most often, you get only two minutes of power.

✔ Some UPS systems also have non-battery-backed-up sockets so that you can plug everything into the UPS directly. Just be sure to plug the monitor and console into the battery-backed-up sockets.

✔ I also recommend plugging any external hard drives into the UPS's battery-backed-up sockets.

✔ Leave the UPS on all the time. Turn it off only when the power is out and the computer has been properly shut down.

✔ In addition to providing emergency power, a UPS provides higher levels of electrical protection for your equipment. Many models offer surge, spike, and dip protection, which keep your PC running smoothly despite any nasties the power company may throw your way.

✔ Also see Chapter 13 for information on having your computer shut down automatically when the power goes out.

Using the UPS (a short play)

Interior upscale kitchen. A thunderclap is heard. The lights flicker and then go out. ROGER, *40ish and nerdy, is left sitting in the dark, his computer still on. The* UPS beeps *once every few seconds.* FELICIA *rushes in. She is pretentious but not insufferably so.*

FELICIA: The power is out! The brioche I put in the toaster oven is ruined! Did you lose that urgent doodle you were creating in Paint?

ROGER: No, darling, I'm still working on it. See? Our UPS has kept the computer console and monitor turned on despite the power outage.

FELICIA: Oh! That explains the beeping.

ROGER: Yes, the UPS beeps when the power has gone out. It does that just in case I don't notice the pitch darkness.

FELICIA: Well, hurry up and print your doodle!

ROGER: Not now, sugarplum! Printing can wait, which is why I didn't connect the printer to the UPS. It's as powerless as the toaster oven.

FELICIA: What can you do? Hurry! The UPS battery won't last forever!

ROGER: Relax, gentle spouse. I shall save to disk, thus. (*He presses Ctrl+S on the keyboard.*) Now I may shut down the computer, assured with the knowledge that my urgent doodle is safely stored on the PC's mass storage system. There. (*He turns off the computer and monitor. He shuts off the UPS and the* beeping *ceases.*) Now we can weather the storm with peace of mind.

Two hours later, after the power is back on, FELICIA and ROGER are sipping wine.

FELICIA: Honey, you certainly demonstrated your Ivy League pedigree with the way you used that UPS.

ROGER: Well, I'm just thankful I read Dan Gookin's book *PCs For Dummies,* from Wiley Publishing, Inc. I think I shall buy more of his books.

FELICIA: Who knew that we could find such happiness, thanks to a computer book?

They canoodle.

Chapter 4

On and Off

· ·

In This Chapter

▶ Starting your PC

▶ Introducing Windows

▶ Locating the various shutdown commands

▶ Turning the computer off

▶ Exploring various non-shutdown options

▶ Restarting Windows

▶ Keeping the PC on all the time

· ·

No doubt about it: Evil computers cannot be turned off. To prove it, I turn to the canon of *Star Trek,* Episode 53: When Scotty tried to turn off the malevolent M5 computer, it actually *killed* the crewman trying to pull the plug. Nope, you just can't turn off an evil computer.

Your PC isn't evil. If it were, you could use Captain Kirk's infallible logic to reason the computer into committing suicide. I regret to tell you, however, that this book doesn't have information on arguing a computer to death. That's because your PC has a power button, which is used to turn the computer both on and off. Although that might sound confusing, this chapter helps clear up the issue.

Turn On Your PC

You turn on the computer this way:

1. **Turn on everything but the console.**

   Everything includes only those items you intend to use, primarily the monitor. If you're not using the scanner or printer, you don't need to turn them on until you need them.

2. **Turn on the console last.**

Or, if everything is plugged into a power strip, just turn on the power strip.

If the console and monitor are plugged into a UPS (which should be kept turned on all the time) and everything else is plugged into a power strip, do this:

1. **Turn on the power strip, which turns on all the computer's external devices, or** *peripherals.*

2. **Press the monitor's power button to turn it on.**

3. **Press the console's power button to turn it on.**

Success is indicated by your computer system coming to life; you can hear the fan whine, and various lights on the console, keyboard, and other devices may flash at you or glow softly. The scanner and printer may whir and grind their servos. Your computing day is at hand.

✔ By turning on the console last, you allow time for the other devices in the computer system to initialize and get ready for work. That way, the console recognizes them faster than when those gizmos are turned on after the console is up and running.

✔ Not all computer devices have their own on–off switches. For example, some USB devices — scanners and disk drives — use the USB port's power. To turn off these devices, you unplug the USB cable, although that's not necessary unless the device is behaving improperly.

✔ Some devices can be left on all the time. For example, the printer may have a special low-power mode that allows you to keep it on all the time while using little energy. It's often better to keep these devices on than to turn them on or off several times a day.

✔ The largest button on the front of the monitor turns it on. Other monitors may have power buttons that aren't physical buttons at all but rather a sweet spot you touch. That sweet spot is often labeled with the universal power button symbol, shown in the margin.

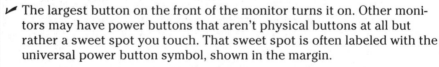

✔ When something doesn't turn on, check to see whether it's plugged in. Confirm that all the cables are properly connected, at both ends.

✔ For times when Windows fails to start smoothly, or whenever the computer goes hinky, consider checking out my book *Troubleshooting & Maintaining Your PC All-In-One For Dummies,* 2nd Edition (Wiley).

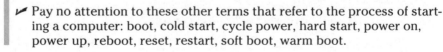

✔ Pay no attention to these other terms that refer to the process of starting a computer: boot, cold start, cycle power, hard start, power on, power up, reboot, reset, restart, soft boot, warm boot.

Windows, Ahoy!

Starting a computer is a hardware thing. But it's software that makes the computer useful. The software that runs the computer directly is called an *operating system.* On most PCs, that operating system is *Windows.* So, after starting your computer's hardware, the next thing you have to deal with is Windows.

The first step to using Windows is to identify yourself. That process is called signing in, logging in, or *loggin on,* depending on the version of Windows installed and on which side of the Mississippi you live. The signing-in process is part of the computer's security. It's a good thing.

In Windows, you identify yourself by choosing your account picture or typing your account name. Then you type a password. Figure 4-1 illustrates the common sign-in or login screen.

Windows 8   Windows 7   Windows Vista

Figure 4-1:
You log in
to Windows
here.

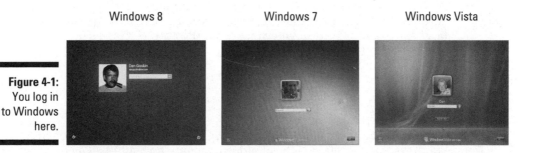

If everything goes well, you're logged in! The next step is to start using your computer, which is covered in Part III.

- ✔ You log in by using an account name, which might be your own name, a nickname, some kind of computer superhero name, or something totally odd, like User117.

- ✔ In Windows 8, you can sign in using your Microsoft Live e-mail address. By doing so, you help coordinate the stuff on your computer with files and such saved on the Internet.

- ✔ If you sign into Windows 8 using your Microsoft Live e-mail address, use that e-mail account's password as your Windows password.

- ✔ The password is designed to ensure that you are who you say you are when you log into the computer.

✔ Both the account name and password were set up when Windows was first configured on your computer. You probably forgot when you did that, but you did do it. If you're using Windows at a large, impersonal organization, the account setup and password were probably preset for you.

✔ When you goof up typing your password, try again.

✔ In Windows 8, you can also use a picture password or type a PIN (personal identification number) to log in. No one uses that flakey option, so I shan't describe it further.

✔ Mind the Caps Lock key on the keyboard! Your password is *case sensitive,* which means that the computer sees uppercase and lowercase letters differently.

Turn Off the Computer

Nothing is more satisfying than turning off a computer by ripping its power cord from the wall. I've done it several times myself. Each time is met with a brief, mirthful smile. Although yanking out the cord works, it's not the best way to turn off a computer.

Finding the shutdown options

Options for turning off your computer are found in a special location in Windows. That location is the Shutdown menu. The Shutdown menu's location varies, depending on which version of Windows burdens your PC. That's the bad news. The good news is that Windows won't relocate the Shutdown menu once you find it.

Windows 8 shutdown options

Shutdown options in Windows 8 are found in two places. Some of the options are accessed from the Settings charm. The rest are accessed by clicking your account picture on the Start screen.

To access the Sleep, Shutdown, and Restart commands, follow these steps:

1. **Summon the charms bar.**

   Move the mouse to the upper-right corner of the screen.

2. **Select the Settings charm.**

3. **Click or touch the Power icon.**

   The three shutdown commands appear in a pop-up menu.

To access the Lock, Sign Out, and Switch User commands, obey these directions:

1. **Display the Start screen.**

   Press the Windows key to instantly summon the Start screen.

2. **Click your account picture.**

   The Lock and Sign Out commands appear on a pop-up menu. Other user names appear in the list as well; choosing one from the menu is how you switch users.

Details on when to use these commands are offered in sections strewn throughout the latter part of this chapter.

The Windows 7 and Windows Vista Shutdown menu

Back in the olden days, when Windows 7 and its older sister Windows Vista ruled the PC planet, all shutdown options were kept in one place. That place was the Shutdown menu, located on the Start button's menu, as shown in Figure 4-2.

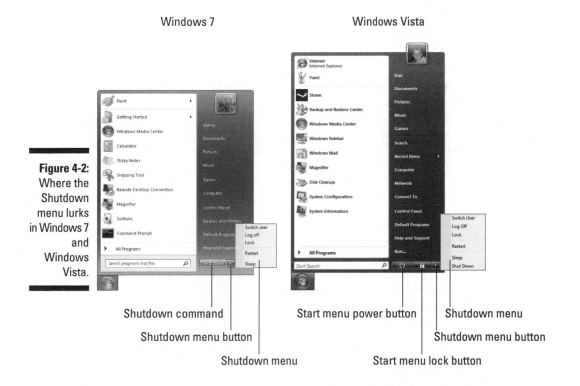

Windows 7   Windows Vista

Figure 4-2: Where the Shutdown menu lurks in Windows 7 and Windows Vista.

Shutdown command

Shutdown menu button

Shutdown menu

Start menu power button

Start menu lock button

Shutdown menu

Shutdown menu button

Regarding that bonus power button (the secret one)

Some PC cases have a true on–off switch in addition to a power button. You can find the on–off switch on the back of the console, usually near the place where the power cord connects to the PC's power supply. The switch is often labeled | and O, for on and off, respectively. Use this button rather than the power button only in times of dire emergency. Also note that the on–off switch must be in the on position for you to use the power button to turn on your computer.

Access the Windows 7 or Windows Vista Shutdown menu by popping up the Start button menu and clicking the Shutdown menu button's triangle (refer to Figure 4-2). Be careful not to click the button(s) next to that menu button, as they do things other than display the Shutdown menu.

If you're still clinging to Windows XP, you'll find shutdown options by clicking the Shutdown button on the Start button menu. You can then use the Turn Off Computer dialog box to choose various shutdown options.

Turning the darn thing off

The proper way to turn off your PC is to choose the Shutdown command. That command goes through all the proper steps of putting various programs to bed, tucking them in nicely, and then turning off the computer. Yes, it really does turn off all by itself.

In Windows 8, follow these steps to shut down the PC:

1. **Summon the charms bar.**
2. **Select the Settings charm.**
3. **Click or touch the Power icon.**
4. **Choose the Shut Down command.**

   The computer turns itself off.

In Windows 7, follow these steps:

1. **Pop-up the Start button menu.**
2. **Click the Shutdown command button.**

   Refer to Figure 4-2 for that button's location.

In Windows Vista, obey these steps to use the Shutdown command:

1. **Pop-up the Start button menu.**

2. **Click the triangle button in the lower-right corner of the Start button menu.**

   The Shutdown menu is displayed, as shown on the right in Figure 4-2.

3. **Choose the Shut Down command.**

In Windows XP, you can still use these directions to turn off your ancient PC:

1. **Pop-up up the Start button menu.**

2. **Choose the Shut Down command.**

3. **In the Turn Off Computer dialog box, click the Turn Off button.**

For all versions of Windows: You may be warned about unsaved files or documents before the shutdown process can be completed. In those cases, cancel the shutdown process; click the Cancel button. Save your stuff. Then shut down the computer again.

✔ After the console turns itself off, go ahead and turn off the other components in your computer system: monitor and scanner and any other external devices. Or, if you have a power strip, simply flip its switch to turn off everything.

✔ It's convenient to flip the power strip button with your foot. It's classy to do so with your toe through a hole in your sock.

✔ The computer may also shut down when you press the console's power button. That button can, however, be reprogrammed to do things other than issue the Shutdown command. In some cases, pressing the power button does nothing. See Chapter 13 for information on changing the power button's function.

✔ In dire times of panic, you can press and hold the console's power button for about three or four seconds, and the computer turns off. Although this trick is a handy one to know, you should use it only when the methods mentioned in this section fail to work.

Reviewing other shutdown options

Windows offers several ways to end your computer day, none of which involve the use of artillery. Here's the gamut of options other than shutting down your PC:

Don't end your computer day: This choice is the one the computer prefers and the one you will invariably make after the computer has full control over your mind. It's *digital demonic possession,* and you'll need a pagan priest and an unblemished goat to rid yourself of the scourge. Seriously: One option for turning the computer off is not to turn it off ever. See the later section "Should You Leave the Computer On All the Time?"

Log off: When several people have accounts on the same computer, you can sign out or log off to keep the computer on, toasty, and ready for someone else to use it. To do so, choose the Log Off option found on the various Shutdown menus. In Windows XP, choose the Log Off button at the bottom of the Start menu, and then click the Log Off button in the Log Off Windows window that appears.

Lock the computer: When you *lock* the computer, you're directing Windows to display the initial logon screen, similar to the ones shown in Figure 4-1. You prevent anyone from seeing what you're doing, as well as keep out anyone who doesn't have an account on your PC.

To lock the computer, press the Win+L key combination, where Win is the Windows key on the computer keyboard and L is the L key. The computer is locked.

Switch users: The Switch User command allows you to temporarily log out so that another user on the same computer can log in. This option is faster than logging out because it doesn't require you to save your stuff or close your programs. When you return (log in again), all your stuff is waiting for you just as you left it.

In Windows 8, choose a user to switch to from your account picture's menu on the Start screen. The Switch users command is found on the Shutdown menu in Windows 7 and Windows Vista. In Windows XP, choose the Log Out command from the Start button menu, and then click the Switch User button in the Log Off Windows dialog box.

Put the computer to sleep: *Sleep mode* is an energy-saving way to not quite turn off the PC. In Sleep mode, Windows saves what you're doing and then puts the computer into a special low-power mode. The computer isn't exactly off, and it restores itself quickly, much faster than either hibernation or a complete shutdown.

The Sleep command is found on the Shutdown menu for Windows 8, 7, and Vista. To put the computer to sleep in Windows XP, click the Shut Down button at the bottom of the Start button menu. In the Turn Off Computer dialog box, click the Stand By button.

To wake the computer from its slumber, you can wiggle the mouse or press a key on the keyboard. Be patient! Sometimes the PC takes a few seconds to wake up.

Put the computer in hibernation: The most dramatic way to save power and not-quite-exactly turn off the PC is to use the Hibernate command. It saves all the computer's memory — everything the system is doing — and then turns off the computer. (It's turned off, not just sleeping). When you turn on the computer again, things return to the way they were. So hibernation not only saves electricity but also provides a faster way to turn the computer off and then on again.

The Hibernation command may need to be activated before it's visible on the Shutdown menu. See Chapter 13.

In Windows XP, you can enter Hibernation mode by choosing Shut Down from the Start button menu. When the Turn Off Computer dialog box appears, press the Shift key, which reveals the Hibernate button. Click that button.

Restart the computer: You need to reset or restart Windows in two instances. First, Windows may direct you to restart after you install something new or change some setting. Second, restarting is a good idea whenever something strange happens. For some reason, a restart clears the computer's head like a good nose blow, and things return to normal.

The Restart command is found on the various Shutdown menus. In Windows XP, restart by popping up the Start button menu and clicking the Shut Down button. Click the Restart button in the Turn Off Computer dialog box.

Here are some things to consider when using these sundry shutdown commands:

✔ Logging yourself off does not turn off the PC.

✔ When you're the only person who has an account on the computer, logging off is an utter waste of time. A better option is to lock the computer; press Win+L.

✔ Lock the computer whenever you need to step away for a bit.

✔ In Win+L, I'm assuming that the L stands for *lock*.

✔ Sleep mode was once known as Stand By mode. Sometimes the term Suspend was used instead. Oh, and Snooze. That, too.

✔ Sleep mode is part of the computer's power management features. See Chapter 13 for more information.

✔ Windows may initiate a restart on its own, such as after an update. If you're lucky, a prompt is displayed, allowing you to click a button to restart the computer.

Should You Leave the Computer On All the Time?

I've been writing about computers for more than 20 years, and this issue has yet to be settled: Should your computer — like the refrigerator or a lava lamp — be left on all the time? Does it waste electricity? Will we ever know *the truth?* Of course not! But people have opinions.

"I want to leave my computer off all the time"

It's an excellent solution, but one that renders nearly all of this book unnecessary.

"I want to leave my computer on all the time"

I say *yes.* If you use your computer often, such as for a home business, or you find yourself turning it on and off several times during the day, just leave it on all the time.

The only time I ever turn off my computers is when I'll be away for longer than a weekend. Even then, I just hibernate the PC rather than turn it off.

Does my method waste electricity? Perhaps, but most computers have Sleep mode and save energy when they're not being used. Modern PCs don't use that much electricity, and having a PC on all the time doesn't raise your electric bill grotesquely, not like a Jacuzzi or a Tesla coil does.

Also, computers enjoy being on all the time. Having that fan whirring keeps the console's innards at a constant temperature, which avoids some of the problems that turning the system off (cooling) and on (heating) again cause.

- ✔ If you use your PC only once a day (during the evening for e-mail, chat, and the Internet, for example), turning it off for the rest of the day is fine.

- ✔ Most businesses leave their computers on all the time, though a medium-size business can save thousands of dollars a year by shutting down their computers overnight. Just a thought.

- ✔ Whatever you do with your PC, always turn off the *monitor* when you're away. Some monitors can sleep just like PCs, but if they don't, turning them off saves electricity.

- ✔ If you leave your computer on all the time, don't put it under a dust cover. You'll suffocate the thing.

Part II
The Nerd's-Eye View

The 5th Wave
By Rich Tennant

"Well, she's fast on the keyboard and knows how to load the printer, but she just sort of plays with the mouse."

In this part . . .

For a moment, dare to pretend that you're a computer nerd. Now imagine that you're looking at a computer. Of course, you see only the hardware, but that hardware beckons you, drawing your attention like a siren lures the captain of a storm-tossed ship into a rocky shoal. Indeed, computer hardware can be alluring; it can entice you, seduce you, overwhelm you with its sweet-smelling, throbbing plastic beauty. Oh, my!

Okay! You can stop pretending that you're a computer nerd now.

This part of the book discusses the true guts of your computer system: its hardware. Although software rules the PC roost, it's the hardware that sets the tone for what the software does. By discovering what computer hardware is and how it fits into the big picture, you get more from your PC. And, yes, it's entirely possible to do that without ever becoming a computer nerd.

Chapter 5

Deep Inside the Console

In This Chapter

▶ Studying the console's insides

▶ Examining the motherboard

▶ Understanding the processor

▶ Checking the time

▶ Knowing about the chipset

▶ Supplying the console with power

You have absolutely no reason to open up the computer console case and peer inside. Just as you probably don't venture under the hood of your car, or probe around the interior of the furnace, or look inside a cat. You can find professionals who are better equipped to deal with such chores. Let them do it.

Then again, you may have a faint recollection of the terms *motherboard, processor, power supply,* and so on. It's possible to use your computer for eons and never really understand or relate to those terms. I'm guessing, however, that you want more from your PC investment than to simply gloss over such specifics. This chapter explains what's what inside the PC's console, and why you should bother to know those details.

Console Guts

When humanoid robots revealed themselves on 1960s TV shows, they displayed their innards as a clutch of wires and blinking lights. The display was believable because, well, you figured a robot's guts would just be an impressive, complex, tangled nest of electronics no one could understand. The same thing applies to your computer's guts — until you know what's what.

Looking under the hood

Buried in your PC's bosom is a maze of mysterious technology, from large metal boxes to tiny pointed and dangerous raw electronics. There's no need to remove the PC's cover to witness such madness, however, because I provide a safe and lovely illustration of what you'd see inside the console, shown in Figure 5-1.

The figure illustrates the PC's internals as though you're looking inside a typical mini-tower console. The front of the computer is on the left. What you don't see in Figure 5-1 are the miles of cables that festoon the console's interior space. Also missing is a thin layer of dust and perhaps some pet hair.

Of all the things wonderful and terrifying inside the console's tummy, three are worthy in the big picture:

✔ The power supply

✔ The disk drive cage

✔ The motherboard

The *power supply* feeds the console that all-important stuff called electricity. You can read more about the power supply in the later section "The Source of PC Power."

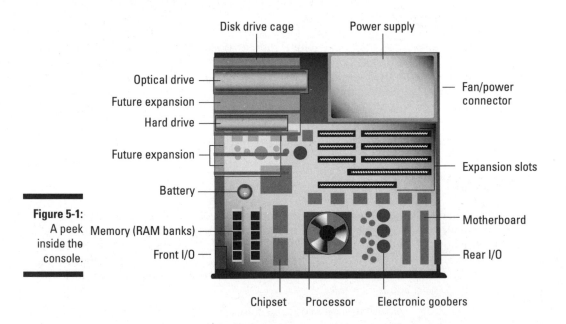

Figure 5-1:
A peek inside the console.

Disk drive cage · Power supply · Optical drive · Future expansion · Hard drive · Future expansion · Battery · Memory (RAM banks) · Front I/O · Fan/power connector · Expansion slots · Motherboard · Rear I/O · Chipset · Processor · Electronic goobers

The *disk drive cage* is a contraption used to house internal hard drives, an optical drive, plus maybe a media card reader. The cage also has room for even more computer storage — the so-called future expansion — usually right behind some knockout panels on the console's front.

Finally, the *motherboard* is the computer's main circuitry board. It's important, as are its many important residents, so I talk about it later in this chapter, starting with the section "The Mother of All Boards."

Going inside the console (not recommended)

There is no sane reason to open your PC's case. Nope. I've owned computers for years without ever popping their hoods. Even when it's a necessary task, such as when performing an upgrade or rescuing a LEGO, I highly recommend that you have someone else do it.

You would probably expect that paragraph would be the end of the topic, but no. I continue writing not because I believe you to be insane, but rather that the console is made easily accessible for a reason; everything inside the PC's case is *modular*. Individual pieces can be replaced or even upgraded without having to toss out the entire console. Modularity is one of the keys to the PC's success as a computer system.

Open the case

If you were going to open the PC's console, which I'm still not recommending, you'd probably follow these general steps:

1. **Start drinking heavily.**

   This step is optional. It's probably best to be slightly sober and perhaps a bit paranoid when you venture inside a computer.

2. **Turn off the computer.**

   Refer to Chapter 4.

3. **There is no Step 3.**

4. **Unplug the console; remove the power cord.**

   Turning off the console isn't enough: You need to unplug the power cord. Heck, hide the power cord in another room.

5. **Move the console out from the wall or locate it in a place where you have room to work.**

   You can unplug some cables if they restrict access to the console, or when replacing an expansion card that has cables attached.

6. **Open the console's case.**

That last step isn't as easy as it sounds. There's no universal way to open a computer console: Some computer cases require a screwdriver and the removal of several screws. Other cases may just pop up, slide off, or swing open. Someone who is good with tools can figure out the operation in a jiffy. And, by "good with tools," I don't mean good with a blowtorch or the jaws of life. Above all, don't force the console open; there is an easy way, if you can find it.

Work inside

Typically, you open the case to do one of three things: add memory, add an expansion card, or replace the PC's battery. Later chapters don't describe any of these options.

Use Figure 5-1 as a general reference for finding things inside the console. Don't be too surprised at the abundance of twisted and tangled cables.

While you work in the console, try to keep one hand touching the case or, preferably, something metal, such as the disk drive cage. That way, your electric potential is the same as the console's and you reduce the chances of generating static electricity — which can damage your computer.

Never plug in the console when the case is open. If you need to test something, close up the case!

Close up the case

When you finish doing whatever motivated you to open the console, close it up! Heed these cautious steps:

1. **Check to ensure that all wires and cables have been properly reconnected.**

2. **Confirm that no tools or parts are left loose inside the case.**

3. **Reattach the lid or console cover.**

4. **Reattach the power cord to the console.**

5. **Turn on the computer.**

6. **Pray that it still works.**

That last step is optional in case you don't believe in a higher, divine being. But why risk it now?

The Mother of All Boards

The largest circuitry board, the *motherboard,* is where the computer's most important electronics dwell. The motherboard is home to the following essential PC components, some of which are illustrated earlier in this chapter (refer to Figure 5-1):

✔ Processor

✔ Chipset

✔ Memory

✔ Battery

✔ Expansion slots

✔ I/O connectors

✔ Electronic goobers

Many of these items have their own sections elsewhere in this chapter. Refer to them for more information. Computer memory is a big deal, so it's covered exclusively in Chapter 6. Expansion slots are covered in Chapter 10.

The *I/O connectors* are simply places on the motherboard where various internal options plug in and communicate with the rest of the computer system. For example, on the motherboard, you find an I/O connector where the internal storage devices plug in and an I/O power connector for electricity from the power supply.

The electronic goobers are those miscellaneous pieces of technology that engineers put on the motherboard to justify their paychecks.

The Processor Rules

It's a common mistake for folks to refer to the computer's processor as its *brain.* That's not true. Software is the brain in a computer; it controls all the hardware, which means that it also controls the processor.

✔ The processor is your PC's main chip. Just about everything else on the motherboard exists to serve the processor.

✔ Another term for a processor is CPU. *CPU* stands for *central processing unit.*

✔ Processors run very hot and therefore require special cooling. If you ever look inside the PC console, you'll notice that the processor wears a tiny fan as a hat. That keeps the processor cool — and stylish.

Understanding the processor's role

Despite its importance, what the processor does is rather simple: First it does basic math — addition, subtraction, division, and multiplication. Second, and most important, the processor can fetch and put information to and from memory. Finally, it can do basic input/output (I/O). That doesn't seem impressive, yet the key to the processor's success is that, unlike your typical brooding teenager, the processor does things *very fast*.

Try to imagine the processor as a combination adding machine and traffic cop, though the traffic is traveling up to 64 lanes wide and at the speed of light.

Naming PC processors

Once upon a time, computer processors were named after famous numbers, like 386 and 8088. The trend now is toward processor names, but not human names, like John or Mary, or even dog names like Rover or Abednego. No, now processors are named after potential science fiction heroes, pharmaceuticals, or sounds made by a baby rhinoceros in distress.

Seriously, the primary processor found in a typical PC is the Intel Core. It is commonly known as Core and has various last names, such as Duo or i7. In fact, you can find a whole lineup of Core processors. Listing them all is pointless in that new variations come out all the time.

✔ Before the Intel Core, the most popular processor in a PC was named Pentium. Some people mistakenly refer to the Core processors as Pentium, but such a faux pas carries no social penalty.

✔ Intel (the company) developed the Intel Core (the processor). Other processor companies exist and make various Core-like processors with various, insignificant names. Truth be told, outside a courtroom, little difference exists between Intel and non-Intel processors. As far as your PC's software is concerned, the processor is the same no matter who made it.

Measuring processor speed

Beyond the name, the truly important yardstick used to judge a processor is its speed, measured in *gigahertz (GHz)*, or billions of cycles per second. The higher that value, the faster the processor.

Typical processor speeds range between 2.0 GHz (slower) and 4.0 GHz (faster). Yep, faster processors cost more. Lots more.

Sadly, speed isn't a realistic gauge of how fast a processor does its processing. Speed is a relative measurement when it comes to computers. So although a Core i7 running at 2.4 GHz is technically slower than a Core i7 running at 3.0 GHz, you probably wouldn't notice the difference between the two.

Discovering your PC's processor

You may not know which processor spins busy inside your PCs thorax, but Windows does! The System window shows a technical inventory, similar to the one shown in Figure 5-2. To summon that window, press Win+Break on your keyboard (that's the Windows key plus the key labeled Break or Pause Break).

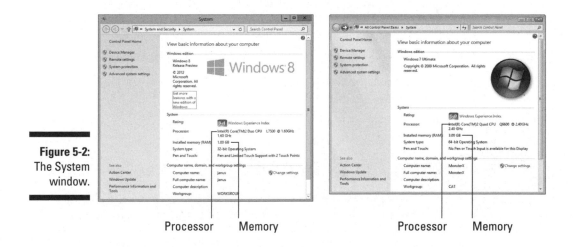

Figure 5-2: The System window.

Processor   Memory   Processor   Memory

In Figure 5-2, the Windows 8 PC sports an Intel Core 2 Duo PC, running at 1.60 GHz. The Windows 7 system uses a Core 2 Quad CPU. It runs at 2.40GHz.

Other information shown in the System window includes the total amount of memory (RAM) available in the computer. The computers shown in Figure 5-2 feature 1GB and 3GB of RAM, respectively. All that information jibes with what I paid for, so my dealer is off the hook.

✔ Not every System window displays information as complete as is shown in Figure 5-2. When Windows doesn't know, it may say something vague, as in "x86 Family."

✔ See Chapter 6 for more information on computer memory.

Your Computer Is Also a Timepiece

All PCs come equipped with internal clocks. Don't look for a dial, and don't bother leaning into the console to hear the thing going "tick-tock." Trust me: The clock exists. Specifically, clock circuitry exists somewhere on the motherboard.

The amazing thing is that the PC keeps track of the time even when you unplug it. That's because the motherboard sports a teensy battery (refer to Figure 5-1). That battery helps the computer hardware keep track of the date and time all the time.

✔ Computers, like humans, need clocks to keep track of time. Computers use clocks for scheduling, to timestamp information and events and generally to prevent everything from happening all at once.

✔ Here's a secret: Computers make lousy clocks. A typical PC loses about a minute or two of time every day. Why? Who knows! Fortunately, the clock is set automatically when your computer is connected to the Internet. See the later section "Using the Internet to set the clock."

✔ On the positive side, the computer's clock is well aware of daylight savings time: Windows automatically jumps the clock forward or backward, and does so without having to know the little ditty "Spring forward, fall back." Or is it the other way around? Whatever — the computer knows and obeys.

Viewing the date and time

Windows reads the PC's hardware clock and displays a software clock for you. In Windows 8, you can see the date and time displayed on the lock screen or when the charms bar (right side of the screen) appears. Otherwise, the date-and-time display shows up in the notification area on the desktop, usually in the lower-right corner of the screen. To see a pop-up clock and calendar, click that time display once.

Setting the clock

The PC's clock is most likely set automatically, unless your computer isn't on speaking terms with the Internet. In that instance, you can set the date and time on your computer by obeying these steps:

1. **Right-click the time display in the notification area on the taskbar.**

   If you don't see the desktop, press the Win+D keyboard shortcut.

2. **From the pop-up menu, choose the command Adjust Date/Time.**

   The Date and Time dialog box appears.

3. **Click the Change Date and Time button.**

   The Date and Time Settings dialog box appears.

4. **Manipulate the controls in the Date and Time Properties dialog box to change or set the date or time.**

5. **Click OK when you're done.**

6. **Before you leave, click the Change time Zone button to ensure that your proper time zone is selected. Click OK when you're done.**

7. **Close the Date and Time dialog box.**

You can also have the computer automatically set time by using something called a *time server* on the Internet. That's covered later in this — oh! Why, it's covered next.

Using the Internet to set the clock

One way to tame the wild computer clock is to have the computer itself automatically synchronize the time with one of the many worldwide time servers. A *time server* is a computer designed to cough up accurate time information for any computer that checks in on the Internet.

Your PC should be configured to automatically set itself to Internet time. To confirm that option, or to set up Internet time, follow these steps:

1. **Right-click the mouse on the date-and-time display in the taskbar's notification area.**

   Use the Win+D keyboard shortcut to visit the desktop and access the taskbar.

2. **Choose the command Adjust Date/Time from the pop-up menu.**

   The Date and Time dialog box shows up.

3. **Click the Internet Time tab in the Date and Time Properties dialog box.**

   If you see the text telling you that the computer is set to automatically synchronize on a scheduled basis, you're set. Skip to Step 7.

4. **Click the Change Settings button.**

   The Internet Time Settings dialog box appears.

5. **Click to place a check mark by the option Synchronize with an Internet Time Server.**

6. **Click the Update Now button to ensure that everything works.**

   When a problem occurs, choose another time server from the Server drop-down list and try again.

7. **Click OK to close the Internet Time Settings dialog box.**

8. **Click OK to close the Date and Time dialog box.**

On Internet time, Windows automatically adjusts the PC's clock whenever you're connected to the Internet. There's nothing else you need to do — ever!

About the PC's Battery

Your PC has an internal battery, which is found clinging to the motherboard. The battery's primary purpose is to help the PC's internal clock keep time even when the computer is turned off or unplugged.

A typical PC battery lasts for about six years, possibly more. You'll know when it dies because the computer's date and time go screwy, or perhaps the PC even has a message telling you that the motherboard's battery needs replacing. You can get a replacement at any Radio Shack.

✔ Yes, you have to open the console's case to get at the battery. Don't expect it to be easy to find, either!

✔ The motherboard's battery is in addition to any other batteries in the computer, such as the main battery used to power a laptop.

The Chipset

Rather than refer to the galaxy of computer chips on the PC's motherboard as The Galaxy of Chips on the PC's Motherboard, computer scientists have devised a single descriptive term. All those chips constitute the chipset.

The *chipset* is what makes up your computer's personality. It contains instructions for operating the basic computer hardware: keyboard, mouse, networking interface, sound, video, and whatever else I can't think of right now.

Different chipsets are available depending on which types of features the computer offers. For example, some motherboards come with advanced graphics in the chipset or maybe wireless networking. The chipset isn't anything you can change, though it was probably referred to in that raft of technical information you didn't read when you first bought the PC.

- Different PCs use different chipsets, depending on which company manufactured the motherboard.

- An older term for the chipset, particularly the main ROM chip in a PC, is *BIOS,* which stands for Basic Input/Output System. There's a BIOS for the keyboard and mouse, one for the video system, one for the network, and so on. Altogether, they make up the *chipset.*

The Source of PC Power

Of all the goodies deep inside the console, one stands out as the least intelligent. That would be the PC's power supply. Although it may not be smart or fast, it is a necessary piece of equipment. The power supply does the following wonderful things for Mr. Computer:

- Brings in electricity from the wall socket and converts the electricity from wild AC current into mild DC current

- Provides electricity to the motherboard and everything living on it

- Provides juice to the internal mechanical disk drives

- Contains fans that help cool the inside of the console

- Contains or is directly connected to the PC's power button

The power supply is also designed to take the brunt of the damage if your computer ever suffers from electrical peril, such as a lightning strike or power surge. In those instances, the power supply is designed to die, sacrificing itself for the good of your PC. *Don't panic!* You can easily have the power supply replaced, at which point you might discover that the rest of your computer is still working fine.

- Thanks to the fan, the power supply is the noisiest part of any PC.

- Power supplies are rated in *watts.* The more internal hardware stuff your PC has — the more disk drives, memory, and expansion cards, for example — the greater the number of watts the power supply should provide. The typical PC has a power supply rated at 150 or 200 watts. More powerful systems may require a power supply upward of 750 watts.

- One way to keep your power supply — and your computer — from potentially going poof! (even in a lightning strike) is to invest in a surge protector, or UPS. Refer to Chapter 3 for details.

Chapter 6

PC Memory

In This Chapter

▶ Understanding memory

▶ Using chips and dips (and DIMMs)

▶ Measuring memory quantity

▶ Discovering how much memory is in your PC

▶ Adding memory to your computer

▶ Understanding virtual memory

▶ Observing weird memory terms

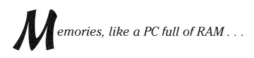

*M*emories, like a PC full of RAM . . .

With plenty of memory installed in the console, your PC has ample elbow room to handle a variety of tasks easily and swiftly. When the computer lacks enough memory, things get cramped worse than a tour bus overflowing with sweaty-drunk PhDs returning from a binger at an all-you-can-eat kimchi bar. But I digress. When it comes to PC memory, more is better.

What Is Computer Memory?

If your computer were a sport, memory would be the field on which competition would take place. Memory is where the action is.

Your computer needs memory because the processor has no storage. Well, it has *some* storage, but not a lot. Basically, the processor works like an old-fashioned calculator but without the paper tape. Computer memory acts like that paper tape to help the processor store information and work on data.

Computer memory is often referred to as *temporary* storage. That's because the memory chips require electricity to maintain their information. So, when you're done creating something in memory, you must *save* that information to long-term storage in the PC's mass storage system. But for working on things, creating stuff, and engaging in general computer activity, memory is where it's at.

- ✔ All computers need memory.

- ✔ Memory is where the processor does its work.

- ✔ The more memory in your PC, the better. With more computer memory on hand, you can work on larger documents, work graphics programs without interminable delays, play games faster, edit video, and boast about having all that memory to your friends.

- ✔ The term *RAM* is used interchangeably with the word *memory*. They're the same thing.

- ✔ RAM stands for *random access memory,* in case you have been working any crossword puzzles lately.

- ✔ Incidentally, more acronyms exist for computer memory types than I care to mention.

- ✔ Turning off the power makes the *contents* of memory go bye-bye. The memory chips themselves aren't destroyed, but without electricity to maintain their contents, the information stored on the chips is lost.

- ✔ Computer memory is *fast*. The processor can scan millions of bytes of memory — the equivalent of Shakespeare's entire folio — in fractions of a second, which is far less time than it took you to trudge through *Hamlet* in the 11th grade.

- ✔ The PC's mass storage system is for long-term storage. See Chapter 7.

- ✔ Memory is reusable. After creating something and saving it, the computer allows that memory to be used again for something else.

- ✔ Yes, Mr. Smartypants, some types of computer memory do not require electricity to maintain information. The problem is that this type of memory isn't fast enough. Only fast RAM, which requires electricity, is best used as temporary storage in your PC.

Tasty Chocolate Memory Chips

Physically, memory dwells on the PC's motherboard, sitting very close to the processor for fast access and ready dispatch. The memory itself resides on a tiny memory expansion card, or *DIMM*. On the DIMM, you find the actual memory chips.

DIMM stands for dual inline memory module, and it's pronounced *jaga-da-wawa*.

TECHNICAL STUFF

Boring details on RAM, ROM, and flash memory

RAM, or *random access memory,* refers to memory that the processor can read from and write to. When you create something in memory, it's created in RAM. RAM is memory and vice versa.

ROM stands for *read-only memory.* The processor can read from ROM, but it cannot write to it or modify it. ROM is permanent, like some members of Congress. ROM chips contain special instructions or other information that the computer uses — important stuff that never changes. For example, the chipset on the

motherboard is in ROM (refer to Chapter 5). The processor can access information stored on a ROM chip, but unlike with RAM, the processor cannot change that information.

Flash memory is a special type of memory that works like both RAM and ROM. Information can be written to flash memory, like RAM, but like ROM the information isn't erased when the power is turned off. Sadly, flash memory isn't as fast as RAM, so don't expect it to replace standard computer memory anytime soon.

No, I'm kidding. It's pronounced "dim."

A typical DIMM is illustrated in Figure 6-1, although in real life you'll find chips on both sides. That's why it's a DIMM and not a SIMM, or single inline memory module.

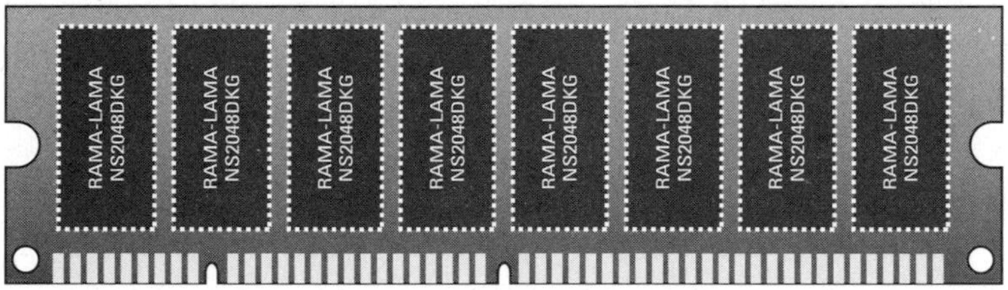

Figure 6-1: A semisweet DIMM.

Each DIMM contains a given chunk of RAM, measured in megabytes or giga-bytes using one of the magical memory quantities of 1, 2, 4, 8, 16, 32, 64, 128, 256, or 512. See the later section "Memory One Byte at a Time" for informa-tion on megabytes and gigabytes. The later sidebar "The holy numbers of computing" features scintillating information on why the memory quantities are measured in powers of two.

A DIMM is plugged into a slot on the motherboard, where it forms a *bank* of memory. So, a PC with 2GB of RAM may have four banks of 512MB DIMMs installed or two banks of 1GB DIMMs. That's all trivial, however. The only time you need to give a rip is when you want to upgrade memory. I'll write more about that task later in the chapter.

- The most common type of memory chip installed in a PC is the DRAM, which stands for *dynamic random access memory*. It's pronounced "dee-ram."
- It's gigabyte, not giggle-byte.
- Other types of memory chips exist, each with a name similar to DRAM, such as EDORAM or BATTERINGRAM or DODGERAM. And then there's DDR2 and GDDR2 and WRAM and RAMA LAMA DING DONG. Most of these are merely marketing terms, designed to make one type of memory sound spiffier than another.

Memory One Byte at a Time

Computer memory is measured by the byte. So what is a byte?

A *byte* is a very tiny storage unit, like a small box. Into that box fits a single character. For example, the word *cerumen* is seven letters (characters) long so it requires seven bytes of storage. That's seven bytes of computer memory, which isn't a lot these days, thanks to inflation.

Individual bytes aren't very useful. It's only when you have lots of bytes that you can store interesting and wonderful things.

Back in the 1970s, having a few thousand bytes of computer storage was *really something!* The Apollo lunar module computer had 2,048 bytes of memory. Today's PCs demand *millions* of bytes just to run the operating system. That works because today's PCs typically have *billions* of bytes of storage available.

Because the words *million* and *billion* represent values too large for the human mind to comprehend, and to keep things lively, computer scientists use special terms to reference large quantities of computer storage. That jargon is shown in Table 6-1.

Table 6-1		Memory Quantities	
Term	*Abbreviation*	*About*	*Actual*
Byte		1 byte	1 byte
Kilobyte	K or KB	1 thousand bytes	1,024 bytes
Megabyte	M or MB	1 million bytes	1,048,576 bytes
Gigabyte	G or GB	1 billion bytes	1,073,741,824 bytes
Terabyte	T or TB	1 trillion bytes	1,099,511,627,776 bytes

The holy numbers of computing

Computer memory comes in given sizes. You see the same numbers over and over:

1, 2, 4, 8, 16, 32, 64, 128, 256, 512, 1024, 2048, 4096, and so on.

Each of these values represents a *power of two* — a scary mathematical concept that you can avoid while still enjoying a fruitful life. To quickly review: $2^0 = 1$, $2^1 = 2$, $2^2 = 4$, $2^3 = 8$, and up to $2^{10} = 1024$ and more, until you get a nosebleed.

These specific values happen because computers count by twos — 1s and 0s — the old binary counting base of song and legend. So, computer memory, which is a binary-like thing, is measured in those same powers of two. RAM chips come in quantities of 256MB or 512MB, for example, or maybe 2GB.

Note that, starting with 1024, the values take on a predictable pattern: 1024 bytes is really 1K; 1024K is really 1M, and 1024M is 1G. So, really, only the first 10 values, 1 through 512, are the magical ones.

Enough of that.

Although it's handy to say "kilobyte" rather than mouth out "1,024 bytes," it's difficult to visualize how much data that is. For comparison, think of a kilobyte (KB) as a page of text from a novel. That's about 1,000 characters.

One *megabyte* (MB) of information is required to store one minute of music in your computer, a medium-resolution photograph, or as much text information in a complete encyclopedia.

The *gigabyte* (GB) is a huge amount of storage — 1 billion bytes. You can store about 30 minutes of high-quality video in a gigabyte.

The *terabyte* (TB) is 1 trillion bytes, or enough RAM to dim the lights when you start the PC. Although I can think of no individual item that requires 1TB of storage, lots of 1GB items abound that fit happily into that 1TB of storage, which is why the term is needed.

A *trilobite* is an extinct arthropod that flourished in the oceans during the Paleozoic era. It has nothing to do with computer memory.

Other trivia:

- The term *giga* is Greek and means *giant*.
- The term *tera* is also Greek. It means *monster!*
- Your computer's long-term mass storage media is also measured in bytes; see Chapter 7.
- A PC running Windows 8 requires at least 1GB of memory to work well. Having 2GB of memory is better.

✔ The PC's processor can access and manipulate trillions and trillions of bytes of memory. Even so, because of various hardware and software limitations, your computer can access only a given amount of RAM. The exact value depends on the motherboard design as well as on the version of Windows.

Memory Q&A

It doesn't matter where I am — greeting people at church, gesturing to my fellow drivers on the freeway, or leaving detox — folks still stop and ask me questions about computer memory. Over the years, I've collected the questions and have distilled the answers in this section. They should help clear up any random access thoughts you may have about computer memory.

"How much memory is in my PC right now?"

You may not know how much RAM resides in your PC's carcass, but the computer knows! Summon the System window to find out: Press Win+Break on the computer keyboard to summon the System window.

The amount of memory (RAM) appears right below the type of processor that lives in your PC. Looking at the value is about all you can do in the System window, so close that window when you've had enough.

"Do I have enough memory?"

If you have to keep on asking this question, the answer is no.

"Does my PC have enough memory?"

Knowing how much memory is in your PC is one thing, but knowing whether that amount is sufficient enough is entirely different.

The amount of memory your PC needs depends on two things. The first, and most important, is the memory requirement of the computer's software. Some programs, such as video-editing programs, require lots of memory. Just check the software's box to see how much memory is needed. For example, the Adobe Premier Pro video-editing program demands 2GB of RAM to run properly.

✔ Generally speaking, all PCs should have at least 1GB of RAM, which is what you need, at minimum, to run Windows.

✔ Here's one sure sign that your PC needs more memory: It slows to a crawl, especially during memory-intensive operations, such as working with graphics.

✔ Not enough memory? You can upgrade! See the upcoming section "Can I add memory to my PC?"

"Can I test whether my PC has enough memory?"

Your computer is designed to function even when it lacks a sufficient amount of memory. To test whether your PC has enough memory installed, make the computer *very* busy, by loading and running several programs simultaneously. I'm talking about *big* programs, such as Photoshop or Word or Excel. While all those programs are running, switch between them by pressing the Alt+Esc key combination.

If you can easily switch between several running programs by using Alt+Esc, your PC most likely has plenty of memory. But if you press Alt+Esc and the system slows down, you hear the hard drives rumbling, and it takes a bit of time for the next program's window to appear, your PC could use more memory.

Close any programs you have opened.

"Can I add memory to my PC?"

You bet! The best thing you can do for your PC is to add memory. It's like putting garlic in a salad. *Bam!* More memory provides an instant boost to the system.

Adding memory to your computer is LEGO-block simple. Well, expensive and scary LEGO-block simple. Knowing how much memory and which type to buy is the tough part. Because of that, I highly recommend that you have a dealer or computer expert do the work for you.

If you opt to perform your own PC memory upgrade, I can recommend Crucial at www.crucial.com. The website uses special software to determine which type of memory you need and how much. You can then buy the memory directly from the site.

"Will the computer ever run out of memory?"

Nope. Unlike the hard drive, which can fill up just like a closet full of shoes and hats, your PC's memory can never truly get full. At one time, back in the dark ages of computing, the "memory full" error was common. That doesn't happen now, thanks to something called virtual memory.

"What is virtual memory?"

Virtual memory is a fake-out. It lets the computer pretend that it has much more memory than it has physical RAM. It does that by swapping out vast swaths of memory to mass storage (the hard drive). Because Windows manages both memory and mass storage, it can keep track of things quite well, by swapping chunks of data back and forth. *Et, voila!* — you never see an "out of memory" error.

Alas, there's trouble in paradise. One problem with virtual memory is that the swapping action slows things down. Although the swapping can happen quickly and often without your noticing, when memory gets tight, virtual memory takes over and things start moving more slowly.

- ✔ The solution to avoiding the use of virtual memory is to pack your PC with as much RAM as it can hold.

- ✔ Windows never says that it's "out of memory." No, you just notice that the hard drive is churning frequently as the memory is swapped into and out of mass storage. Oh, and things tend to slow down dramatically.

- ✔ You have no reason to mess with the virtual memory settings in your computer. Windows does an excellent job of managing them for you.

"What is video memory?"

Memory used by your PC's video system is known as *video memory*. Specifically, memory chips live on the display adapter expansion card. Those memory chips are used for the computer's video output and help you see higher resolutions, more colors, 3D graphics, bigger and uglier aliens, and girlie pictures that your husband downloads from the Internet late at night but says that he doesn't.

As with regular computer memory, you can upgrade video memory if your PC's display adapter has room. See Chapter 8 for more information on display adapters.

"What about shared video memory?"

Shared video memory is used on some computers to save money. What happens is that the PC lacks true video memory and instead borrows some main memory for use in displaying graphics. This strategy is fine for simple home computers but not nearly good enough to play cutting-edge games or to use photo-editing software.

Chapter 7

Mass Storage

· ·

In This Chapter

▶ Understanding mass storage

▶ Recognizing the main storage device

▶ Working with removable storage

▶ Inserting and removing media

▶ Exploring external storage

▶ Using storage media in Windows

· ·

*O*utside of the computer realm, *mass storage* might refer to a file cabinet in Father Darby's office. Or it could be something related to Einstein's Theory of Relativity. Maybe it explains what's happening to my body's mid-section? Those are all good speculations, but within the computer realm, *mass storage* means something entirely different, something it takes an entire chapter to explain.

What Is Mass Storage?

All computer storage can be classified in two ways: temporary and long-term. The work gets done in temporary storage. That's computer memory, or RAM. The work is saved in long-term storage. That's mass storage.

Mass storage is permanent storage. It's required for keeping information for the long term, like you're supposed to keep your tax records but don't because, well, what the government doesn't know . . .

But mass storage is more than just a shoebox at the bottom of a closet. On your PC, mass storage is where the operating system is located, where all your PC programs are kept, and where you keep the stuff you create and save.

✔ All PCs require mass storage.

✔ Any time you use the Save command, you're putting information into mass storage. That information is transferred from computer memory (RAM) to long-term storage.

✔ When you use the Open command, you're taking information out of long-term storage and copying it to computer memory. That's because information can only be examined, used, changed, or created in computer memory.

✔ The computer's operating system, Windows, is in charge of managing both memory and mass storage.

✔ See Chapter 6 for information on computer memory, or temporary storage.

Surveying the storage media landscape

In the olden days, mass storage was referred to as the computer's "disk drives." Today, mass storage consists of more than just spinning disks, although the term *disk drive* is still used.

Mass storage can be classified into two types: nonremovable and removable. The nonremovable devices primarily dwell inside the PC console. They include:

Hard disk drive: The hard drive is the computer's traditional mass storage device.

Solid-state drive (SSD): An SSD is essentially a large-capacity media card, albeit one designed to serve as the computer's primary mass storage device. SSDs are fast but too expensive to be ubiquitous.

Pretty much every other type of mass storage available to a PC can be removed:

Optical drive: An optical drive is used to access optical discs, CDs, and DVDs.

Media card: The media card reader accesses memory cards. This is the same storage type used by digital cameras and other portable gizmos.

Thumb drive: Thumb drives are solid-state mass storage devices, with similar electronics to media cards but designed as removable computer storage.

Later sections in this chapter go into detail on these various forms of storage.

✔ Mass storage can be internal or external. Internal storage is mounted inside the console. External storage is attached to the console, typically by using a USB cable.

✔ Storage media capacity is measured in bytes. Refer to Chapter 6 for more information on bytes, megabytes, gigabytes, and other obnoxious terms.

Reviewing mass storage technical terms

The following terms may rear their ugly heads when dealing with mass storage. You have no sane reason to know this stuff, but here's the short list anyway:

Media: The media is where information is recorded. Media is the disk in a disk drive or the CD or DVD in an optical drive. For a media card, media is the card itself, though some humans may insist that it's the *flash memory* inside the media card. Nerds.

Drive: The drive mechanism reads the media. It spins the hard disk or optical disc so that information can be read from or written to the media. For a media card, the drive is the gizmo that accesses the information stored on the media card's flash memory chip.

Interface: The interface is a general term applied to both the hardware and software used to transfer information between the storage media and the rest of the computer.

The most important thing to remember is that the media isn't the drive; the drive reads the media. The confusion comes because some mass storage devices, such as the hard drive or a thumb drive, combine both drive and media.

✔ The current interface standard for internal mass storage (hard drives, optical drives, and SSDs) is *SATA*, which stands for Serial Advanced Technology Attachment.

✔ Some internal storage, such as media card readers, uses USB as the interface.

✔ For external storage, the interface standards include USB, IEEE, and eSATA. See Chapter 10 for scintillating details.

Your PCs Primary Storage Media

Of all the storage media available to your PC, one has to be the head honcho, the big cheese, the A-number-one. The PC's primary storage media is where the operating system dwells, along with all the programs installed on the computer — and is also the media to which those programs prefer to save the stuff you create.

- ✔ Your PC's primary storage media is either the traditional hard drive or the newer SSD.

- ✔ The primary storage media cannot be removed from the computer. It's fixed, as in "nonremovable," not fixed as in "was broken but now it's not."

- ✔ The PC's primary storage media is known as *drive C* or *the C drive*. See the section "Permanent Storage ABCs," later in this chapter, for an explanation.

- ✔ The primary storage media is also known as the *boot disk*. That's the media from which the operating system is loaded when the computer first starts.

- ✔ The operating system could also be loaded from an optical disc, providing that such a disc is inserted into an optical drive when the PC first starts. A prompt appears on the screen, asking whether you want to start (boot) the computer from the CD/DVD. Press the Enter key to do so. Otherwise, the computer starts up as it normally would.

Understanding the Hard Drive

The traditional primary storage media on a PC is the hard drive, or hard disk drive. For decades, hard drives have offered computer users copious amounts of storage and fast access at a reasonable price.

Hard drives are measured by their capacity, and the standard computer unit of a *byte* is the yardstick. So much information can be stored on a hard drive that the bytes have to be counted by the billions, or gigabytes. A typical PC hard drive can store between 120GB and 500GB of information — or more.

- ✔ The hard drive is simply a storage device. It isn't *everything* inside the console.

- ✔ The primary hard drive dwells in the PC console. Most PCs also have a second hard drive, and some have external hard drives.

- ✔ See the later section "External Storage" for information on external hard drives.

Introducing the SSD

The big issue with hard drives is that they're mechanical. Because they spin, they can break. To fix that problem, the SSD, or solid-state drive, was developed.

The storage media on an SSD is similar to computer memory. It's like a giant media card that you can use as the primary mass storage device in your PC. Because the SSD is fully electronic, it's also very fast.

Beyond being fast, other advantages of an SSD are that it uses less power and is quite reliable. The primary disadvantage to the SSD is price; the typical SSD costs about six times more than a comparable hard drive. Also, hard drives still have a higher storage capacity than your run-of-the-mill SSD.

> ✔ Currently, having an SSD in a desktop PC is something of a novelty. SSDs are more commonly found on laptops, where their light weight and low power can be an advantage worthy of a higher price.

> ✔ As far as use is concerned, you use an SSD just as you would a hard drive. There's only one caveat:

> ✔ SSDs don't need defragmenting. Windows won't even let you try to defragment an SSD. However, if you could defragment an SSD, you might shorten the device's lifespan.

Removable Storage

If there were no such thing as removable mass storage on a PC, some hacker would invent it. Back in the early days, people seriously wanted to remove their PC's hard drives. That desire is similar to pulling the engine from one car just so you can stick it in another car. Silly, but people wanted it.

To sate those removable storage desires, the typical PC comes with a host of drives into which you can plug and unplug various forms of removable storage media. You can use that media to easily share your stuff with others, create safety copies, or just amaze your friends because you have a thumb drive that looks like SpongeBob SquarePants.

Exploring removable storage

Scientists have discovered three forms of removable PC storage:

✔ Optical drives, which use optical discs

✔ Media drives, which use memory cards

✔ Thumb drives, which use severed human digits

All about optical discs

An optical disc is circular plastic, about 5 inches in diameter, and coated with a Mylar film on which data is stored. All in all, it's ho-hum — so ho-hum that you can't readily tell the difference between CD and DVD optical discs by looking at them.

Other than its boring physical description, an optical disc can be rated by its capacity. As you would suspect, a DVD holds more information than a plain ol' CD. Here are some stats:

- ✔ DVD is an acronym for Digital Versatile Disc. Or it may be Digital Video Disc. Whatever.

- ✔ CD stands for Compact Disc.

- ✔ A typical CD holds as much as 640MB of data or 80 minutes of music.

- ✔ A DVD is capable of storing 4GB of information on one side of a disc, or 8GB on one side of a dual-layer (DL) disc.

- ✔ A Blu-ray disc can store as much as 25GB on a single side of the disc or 50GB on a dual-layer (DL) disc. Even so, Blu-ray discs are used mainly for videos.

- ✔ The British spelling of *disc* is used for historical reasons, most likely because it was part of some elaborate palindrome that has long since been forgotten.

I'm just kidding on that last item: Thumb drives are their own storage gizmos.

The PC's primary form of removable mass storage is its optical drive. The purpose of the optical drive is to let your PC access removable media in the form of optical discs, CDs, and DVDs. New software is often installed on your PC by using an optical disc.

I use the term *media card* to describe the various memory cards, sticks, and wafers commonly used with portable electronic devices. The cards themselves come in a variety of shapes and are referred to by a host of different names. Because the cards are used primarily by portable devices to store media (pictures, music, video), the generic term *media card* seems apt.

Thumb drives get their name because of the shape. They use the same type of flash memory storage as media cards, but a thumb drive is designed to plug directly into a computer's USB port.

- ✔ Removable media, such as optical discs, media cards, and thumb drives, are used for regular PC storage, to help transfer files between computers and portable electronic gizmos, for backups, or for a bunch of other interesting tasks.

- ✔ You can also use the PC's optical drive to create, or *burn,* your own optical discs. It's a big topic, so Chapter 19 is devoted to the subject.

- ✔ The typical PC has at least one optical drive installed.

- ✔ Optical drives are available that can read high-capacity Blu-ray discs, but they're not yet considered standard PC drives.

✓ If your PC lacks the capability to read media cards, you can add an
external media card reader by using a USB port. See Chapter 10.

Identifying removable storage drives

Although the media may be removable in removable storage, the drive that
reads the media is not. The drive is found lurking inside your PC console,
with its face popping out in front for easy access.

Figure 7-1 illustrates the typical optical drive interface. It may be readily
apparent on the front of the console or hidden behind a door or slide.

Recordable (rewritable) disc logo DVD logo Disc tray CD logo

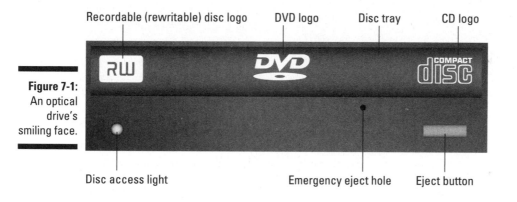

Figure 7-1:
An optical
drive's
smiling face.

Disc access light Emergency eject hole Eject button

The key elements of the drive are the disc tray, which slides out to accept a
disc, and the Eject button, which pops out the tray. Instead of a tray, some
drives may have a slot into which you jam the disc.

To use the media card type of removable storage, your PC must come
equipped with a *media card reader*. The most common reader is the 19-in-1,
which contains cubbyholes for all types of media cards, as shown in Figure 7-2.

SmartMedia or Secure Digital or
xD Picture Card MultiMediaCard

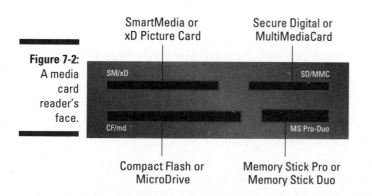

Figure 7-2:
A media
card
reader's
face.

Compact Flash or Memory Stick Pro or
MicroDrive Memory Stick Duo

Optical drive tattoos

In addition to its button, light, and tray, the optical drive might be adorned with various tattoos (refer to Figure 7-1). Rather than be an empty trend, each tattoo helps explain which types of disc the optical drive can read. Here's a list of the terms you might see:

DVD: The drive can read both CD and DVD discs. The logo is shown earlier, in Figure 7-1.

Disc: The drive can read CDs. Even when the Compact Disc logo (refer to Figure 7-1) doesn't appear on a DVD drive, that DVD drive can still read CDs.

Blu-ray Disc: The drive can read high-capacity Blu-ray discs as well as DVDs and CDs.

RW: The drive is capable of creating rewritable discs.

DL: The DVD drive can read dual-layer discs. The label *R DL* means that it can also create dual-layer discs.

R: A single *R* indicates a drive that can create optical discs. The R may be suffixed with a + or − or the ± thing, which means that you can create discs in the + or − (or both) formats.

RAM: The DVD drive can read or create the antique DVD-RAM disc format.

The typical media card reader contains four slots, which, surprisingly, let you access as many as 19 types of media cards — hence the 19-in-1 name. The reader is labeled, as shown in Figure 7-2, though you can pretty much figure out which card goes in which hole by its size.

The only other item of interest on both an optical drive and media card reader is the light that blinks when the drive is in use. Don't let the thing freak you out.

- ✔ The optical drive is represented by a single drive letter and icon in Windows. Similarly, each hole in the media card reader is represented by a drive letter. See the later section "Permanent Storage ABCs" for more info.

- ✔ If your PC lacks an internal media card reader, you can buy an über cheap external media card reader and easily attach it to your PC by using a USB port.

- ✔ Some PCs sport single-media drives, such as a single SD memory card slot. The slot is labeled according to which media card it eats.

- ✔ Optical drives feature a teensy hole (refer to Figure 7-1), which is used to eject a stubborn disc or to open the tray when the drive isn't functioning or is turned off. You simply jab a bent paper clip into the hole, press, and the tray pops open or the disc pushes itself out.

Inserting removable media

The term *removable* implies the ability to both remove and insert media. After all, once you get the media out, you'll probably want to put it back in again at some point in the future.

Once inserted, the removable media is accessed on your computer system just like any other mass storage. It's given a drive letter, and the files and whatnot on that media are made instantly available for use.

Stick an optical disc into an optical drive

Generally speaking, the disc is always inserted label side up. On an all-in-one PC, the disk is inserted vertically, with the label facing toward you. Aside from that, how you stick the disc into the drive depends on how the drive eats discs:

Tray: Press the drive's Eject button, which pops out the tray (often called a *drink holder* in computer humor). Drop the disc into the tray, label side up. Gently nudge the tray back into the computer. The tray slides back in the rest of the way on its own.

Slide in: Push the disc (label side up) into the slot. A gremlin inside the drive eventually grabs the disc and pulls it in all the way.

What happens after you insert the disc depends on the disc's content. You may see a prompt to install software, play a movie, or play or import music — or sometimes you don't see anything. In that case, to find out what to do next, you have to heed whatever directions came with the optical disc.

Some CDs and DVDs are shapes other than round. These discs work fine in the tray type of optical drive, but don't insert them into the slide-in type of drive.

Insert a media card or thumb drive

To use a media card, just jab it into the proper card slot on the media card reader. Media cards are inserted label side up.

Likewise, to add a thumb drive to your PC's storage system, plug the thumb drive into an available USB port. The drive plugs in only one way and odds are pretty good that your first attempt will be wrong, so just flip over the thumb drive and try it that way first.

Don't force a media card into a slot! If the media card doesn't fit into one slot, try another.

Ejecting removable media

You cannot just yank media — even removable media — out of a computer. Although nothing prevents you from being naughty and doing so, you run the risk of damaging the information stored on the media, not to mention having to endure a nasty warning message from Windows. That's the worst part.

Follow these steps to properly and politely remove media:

1. **Ensure that you're done using the media.**

   Be sure that none of your programs or windows are accessing information on the removable media — optical disc, media card, or thumb drive.

2. **Press the Win+E keyboard shortcut.**

   Win is the Windows key. After pressing Win+E, you'll see a Windows Explorer window, which displays the Computer or My Computer window. That window lists all your PC's mass storage devices, including removable media.

3. **Click to select the removable media's drive icon.**

   Just click once; you want to select the icon, not open it.

   It's not always obvious which icon in the Computer window represents a media card or thumb drive. Sometimes, you can tell because the name below the icon is something other than Removable Disk.

4. **Click the Eject button on the toolbar.**

5. **Remove or detach the media card or thumb drive.**

   Optical drives spit out the disc automatically.

Store the media in a safe location when you're not using it.

You may be tempted to eject an optical disc by punching the Eject button on the front of the drive. Don't ever punch a computer! If Windows is using the drive, you may see an ugly error message on the screen when you try to eject a disc this way.

External Storage

Your PC's mass storage isn't limited to what's available inside the console. Using the smarts of the USB port, you can expand your computer system externally. You can attach peripheral hard drives, optical drives, flash drives, or media card readers to your heart's (and wallet's) content. You can even use your PC to access storage on the Internet.

See Chapter 10 for specific information on using the USB port.

Adding external storage

To add another mass storage drive to your computer, simply plug it in. What can you add? An external hard drive, an optical drive, a media card reader — you name it. The device attaches to the console by using a USB cable. If the device also requires power, plug the thing into the wall — or better, into a UPS. (See Chapter 3.)

Assuming that the device has power, works, and is properly connected, Windows instantly recognizes it. The media is added to your computer system's mass storage inventory, showing up in the Computer window. You're ready to go.

✔ One of the most common and useful types of external storage to add is an external hard drive. You may not need the extra storage for your normal work, but it comes in handy for making a backup copy. See Chapter 18.

✔ For technical information on setting up a hard drive, including information on partitions and all that nonsense, refer to my book *Troubleshooting & Maintaining Your PC All-In-One For Dummies,* 2nd Edition (Wiley). Look for it in the Long Title section of your favorite book store.

✔ Although you can easily unplug any USB device from the PC at any time, I don't recommend doing so for external storage. For removing the media, follow the directions earlier in this chapter in the section "Ejecting removable media." But see Chapter 10 for specific directions on removing the storage device (drive) itself.

Exploring the cloud (Internet storage)

The Internet is brimming with opportunities to store your files, graphics, documents, music, porn, and whatever other digital information. You need just two things to make Internet storage happen: A fast, broadband Internet connection, and access to an Internet-based storage system.

The weird part about all this: The term *cloud* is used to refer to Internet storage. What does it mean? Is it a real cloud? Is there a humidity issue? I have no idea.

With Windows 8, Microsoft has introduced a cloud-based storage system called SkyDrive. Once you set it up, you can access the SkyDrive directly from certain Microsoft products, even from the Open or Save As screens. Otherwise, you can visit your Internet files on the web at `http://skydrive.live.com`.

Google's Internet storage solution is called Google Drive. Unlike SkyDrive, Google Drive maps right into your PC's storage system, appearing as a folder along with the rest of your digital stuff. Visit `http://drive.google.com` to get started with a Google Drive.

Another Internet storage system is Dropbox. Like Google Drive, Dropbox maps its Internet storage to a folder on your computer, which makes it easy to use. Visit `www.dropbox.com/home` for details.

✔ Files you copy to and from Internet storage are available to any other computer, mobile device, or digital psychic who has Internet access. That's the whole point of cloud storage; your stuff is available wherever you can access the Internet.

✔ One drawback to cloud storage is limited storage capacity. That can be addressed if you're willing to pay for more Internet storage.

✔ The Windows SkyDrive can also be accessed from the Start screen in Windows 8 by clicking or touching the SkyDrive tile.

✔ Both Google Drive and Dropbox are accessible through teensy-weensy icons on the desktop's notification area. Press Win+D to see the desktop in Windows 8.

✔ See Chapter 16 for more information on folders. When you copy files to an Internet folder on your PC, those files are synchronized with the cloud. They're available to you from any other computer with Internet access — well, providing you log in to the cloud to access your files.

Permanent Storage ABCs

Windows displays all the computer's permanent storage devices in one central location, a place called the Computer window, shown in Figure 7-3.

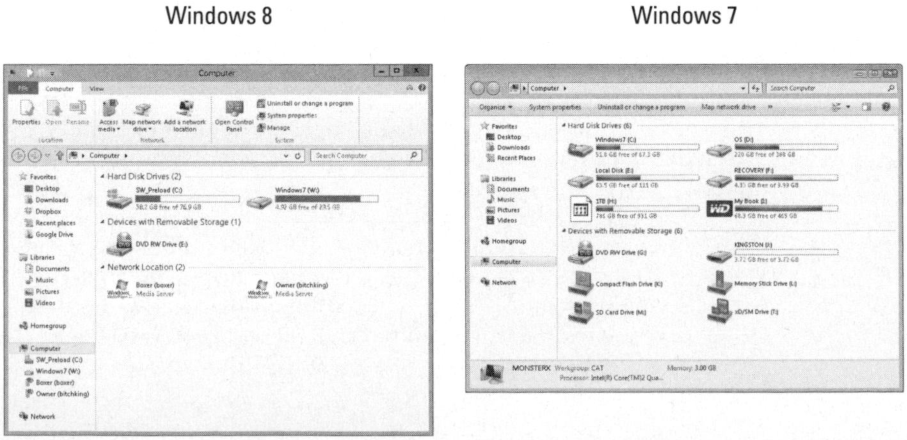

Windows 8   Windows 7

Figure 7-3: Assorted storage devices in the Computer window.

To see the Computer window, press the Win+E keyboard shortcut. You see the storage devices available to your computer, similar to what's shown in the figure.

In Figure 7-3, the storage devices are organized by categories. The categories are Hard Disk Drives, Devices with Removable Storage, and Network Location. To see the storage devices listed by drive letter, which is more useful, right-click in the window and choose the command Group By⇨(None). Then, to sort the storage devices alphabetically, right-click in the window and choose Sort By⇨Name.

> ✔ The Computer window can be accessed also by choosing the Computer command from the Start button menu. (That command is unavailable in Windows 8.)
>
> ✔ In Windows XP, the window is titled My Computer. Yeah, Windows XP was going through the "terrible twos."
>
> ✔ Mass storage available on a computer network might also appear in the Computer window. See Part IV for more information on networking.

Identifying mass storage devices

To keep your mass storage devices honest, the computer requires three forms of ID: an icon, a name, and a drive letter.

Unique icons are used to represent the various types of mass storage devices. You'll see icons for a hard drive, an optical drive, and various removable drives. The primary mass storage device, the one from which the operating system is stored, is shown with a Windows flag on its icon.

The storage device's name can help identify the storage media, though the name isn't used much in Windows. I've seen primary mass storage (hard drives) named Windows 7, which is helpful, but not every computer names the primary mass storage drive that way.

The most important aspect of the storage device's descriptions is the drive letter, covered in the following section.

Assigning drive letters

Mass storage devices in Windows are referred to by letters of the alphabet, from A to Z. I assume in Russian, the drive letters go from A to Я, and in Greek the range is most likely A to Ω. Knowing the drive letter is how you access the media and the information stored there.

Although each PC's mass storage setup is different, Windows follows a set of rules regarding how the drive letters are assigned. Here's the skinny:

Drive A: On a PC, drive A is the first floppy disk drive, which is how the first IBM PC was configured. Because floppy drives are no longer used, drive letter A is no longer used — unless you attach an external floppy drive to your PC.

Drive B: The letter *B* is reserved for the PC's second floppy drive, whether it has one or not. Few did, even back in the early days.

Drive C: The letter *C* represents the PC's primary storage media, typically the first hard drive. That media is the drive where Windows dwells, though that's not a hard-and-fast rule.

After letter *C,* the storage media in a PC receive drive letter assignments based on media type and whether the storage is internal or external. Here are the rules:

✔ Any additional internal storage is assigned the next letter of the alphabet after *C.* So, if you have a second internal hard drive, it becomes drive D. (Most PCs use drive D as their recovery drive.) A third internal hard drive would be drive E.

✔ The internal optical drive is given the next drive letter after the last internal hard drive has been given a letter. Any additional internal optical drives are given the next letter (or letters) of the alphabet.

✔ After the optical drive, any internal media card readers are given the next few drive letters.

✔ After all internal storage has been assigned letters, Windows begins assigning letters to external storage devices in the order in which they're found when the PC was first turned on or when the drives were attached. Each new storage device is given the next letter in the alphabet.

Not every PC will have the same drive letter assignments. For example, on your PC, drive D may be the optical drive, but that doesn't mean that drive D on *all* PCs is the optical drive.

Make a note of your PC's disk drive assignments on the printable cheat sheet available for download at www.dummies.com/cheatsheet/pcs.

Chapter 8

Merry Monitor Mayhem

In This Chapter

▶ Learning about the monitor

▶ Understanding the display adapter

▶ Adjusting the monitor

▶ Adding a second monitor

▶ Adjusting the resolution

▶ Using a screen saver

Contrary to what Hollywood may have led you to believe, text makes no noise when it appears on a computer screen. Text also appears rather quickly, not one letter at a time. If you really want a noisy computer, you need to return to the deafening days of the teletype, which served as the main input and output gizmo for the ancient, steam-powered mainframe computers of the 1960s. Things today are much better, and quieter.

The computer's main output gizmo is the monitor. The thing that drives the monitor is the PC's video system, which is rather spritely, full of color, and far quieter than an old teletype. It also wastes a lot less paper. This chapter covers the computer monitor, as well as the electronics and software that control the monitor.

The PC's Graphics System

Those folks who use their computers while hunched over the keyboard typing rarely appreciate the beauty and elegance of the PC's graphics system. That's sad because the computer's monitor is the thing most people stare at while using a computer. Sure, it loves the attention, but the monitor is only the visible half of the computer's video system. Inside the PC console dwells the other half, a sophisticated bit of electronics called the *display adapter*.

That's correct: The monitor is the dumb part. All it does is display information.

The display adapter is the heart of the PC's display system. It tells the monitor what to display and where, plus how many colors to use and the overall resolution of the image. The display adapter determines your PC's graphics potential.

Understanding PC graphics

Figure 8-1 illustrates the PC graphics system, showing both the monitor and the display adapter. The monitor and the display adapter are two separate things — even on an all-in-one PC.

The display adapter circuitry usually lives on an expansion card, which is plugged into the console's motherboard. It's not free-floating in space, as shown in the figure. It could also be part of the motherboard. A cable connects that circuitry to the monitor, as illustrated in the figure. The cable can also be internal, which is the case with an all-in-one PC.

Two additional cables might be found on the typical PC monitor. First, every monitor requires a cable that plugs into a power socket. Second, touchscreen monitors feature a USB cable. That connection is required for the PC to interpret how you smear, smudge, and poke at the screen with your fingers.

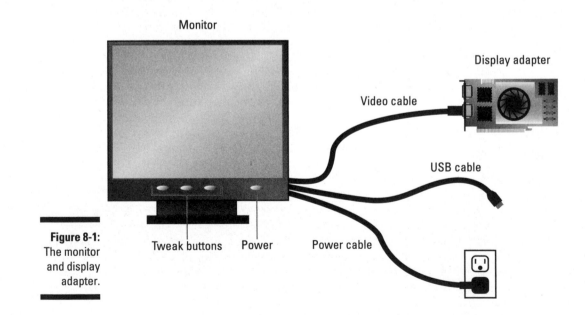

Monitor

Display adapter

Video cable

USB cable

Figure 8-1: The monitor and display adapter.

Tweak buttons   Power   Power cable

Not shown in Figure 8-1 is the software that drives the video hardware. The software is part of Windows, which tells the display adapter what kind of graphical goodness to toss up on the monitor. As a human, you use that software (from Windows) to control various aspects of the display, as covered elsewhere in this chapter.

✔ The display adapter is also known as a *video card*.

✔ The term *integrated video* is often used to describe a display adapter that's part of the motherboard, not a separate expansion card.

✔ You can have more than one monitor attached to your PC. See the section "Adding a second monitor," later in this chapter.

✔ The video system is the computer's standard output device.

Minding the monitor

The most common type of PC monitor is the LCD monitor, where LCD stands for *liquid crystal display,* not a hallucinogenic.

LCD monitors are flat. They're also thin, and they don't use much power, which keeps the bearded, sandal-wearing Seattle crowd happy.

A special type of LCD monitor is the touchscreen. It works like any other monitor, but it also has the capability to read locations where you physically touch the screen. A monitor that accepts more than a single touch at a time is a *multitouch* monitor.

✔ Windows 8 is the first major release of Windows to take direct advantage of multitouch monitors. Even so, you can still use Windows 8 on a normal LCD monitor, though you'll be bored.

✔ Before LCD monitors took over the world, computers used bulky, hot, power-hogging, glass-faced *CRT* monitors. I don't think you can even buy a new CRT monitor these days.

✔ CRT stands for *cathode ray tube,* not *catheter* ray tube.

✔ It's popular, and often economical, to use an HDTV as your PC's monitor. In fact, many large-format LCD and plasma TVs feature a computer input, into which you can plug the console's monitor cable. Gamers love the big screens, but that might just be the Red Bull talking.

✔ You don't need to have the same brand of computer and monitor. You can mix and match. You can even keep your old PC's monitor for use with a new console — as long as the monitor is in good shape, why not?

Monitor-screen-display jargon

Where does text appear? Is it on the monitor? On the screen? What is the display? Sadly, several confusing terms are often used interchangeably to refer to the stuff the computer displays. Here's a handy lexicon for you:

✔ The *monitor* is the box.

✔ The *screen* is the part of the monitor on which information is displayed.

✔ The *display* is the information that appears on the screen.

These are the terms as I use them. Other folks, manuals, and web pages mix and match them to mean whatever. In this book, however, I pretend to use these terms consistently.

Discovering the display adapter

The smarter and most important half of the PC's display system is the graphics hardware itself, known as the *display adapter*. This circuitry runs the monitor and controls the image that the monitor displays.

Of all PC hardware, display adapters have the most interesting and confusing array of names, numbers, and designations. Ignore them. Instead, you should concentrate on two characteristics of all graphics adapters: the amount of graphics memory and the GPU, or graphics processing unit.

Graphics memory

PC graphics require special memory that's separate from the computer's main memory. This memory is known as *video RAM,* or *VRAM.* The more video memory, the more colors and high resolutions and fancier tricks the display adapter is capable of.

Display adapters can have from 0M (no memory) to 1024MB (1 gigabyte) and beyond. Even so, more video memory isn't necessarily better. The price is worthwhile only when applications — especially games and photo-editing software — demand more memory or can take advantage of the extra video memory. Otherwise, the 32MB to 512MB of video RAM in a typical PC is enough.

GPU

Display adapters feature their own processor, a second processor to the computer's main processor. The GPU is specially geared toward graphical operations. It allows the display adapter to handle all that ugly graphics math, which means that images appear with more pep and vigor than if the PC's main processor were burdened with the graphics task.

The variety of GPUs, names, numbers, and nonsense is seemingly endless. Ignore all that feldercarb. The software you use offers GPU recommendations on the side of the box, which is what you should go by when it comes to ensuring that your PC's display adapter is up to snuff.

✔ Touchscreen monitors don't use the display adapter to interpret touch input. The monitor's USB cable feeds that information directly to the console. (Refer to Figure 8-1.)

✔ The more memory the display adapter has, the higher the resolutions it can support and the more colors it can display at those higher resolutions.

✔ Some video adapters share memory with main memory, such as adapters listed with 0MB of video memory. For anyone interested in playing games or creating computer graphics, such as setup is a bad deal.

✔ You can always upgrade your PC's video adapter. In some cases, you can even add more memory directly to the adapter. Well, you can have someone else do it for you; you don't have to upgrade anything yourself.

✔ Refer to Chapter 10 for more information on expansion slots, which is how the display adapter attaches to the PC's motherboard.

✔ See Chapter 6 for more information on computer memory.

✔ Many display adapters are advertised as supporting 3D graphics or having a physics engine. Note that these features work only if your software supports them. If so, the side of the software box should say so.

Descriptive Display Data

Yes, the PC's monitor displays wonderful graphical stuff, but when you boil it down to the basics, it's merely a peripheral. Yeah, it's an important peripheral, a vital part of the basic computer system. But aside from looking at the monitor, you don't spend much time pressing its buttons or studying it intently. When you do, the information in this section proves handy.

Measuring a monitor

Monitors are judged primarily by their picture size, measured on a diagonal, just like a TV set. And just as TVs have undergone a widescreen revolution, so have computer monitors. Sizes for PC monitors were once rather small, but today you commonly see "cinema" monitors rated at 21-inches diagonal and higher.

Another descriptive characteristic of a monitor is its *aspect ratio,* or the relationship between the monitor's width to its height. Traditionally, computer monitors used the *Academy Standard* aspect ratio of 4:3. That's four units of width for three units of height.

Today's widescreen monitors sport aspect ratios hovering around 16:9; the screen is 16 units wide for every 9 units in height. Figure 8-2 illustrates how monitors are measured diagonally as well as compares the aspect ratios between the traditional monitor and the newer, widescreen monitors.

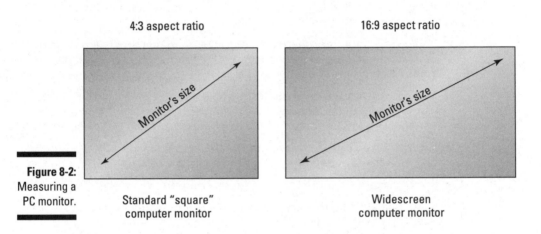

4:3 aspect ratio

16:9 aspect ratio

Monitor's size

Monitor's size

Figure 8-2:
Measuring a
PC monitor.

Standard "square"
computer monitor

Widescreen
computer monitor

If you have a touchscreen monitor, it's measured by the number of times you can simultaneously touch the screen. If the monitor can read multiple touches simultaneously, you have a multitouch monitor. If the monitor can read two separate touches, it's a two-point multitouch monitor.

- ✔ To get the most from Windows 8, you need a five-point multitouch monitor.

- ✔ Monitors also feature a swath of buttons that I hope are right on the front, where they're handy. If not, look for the buttons on the monitor's sides or bottom or even behind a door or panel on the front. The most important button is the power button, which is how you turn the monitor on and off.

- ✔ Other features that have found their way onto modern PC monitors include integrated stereo speakers and cameras. Generally, these devices are adequate but better options for speakers and PC video exist.

Connecting to the PC

Don't let Figure 8-1 fool you: More than one way exists for connecting a monitor to a PC. In fact, three common methods are known to computer scientists. Most monitors come with these separate connectors, to which you attach a specific cable that plugs into your PC's display adapter:

- ✔ **VGA:** The oldest of the video connectors, VGA uses a D-shaped connector with 15 holes. On many consoles, the connector is colored cyan or blue.

- ✔ **DVI:** The most common connector, a DVI connector is white, rectangular, and the best way to connect an LCD monitor to a display adapter.

- ✔ **HDMI:** This connector allows you to use a high-end HDTV as a monitor. It's the same connector used to attach other gizmos (Blu-ray players and video game consoles, for example) to big-screen TVs.

To make the connection, you choose the proper cable type, plug one end into the monitor, and plug the other end into the console.

For monitors that have only one cable type, you may need to use an adapter to attach the cable to the console. For example, you would use a DVI-to-VGA adapter if your console had only VGA input. Such adapters usually come with the monitor.

Reading monitor messages

Forget about the computer's messages; monitors are capable of displaying their own information. Sometimes that information is summoned forth to adjust the display, as covered in the next section. Other times, the text is informative, explaining that the monitor is turned on and ready but is not receiving a signal from the PC.

Various types of messages appear when the monitor is on but not receiving a signal. They range from the descriptive No Signal to the vague Power Save Mode. Other text messages with a similar connotation may pop up, including Where's my juice? and The printer is a jerk.

These messages are nothing to be alarmed about: The monitor pops to life properly when you turn on the console and the video signal is restored.

Adjusting the display

Tuning a computer monitor isn't the chore it once was. Today's LCD monitors are fairly stable and their display is consistent. Out of pity, however, manufacturers have made a few things available that you can tune and tweak, should the need arise. The only ordeal is working the silly onscreen display by manipulating various buttons on the monitor.

The first step to adjusting the display is figuring out which of the monitor's buttons summons the onscreen menu. If the button isn't obvious, just press any button and the menu may pop up.

After the menu is displayed, use the monitor's buttons to navigate the menu and change various settings. The buttons are labeled with various symbols and hieroglyphs: You may find four directional arrows, or only two arrows and then a + and – symbols. Because nobody will ever fully understand how the symbol buttons work, I'm curious as to why the manufacturers tried to label them at all.

The settings you can adjust depend on the monitor, but often include items such as brightness, contrast, color temperature, and volume (if the monitor features speakers). I wish I could be more specific, but I'd have to fill the entire chapter with details for each monitor because they're all so different.

When you're done messing with the display and adjusting the monitor, either choose an Exit menu item or just wait long enough and the onscreen display will vanish.

✔ The monitor's onscreen menu is displayed by the monitor itself, not Windows. You won't be able to use the computer's keyboard or mouse to work the menu.

✔ Monitor buttons are most often found on the bottom of the monitor below the screen, or on the monitor's edges. Look under the bottom edge or on the right edge.

Windows Controls What You See

Don't look now, but the thing controlling what you see on the computer's monitor isn't the monitor. It isn't even the display adapter. Nope, the thing in charge is software, and the software that controls what you see on the monitor is Windows itself. This section describes how to use Windows to control what you see on the screen.

✔ Additional control over your display may be available by using custom software that came with your PC's display adapter. For example, ATI adapters come with a special control center that you can access from the taskbar's notification area.

✔ The specific software that controls the display is something called the *video driver.* It is not a computer car simulator.

Adding a second monitor

Some versions of Windows allow you to enjoy a second monitor on your PC. As long as your computer's video hardware can support two monitors, you too can enjoy the dueling monitors feature. The trick is to see whether the console's derrière features two display ports. If so, you're in business.

After connecting the second monitor, you need to use Windows to configure the monitors. Obey these steps:

1. **Right-click the mouse on the desktop.**

   Right-click a blank part of the desktop, not any icon or window.

   In Windows 8, press the Win+D keyboard shortcut to see the desktop.

2. **Choose the Screen Resolution command from the pop-up menu.**

   In Windows Vista, you need to choose the Personalize command and then choose the Display Settings option.

   The Screen Resolution dialog box appears, similar to what's shown in Figure 8-3.

3. **If you don't see the second monitor displayed in the dialog box, click the Detect button.**

   If you still don't see the second monitor after clicking the Detect button, your computer system (hardware or software) isn't capable of using two monitors.

4. **From the menu button next to Multiple Displays, choose the option Extend These Displays.**

   In Windows Vista, put a check mark by the option Extend the Desktop onto This Monitor.

5. **(Optional) Configure the second display.**

   Instructions for setting resolution and colors are found elsewhere in this chapter.

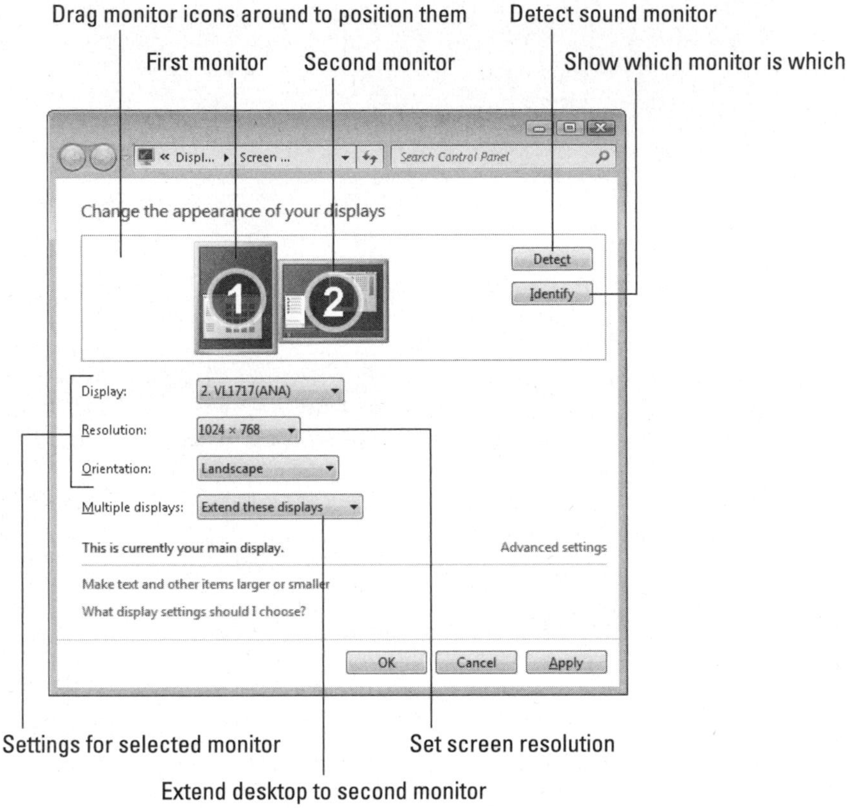

Drag monitor icons around to position them   Detect sound monitor

First monitor   Second monitor   Show which monitor is which

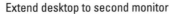

Figure 8-3:
Set screen
resolution
and dual
monitors
here.

Settings for selected monitor   Set screen resolution

Extend desktop to second monitor

6. **Use the mouse to adjust the two monitor preview icons so that they line up onscreen as they do in the real world.**

7. **Click OK.**

The two monitors share the desktop, but the taskbar stays on only the main monitor. Otherwise, you can use both monitors in Windows as if your PC had one, huge monitor.

✔ The versions of Windows that don't support the dual monitor features are the Home and other cheap releases.

✔ In Windows 7 and Windows Vista, icons stick to only the first monitor's desktop. If you place any icons on the second monitor's desktop, they hop back to the first monitor when you restart the PC.

✔ In Windows 8, the taskbar appears on both monitors. You can also access the hot corner shortcuts (for the Start screen, charms bar, and recent programs) from either monitor.

Setting display size (resolution)

The monitor's physical dimensions cannot change, but you can control the amount of stuff you see on the screen by adjusting the screen *resolution.* That's the number of dots, or *pixels,* the monitor displays, measuring horizontally by vertically.

To set the screen's resolution, follow these steps:

1. **Right-click the desktop and choose the Screen Resolution command from the pop-up menu.**

   In Windows Vista, right-click the desktop, choose Personalization, and then, from the Personalization window, choose Display Settings.

   The Screen Resolution dialog box appears (refer to Figure 8-3).

2. **Click the Resolution menu button.**

   If the button is unclickable, the monitor has a fixed resolution and cannot be changed. Reward yourself with a cookie.

3. **Use the slider gizmo to set the resolution.**

   As you adjust the slider, the preview monitor in the Screen Resolution dialog box adjusts the size to reflect how things will appear on the screen.

   The recommended resolution is the option that works best for your PC's combination of monitor and display adapter.

4. **Click the Resolution button again to lock in your choice.**

5. **Click the Apply button to try out the new resolution.**

6. **Click the OK or Keep Changes to accept the new resolution.**

The maximum resolution and color settings depend on the amount of video memory available to the display adapter. Resolution isn't based on the monitor's size.

- ✔ *Pixel* is a contraction of *picture element.* On a computer display, a *pixel* is a single dot of color.

- ✔ Some computer games automatically change the monitor's resolution to allow the games to be played. This change is okay, and the resolution should return to normal after you play the game.

Saving the screen

A *screen saver* is an image or animation that appears on the monitor after a given period of inactivity. After your computer sits there, lonely and feeling ignored, for 30 minutes or whatever, a pleasant image or animation appears on the monitor. It's jocular.

Screen savers actually have a serious history. When the old CRT (glass) monitors were popular, images could *burn* into the screen's phosphor, rendering the monitor less-than desirable. The screen saver would kick in to literally save the screen from the perils of phosphor burn-in. Today, they remain as an amusement, but also as a form of security.

To set up your computer to display a screen saver, obey these steps:

1. **Right-click the desktop and choose the Personalize command.**

2. **Choose the Screen Saver item in the Personalization window.**

   The Screen Saver Settings dialog box appears.

3. **Choose a screen saver from the Screen Saver area.**

   The screen saver is previewed in the tiny monitor window.

4. **Click the Settings button to adjust any options for the individual screen saver you chose.**

   The options vary, depending on the screen saver.

5. **Enter the number of minutes to wait before the screen saver kicks in.**

6. **For extra security, put a check mark by the option On Resume, Display Logon Screen.**

7. **Click the OK button, and then close the Personalization window as well.**

After you haven't touched the mouse or keyboard for the given length of time, the screen saver appears on your monitor. To dismiss the screen saver, and return to Windows, press a key on the keyboard or jiggle the computer mouse.

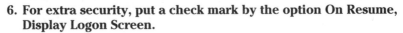

✔ To disable the screen saver, choose (None) from the screen saver menu button.

✔ Beware of downloading screen savers from the Internet. Although some are legitimate, most are invasive ads or programs that are impossible to uninstall or remove. If you download this type of screen saver, you're pretty much stuck with it. Be careful!

✔ You may never see the screen saver, especially if you're using the PC's power management system to put the monitor to sleep. See Chapter 13 for more information.

Chapter 9

Input This!

In This Chapter

▶ Understanding the keyboard

▶ Using specific keys

▶ Controlling the keyboard in Windows

▶ Getting to know the mouse

▶ Working with the mouse in Windows

▶ Changing mouse behavior

▶ Touching the screen

*O*ur history is blessed with famous duos, legendary teams who add spice to our life and depth to our culture. Think of bacon and eggs, death and taxes, Batman and Robin. Memorable things come in twos, and your computer is no exception. Its two input buddies are the keyboard and mouse. They may not taste good, they're not inevitable, and they don't dress up and fight crime. But they do help you provide important input to your PC.

Joining the duo is a third member, touch input. It's sort of like Batgirl to the dynamic duo; you may doubt the impact touch has on the input efforts of the keyboard and mouse, but it's a cute option that has its purpose.

Meet Mr. Keyboard

To understand the PC keyboard, you have to know its history. Without boring you too severely, the keyboard spawns from the shotgun marriage between the electric typewriter and the calculator. Or perhaps it was a teleporter accident? Regardless, you'll be spending a lot of time using the computer's primary input device, the keyboard.

Attaching a keyboard

The PC keyboard plugs into the console by using a USB port. Some older keyboards use the specific keyboard port on the console. Simple, but:

Do not attach a PC keyboard to the keyboard port unless the console is turned off! Attaching a keyboard to the keyboard port with the system on may damage the computer.USB keyboards, however, can be plugged in and unplugged at will.

✔ Wireless keyboards are available. Some use wireless receivers that attach to the USB or keyboard port. Others are Bluetooth keyboards. See Chapter 22 for information on Bluetooth.

✔ See Chapter 2 for the specifics of the keyboard and USB ports on the console.

✔ You'll need batteries to charge a wireless keyboard.

Examining the typical PC keyboard

There's no such thing as a typical PC keyboard. Each manufacturer likes to customize things a tad, plus special keyboards have *even more* buttons than standard keyboards. But if there were a typical PC keyboard, it would look like the model shown in Figure 9-1.

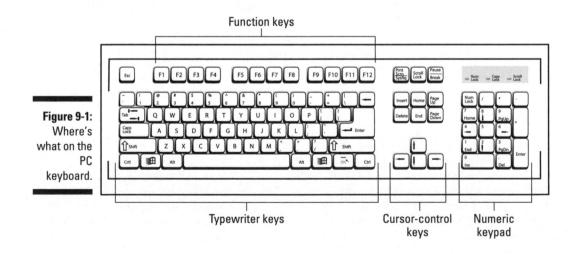

Figure 9-1: Where's what on the PC keyboard.

You can safely divide the typical PC keyboard into four areas, shown in Figure 9-1:

Function keys: These keys are positioned near the top of the keyboard. They're labeled F1, F2, F3, and so on, up to F11 and F12. They're also called *F-keys,* where F stands for *function,* not anything naughty.

Typewriter keys: These keys are the same types of keys you would find on an old typewriter — letters, numbers, and punctuation symbols. They're often called *alphanumeric* keys by humans too young to remember typewriters.

Cursor-control keys: Also called *arrow keys,* this clutch of keys is used primarily for text editing.

Numeric keypad: Borrowing a lot from a calculator, the numeric keyboard makes entering numbers quick and easy.

These four areas are common to all PC keyboards. Again, the keyboard you use may have more keys with custom functions. Such variations are mentioned elsewhere in this chapter.

✔ The *cursor* is the blinking goober on the screen that shows you where the characters you type appear. As though *cursor* isn't weird enough, the blinking doodad is also called an *insertion pointer.*

✔ See the section "Changing keyboard behavior keys," later in this chapter, for more information on how the numeric keypad can go all schizo.

✔ PC keyboards use the Enter key. Macintosh keyboards have a Return key.

✔ No "Any" key appears on the keyboard. When you're prompted to "Press any key" do what I do: Press the spacebar.

✔ If you're really old — and I mean ancient — you must remember that a computer keyboard has 1 and 0 keys. Don't type a lowercase *l* to represent the numeral 1 or a capital letter *O* for the numeral 0.

Using modifier keys

Four keys on the computer keyboard qualify as shift keys, though only one is named Shift. The other three are Ctrl, Alt, and Win. Rather than call them all *shift keys,* the term *modifier keys* seems more appropriate.

"Must I learn to type to use a computer?"

The short answer: No, you don't need to touch-type to use a computer. Plenty of computer users hunt and peck. In fact, most programmers don't know how to type, but that brings up an interesting story: A computer software developer once halted all development and had his programmers learn how to touch-type. It took two whole weeks, but afterward, they all got their work done much faster and had more time available to break away and play those all-important computer games.

As a bonus to owning a computer, you can have it teach you how to type. The Mavis Beacon Teaches Typing software package does just that. Other packages are available, but I personally enjoy saying the name Mavis Beacon.

A modifier key works in combination with other keys: You hold down a modifier key and then press another key on the keyboard. What happens then depends on the keys you press and how the program you're using reacts to the key combination.

You use the keys like this: Press and hold down the modifier key, and then tap the key it's modifying. Release the modifier key.

For example, to use the keyboard shortcut for the Save command, you press and hold down the Ctrl key and tap S; release both keys. That key combination is written as Ctrl+S. To close a window on the display, you hold down the Alt key and press the F4 key, written as Alt+F4.

- ✔ The Shift key is used to make capital letters or to access the punctuation and other symbols on the number keys and other keys. That's how you can create the %@#^ characters that come in handy for cursing in comic strips.
- ✔ Ctrl is pronounced "control." It's the *control* key.
- ✔ Alt is the *alternate* key.
- ✔ Win is the Windows key, adorned with the Windows logo.
- ✔ Most of the time, pressing a modifier key by itself does nothing. However, when pressed by itself, the Win key displays the Windows 8 Start screen or, in older versions of Windows, pops up the Start button menu. Pressing the Alt key by itself activates menu bar shortcuts in some programs.

- ✔ Keyboard shortcuts are written using capital letters. So even though you may see Ctrl+S or Alt+S with a capital *S*, for example, it doesn't mean that you must press Ctrl+Shift+S or Alt+Shift+S. The *S* is written in uppercase simply because Ctrl+s looks like a typesetting error.

✔ Multiple modifier keys are also used together, as in Shift+Ctrl+F6 and Ctrl+Shift+Alt+C. Just remember to press and hold down both modifier keys first and then tap the other key. Release all the keys together.

✔ Some technical manuals use the notation ^Y rather than Ctrl+Y. This term means the same thing: Hold down the Ctrl key, press Y, and release the Ctrl key. The ^ symbol is the traditional computer symbol for the Control key.

Changing keyboard behavior keys

Three keys on the PC keyboard change how certain parts of the keyboard behave. I call them the Lock keys. Behold:

Caps Lock: This key works like holding down the Shift key, but it works only with the letter keys. (Think *Caps* as in *capital* letters.) Press Caps Lock again, and the letters return to their normal, lowercase state.

Num Lock: Pressing this key makes the numeric keypad on the right side of the keyboard produce numbers. Press this key again, and you can use the numeric keypad for text editing; the numeric keypad is labeled with both numbers and arrow key symbols.

Scroll Lock: This key has no purpose. Well, some spreadsheets use it to reverse the function of the cursor keys (which move the spreadsheet rather than the cell highlight), but that doesn't count.

Strange keyboard abbreviations

The key caps are only so big, so some key names have to be scrunched down to fit. Here's your guide to some of the more oddly named keys and what they mean:

✔ Print Screen is also known as PrtSc, PrScr, or Print Scrn.

✔ Scr Lk is the Scroll Lock key.

✔ Page Up and Page Down are sometimes written as PgUp and PgDn on the numeric keypad.

✔ Insert and Delete may appear as Ins and Del on the numeric keypad.

✔ SysRq means System Request, and it has no purpose.

When a lock key is on, a corresponding light appears on the keyboard. The light may be on the keyboard or on the key itself. The light is your clue that a lock key's feature is turned on.

✔ Caps Lock affects only the keys A through Z; it doesn't affect any other keys.

✔ If you type This Text Looks Like A Ransom Note and it appears as tHIS tEXT lOOKS lIKE a rANSOM nOTE, the Caps Lock key is inadvertently turned on. Press it once and then try typing your stuff again.

✔ If you press the Shift key while Caps Lock is on, the letter keys return to normal. (Shift kind of cancels out Caps Lock.)

Touring the most useful keys

All keys are created equal, but some keys are more equal than others. I find the following to be the most useful keys on the keyboard.

 You'll find two Enter keys on the typical PC keyboard. They're duplicates. You press the Enter key to accept input, to end a paragraph in a word processor, to open a highlighted icon, or to "click" the OK button in a dialog box.

 The Escape key is labeled Esc, but it means Escape. Pressing the key doesn't immediately take you to some luscious tropical locale complete with refreshing beverage. Nope, pressing the Esc key is the same as clicking Cancel in a dialog box.

 Don't bother looking on the keyboard: It has no Help key. Instead, whenever you need help in Windows, whack the F1 key. F1 equals help. Commit that to memory.

 The Tab key is used in two ways on your computer, neither of which generates the diet cola beverage. In a word processor, the Tab key is used to indent paragraphs or line up text. In a dialog box, the Tab key moves focus between the various graphical gizmos.

✔ Use Tab rather than Enter when you're filling in a form. For example, press the Tab key to hop between the First Name and Last Name fields.

✔ The Tab key often has two arrows on it — one pointing to the left and the other to the right. These arrows may be in addition to the word *Tab*, or they may be on there by themselves to confuse you.

✔ The arrows on the Tab key go both ways because Shift+Tab is a valid key combination. For example, pressing Shift+Tab in a dialog box moves you "backward" through the options.

Understanding strange keys

Arguably, all keys on a computer keyboard are strange. I mean, how many times do you use the { and } characters when you type? Beyond the weirdo character keys, some keys may have you really scratching your head. Here's the list:

 The Break key shares a keycap with the Pause key. It's not used any more, which is good because it should have been spelled *Brake* in the first place.

 Some games may use the Pause key to temporarily suspend the action, but it's not a consistent thing. Many games now use the P key to pause.

 The backslash (\) leans to the left. Don't confuse it with the forward slash key, which leans to the right (/).

The Print Screen key, also named PrtSc, takes a snapshot of the Windows desktop, saving the image in the Windows Clipboard. You can then paste that image into any program that lets you paste a graphical image. The key has nothing to do with the computer printer. (Well, not anymore.)

The AltGr, or Alt Graph, key is used on non-U.S. keyboards to help non-English–speaking humans access characters specific to their non-English language.

Some international keyboards sport a euro currency symbol, often found sharing the 4 key with the dollar sign. That key will be a collector's item in a few years.

The System Request key shares its roost with the Print Screen key. It does nothing.

 This booger is the Context key. It resides between the right Windows and Ctrl keys. Pressing this key displays the shortcut menu for whatever item is selected on the screen — the same as right-clicking the mouse when something is selected. No one in recorded computer history has ever used this key.

Understanding keys for math

 No matter how hard you look, you won't find a × or ÷ key on the computer keyboard. That's because computer math doesn't involve multiplication or division.

Special keys on some keyboards

Any keys beyond the standard 104 keys (see Figure 9-1) on your PC's keyboard are probably custom keys, added by the keyboard manufacturer because they look cool or the manufacturer figured that you needed special functions such as volume control, play/pause, start e-mail, or what-have-you. The buttons can do anything because they're nonstandard.

When you have a nonstandard keyboard, you most likely also find a special program that came with your computer. That program controls the keyboard's special buttons, sometimes allowing their functions to be reassigned. Look for the special program in the Control Panel.

Just kidding. Computers take advantage of character symbols to carry out various mathematical operations. To help you remember the symbols, the keyboard designers clustered them on the numeric keypad, where most of the math stuff takes place anyway. Here's the list:

- ✔ + is for addition.
- ✔ – is for subtraction.
- ✔ * is for multiplication.
- ✔ / is for division.

You use the asterisk (*), not the lowercase *x,* for multiplication.

Controlling the keyboard in Windows

If you plan to write a lot of fast-paced theatrical drama on your computer, you'll probably write the word *Aaaaaaaaaaaaaaa* a lot. To do so, you press and hold the A key. After a delay, the A key repeats itself, spewing out the letter *A* like water from a fire hose. You can control both the delay and how fast the character repeats itself by using the Keyboard Properties dialog box in Windows, shown in Figure 9-2.

To open the Keyboard Properties dialog box, follow these steps:

1. **Open the Control Panel window.**

   See Chapter 14 if you need help finding the Control Panel window.

2. **On the View By menu, near the upper-right corner of the window, choose Large icons.**

3. **Click the Keyboard icon to display the Keyboard Properties dialog box.**

4. **Use the mouse to manipulate the sliders in the dialog box to set the rates, and then test out the rates in the text box that's provided.**

5. **Click the OK button only when you're happy.**

   You might want to change Control Panel view back to Category view before you close its window.

6. **Close the Control Panel window when you're done.**

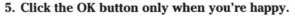

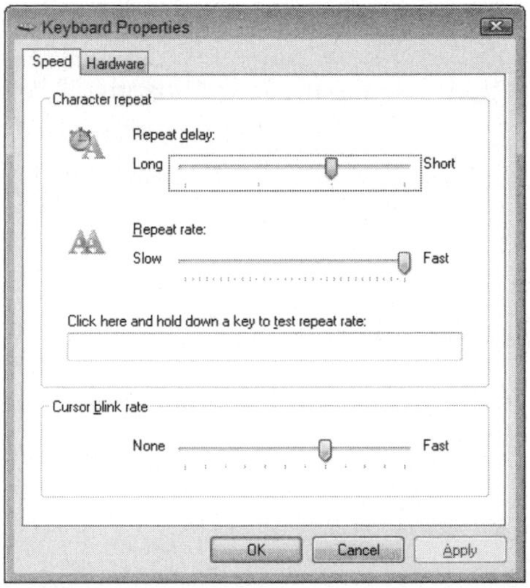

Figure 9-2:
Control the
keyboard
here.

Say "Eeek!" to the Mouse

Your computer's mouse is an *input* device. Although the keyboard (another input device) can do almost anything, you need a mouse to control the glorious graphical goodness of an operating system such as Windows.

Connecting the mouse

The computer mouse connects to the console by using a USB port. Some older mouse models may use the specific mouse port.

The mouse usually rests to the right of the keyboard, with its tail pointing back to the computer. The flat part of the mouse goes on the bottom.

You need space to roll the mouse around, usually a swath of desktop real estate about the size of this book. Or the size of a mouse pad, which is why mouse pads are popular.

✔ Wireless mice don't use cables to connect to the console. Instead, they use a base station or similar gizmo, typically attached to the console's USB or mouse port. A wireless Bluetooth mouse may not require a connector because it uses a Bluetooth receiver internal to the console.

✔ A wireless mouse requires power, which probably comes in the form of batteries. They must be replaced or recharged occasionally, or else the mouse doesn't work.

✔ You can also set the mouse on the left side of the keyboard if you're left-handed. See the section "Use the mouse left-handed," later in this chapter.

✔ See Chapter 2 for more information about where the mouse plugs into the PC console.

Reviewing basic mouse parts

A typical computer mouse is shown in Figure 9-3, where the basic and important mouse features are illustrated.

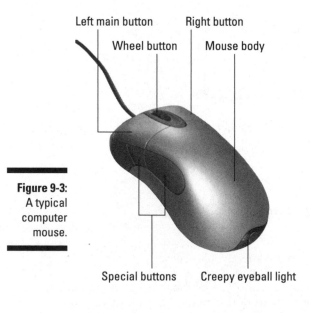

Left main button   Right button

   Wheel button   Mouse body

Figure 9-3:
A typical
computer
mouse.

Special buttons   Creepy eyeball light

Mouse body: The mouse is about the size of a bar of soap. You rest your palm on its body and use your fingers to manipulate the mouse buttons.

Left (main) button: The left button, which falls under your right hand's index finger, is the *main* button. That's the button you click the most.

Wheel button: The center, or wheel, button can be pressed like the left and right buttons, and it can be rolled back and forth. Some wheels can even be tilted from side to side.

Right button: The right button is used for special operations, although right-clicking mostly pops up a shortcut menu.

Special buttons: Some mice come with special buttons, which can be used for Internet navigation or assigned specific functions by using special software (see "Controlling the Mouse in Windows," later in this chapter).

On the mouse's belly, you find its method of motion detection, which is either a light or a laser. Older mice used a hard rubber rolly-ball. Those mechanical mice were more difficult to keep clean and required a mouse pad to get the best traction.

Exploring mouse species

The variety of computer mice seems endless. They have different styles and shapes, special buttons, and unique features designed to drive the mildest of nerds into a technogeek frenzy.

A popular mouse variation is the *trackball,* which is like an upside-down mouse. Rather than roll the mouse around, you use your thumb or index finger to roll a ball on top of the mouse. The whole contraption stays stationary, so it doesn't need nearly as much room and its cord never gets tangled. This type of mouse is preferred by graphical artists because it's often more precise than the traditional "soap-on-a-rope" mouse.

Another mouse mutation enjoyed by the artistic type is the *stylus* mouse, which looks like a pen and draws on a special pad or right on the screen. This mouse is also pressure sensitive, which is wonderful for use in painting and graphics applications.

Finally, those *cordless 3D* mice can be pointed at the computer screen like a TV remote. Those things give me the willies.

Moving the mouse

The computer's mouse controls a graphical mouse pointer on the screen, as shown in the margin. Roll the mouse around on your desktop, and the pointer on the screen moves in a similar manner. Roll the mouse left, and the pointer moves left; roll it in circles, and the pointer mimics that action. Tickle the mouse, the pointer laughs.

Moving the mouse and clicking the buttons — that's how the mouse works with the computer. Specific names are given to those actions. Here's a list:

Point: When you're told to "point the mouse," you move the mouse on the desktop, which moves the mouse pointer on the screen to point at something interesting (or not).

Click: A *click* is a press of the main (left) mouse button — press and release. It makes a clicking sound (if you lean in to the mouse closely enough).

Right-click: This action is the same as a click, but with the right mouse button.

Double-click: A double-click is two clicks of the mouse in a row without moving the mouse. The clicks don't need to be *really* fast, and you can adjust the click time, as covered later in this chapter in the "Fix double-click" section.

Drag: The drag operation is a multistep process. Point the mouse at the thing you want to drag, a graphical object or an icon. Press and hold down the mouse's button, and then move the mouse to move the object on the screen. Keep the mouse button down until you're finished moving the mouse. Release the mouse button to "drop" whatever you moved.

Right-drag: This action is the same as a drag, but the mouse's right button is used instead.

Ctrl+drag: This action is the same as a drag, though you also press the Ctrl key on the keyboard while you drag around a graphical doodad.

Shift+drag: This action is just like a Ctrl+drag, but the Shift key is used instead.

The best way to learn how to use a computer mouse is to play a computer card game, such as Solitaire or FreeCell (both of which come with Windows). You should have the mouse mastered in only a few frustrating hours.

Controlling the mouse in Windows

In Windows, the mouse is controlled, manipulated, and teased by using the Mouse Properties dialog box, which lies buried in the Control Panel. To visit the dialog box, heed these directions:

1. **Open the Control Panel.**

   Refer to Chapter 14 for specific directions.

   In Windows Vista, choose Control Panel Home on the left side of the window. Then you can click the Mouse link under the Hardware and Sound heading.

2. **Choose Hardware and Sound.**

   If you don't see the Hardware and Sound category, choose the Category view from the upper-right corner of the Control Panel window.

3. **Click the Mouse link, found under the Devices and Printers heading.**

   Lo and behold: the Mouse dialog box.

The Mouse Properties dialog box controls the mouse's look and behavior. It may also feature custom tabs that deal with special features particular to your mouse.

The following sections assume that the Mouse Properties dialog box is open on the screen.

Make the pointer easier to find

To help you locate a wayward mouse pointer, use the Pointer Options tab in the Mouse Properties dialog box. The options in the Visibility area, near the bottom of the dialog box, can come in handy, especially on larger displays or when the screen is particularly busy.

- ✔ **Snap To:** This option jumps the mouse pointer to the main button in any dialog box that appears.

- ✔ **Display Pointer Trails:** This option spawns a comet trail of mouse pointers as you move the mouse about. Jiggling or circling the mouse makes lots of visual racket, which allows you to quickly locate the mouse pointer.

- ✔ **Show Location/Ctrl Key:** This option allows you to find the mouse pointer by tapping either Ctrl key on the keyboard. When you do, a radar-like circle appears, by zeroing in on the cursor's location.

Another way to make the pointer more visible is to choose a more visible mouse pointer: Click the Pointers tab in the Mouse Properties dialog box. Use the options there to choose a different look or size for the mouse pointer.

Fix double-click

If you can't seem to double-click, one of two things is happening: You're moving the mouse pointer a little between clicks or the double-click rate is set too fast for human fingers to manage.

The *double-click rate* is set in the Mouse Properties dialog box, on either the Buttons tab or the Activities tab, in the Double-Click Speed area. Practice your double-clicking on the tiny folder icon off to the right. Use the Slow-Fast slider to adjust the double-click speed to better match your click-click timing.

Use the mouse left-handed

In Windows, you can adjust the mouse for southpaw use on the Buttons tab. Put a check mark by the box labeled Switch Primary and Secondary Buttons. That way, the main mouse button is under your left index finger.

With some mice, the buttons must be assigned in the Pointers tab, by choosing actions for the Left and Right mouse buttons separately.

This book and all computer documentation assume that the left mouse button is the main button. *Right-clicks* are clicks of the right mouse button. If you tell Windows to use the left-handed mouse, these buttons are reversed. A right-click is then a left-click.

Left-handed mice are available, designed to fit your left hand better than all those biased, right-hand-oriented mice on the market.

Touchscreen Input

In the world of Windows 8, a touchscreen monitor becomes handy as yet another input device. Rather than randomly stab at the screen and hope to get some action out of Windows, you can use these finely honed touchscreen techniques:

Touch: The simplest way to manipulate the touchscreen is to touch it. You touch an object, an icon, a control, a menu item, a doodad, and so on. The touch operation is similar to a mouse click. It may also be referred to as a *tap* or *press*.

Double-tap: Touch the screen twice in the same location. Double-tapping can be used to zoom in on an image or a map, but it can also zoom out. Because of the double-tap's dual nature, I recommend using the *pinch* or *spread* operation instead when you want to zoom.

Long-press: A long-press occurs when you touch part of the screen and hold your finger down. Depending on what you're doing, a pop-up menu may appear, or the item you're long-pressing may get "picked up" so that you can drag (move) it around after a long-press. *Long-press* might also be referred to as *touch and hold.*

Swipe: To swipe, you touch your finger on one spot and then drag it to another spot. Swipes can go up, down, left, or right, which moves the touch-screen content in the direction you swipe your finger. A swipe can be fast or slow, and it can also involve more than a single finger. It's also called a *flick* or *slide.*

Pinch: A pinch involves two fingers, which start out separated and then are brought together. The effect is used to *zoom out,* to reduce the size of an image or see more of a map.

Spread: The opposite of *pinch* is *spread.* You start out with your fingers together and then spread them. The spread is used to *zoom in,* to enlarge an image or see more detail on a map.

Rotate: A few apps let you rotate an image on the screen by touching with two fingers and twisting them around a center point. Think of turning a combination lock on a safe, and you get the rotate operation.

You can't manipulate the touchscreen while wearing gloves unless they're gloves specially designed for using electronic touchscreens, such as the gloves that Batman wears.

Chapter 10

System Expansion

In This Chapter

▶ Understanding ports

▶ Using the USB port

▶ Adding and removing USB gizmos

▶ Adding even more USB ports

▶ Hanging on to older PC ports

▶ Using expansion cards

*I*t's relatively easy for a human being to expand. I'm expanding all the time! Of course, the expansion I'm experiencing doesn't add new options or features to my system, at least not new features I'm eager to have. With a PC, however, such expansion is both possible and desirable. Indeed, you have at your disposal many beneficial ways to expand your computer system, none of which involves adult beverages, donuts, or pizza.

It's a Port

PCs have always been adorned with various connectors, into which are plugged cables used for expanding the computer system. Those connectors are known by various technical names, though they're commonly called *holes, jacks,* and *ports.* Of those terms, port is the best.

A port is more than a hole. It defines the shape of the hole and its connector, the type of devices that can be plugged in, and all sorts of technology required to control the device being connected. It's a big deal.

The PC's console features a host of ports into which a variety of devices can be attached. The goal is to expand the computer system.

✔ Officially, a *port* is a place on the computer where information can be sent or received or both. It's also a dessert wine.

✔ In the past, PCs had specific ports for specific tasks. Those various ports have been eliminated over the years, replaced with more versatile ports such as the USB port.

✔ If your PC still features some of the older ports, they're known as *legacy ports.* See the later section "Legacy Ports" for details.

✔ Also refer to Chapter 3 for information on finding the various PC ports.

USB, a Most Versatile Port

The most popular and useful port on your PC is the USB port, where the *U* stands for *universal* and means that this port can be used to *plug* in an entire universe of peripherals. I could also make up that the *S* in USB stands for cinchy, but cinchy is spelled with a *C,* so that one won't fly.

Since I brought it up, USB stands for Universal Serial Bus. Pronounce it letters-only: "yoo-ess-bee."

The variety of USB devices is legion: printers, speakers, headsets, joysticks, scanners, digital cameras, video cameras, webcams, disk drives, media storage, keyboards, networking gizmos, pointing devices, tiny fans, lamps, tanning beds, time machines — the list goes on and on. More and more USB devices are appearing every day.

The best news about USB? It's *easy.* Just plug in the gizmo. Often, that's all you need to do!

✔ USB ports, as well as USB devices, sport the USB symbol, shown in the margin.

✔ To see what the USB hole looks like, see Chapter 2.

✔ The most popular USB standard is 2.0. USB 3.0 devices are available, which are many times faster. If your PC has USB 3.0, do yourself a favor and find some USB 3.0 gizmos — and some USB cables. Otherwise, most USB 3.0 devices can be used on older USB ports, although they don't run as fast.

Understanding USB cables

Whereas a few USB devices attach directly to the computer, such as a USB thumb drive, most USB devices need cables. The name of the cable is, surprisingly, *USB cable.*

The IEEE port

About the time the USB port was taking over the computer world, a second, "universal" computer port standard appeared. Sadly, this port lacks a clever acronym. Instead, it's named the IEEE port or IEEE 1394 port (after the technical standard) or the 1394 port. It was once known as i.LINK in the Macintosh world, and it's also known as the FireWire port. No matter what you call it, it's the same port.

The IEEE port works similarly to the USB port: IEEE devices can be plugged and unplugged at any time, just like USB gizmos. You can find IEEE hubs, just as you can find USB hubs. Sadly, IEEE never caught on as well as USB, so today IEEE is kind of rare, especially on the PC scene. And that's too bad, because IEEE is pronounced with the same sound you make when you spill hot coffee in your lap.

USB cables are judged by their length and the type of connector on each end.

As far as length goes, you can get a USB cable up to 3 or 4 meters long. Any longer and you'd probably want me to specify the length in feet instead of meters. But seriously, the signal may be compromised after about 15 feet or so.

A standard USB cable has two different ends, dubbed A and B, illustrated in Figure 10-1. The A end is flat, and it plugs into the console or a USB hub. The B end has a trapezoidal shape and plugs into the USB device.

You may also see mini- and micro-USB connectors on portable devices, such as cellphones and video cameras. The cables used to connect these devices to your PC feature a mini- or micro-USB connector for the device but a standard A connector for the PC.

Figure 10-1:
The A and B ends of a USB cable.

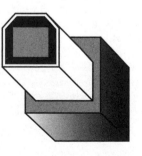
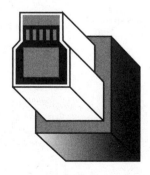

A end   B end   B end (USB 3.0)

> ✔ You can use a standard USB cable with a USB 3.0 device, though the data transfer won't take place at USB 3.0 speeds. Do yourself a favor and get a USB 3.0 cable.
>
> ✔ The A end of a USB 3.0 contains a blue "tongue"; it's black for a standard (non-USB 3.0) cable.
>
> ✔ Special USB extension cables are available with two A ends, so try not to confuse them with the standard A-B cables.

Connecting a USB device

One reason that the USB port took over the world is that it's smart. Dumb things never take over the world. That's why you don't see any cheese-flavored gelato. But I digress.

Adding a USB device to your computer is easy: Just plug it in. You don't need to turn off the computer first, and most of the time you don't need to install special software. When you plug in a USB device, Windows instantly recognizes it and configures the device for you.

Of course, it pays to read the directions! Some USB gizmos require that you first install software before connecting the device. The only way to tell is to read the quick-setup guide or the manual that came with the USB device.

There may be some on-screen activity when you attach a USB device. You might see a pop-up window or information saying that a driver is being installed. The *driver* is the software Windows uses to interface with the device. It's installed automatically.

Using USB-powered gizmos

Another advantage of USB is that many types of USB devices don't require separate power cords. Instead, they use the power supplied by the USB port, making them *USB-powered* devices.

When you have a USB-powered device, you need to plug it into one of two places: directly into the console or into a USB-powered hub. When you don't plug the device into the console or a USB-powered hub, it doesn't work properly. See the section "Expanding the USB universe with hubs," a little later in this chapter, for information on powered-versus-unpowered hubs.

> ✔ Some folks are uncomfortable that USB-powered devices lack an on–off switch. It's fine to leave the device on, as long as you keep the computer on. But, if you really, *really* want to turn the gizmo off, simply unplug the USB cable.
>
> ✔ USB devices that require lots of power, such as printers and certain external storage devices, use their own power cords.

Removing a USB device

Removing a USB device is cinchy: Just unplug it. That's it!

Well, that's it unless that device is storage media, such as an external disk drive or a thumb drive. In that case, you must officially *unmount* the gizmo before you unplug it. Here's how:

1. **Summon the Computer window.**

   Press the Win+E key combination to display a Windows Explorer window, honed in on the Computer window. You'll see a list of all your PC's storage devices, plus maybe some network locations.

2. **Right-click the external storage device's icon.**

   A pop-up menu appears.

3. **From the pop-up menu, choose the command Eject or Safely Remove.**

   Windows displays a message (in the notification area), informing you that the device can be safely removed.

4. **Disconnect the external storage device.**

If you see an error message, the storage device is either busy or being used. You have to wait and try again. If the error is persistent, you should turn off the computer, detach the device, and then restart the computer.

Refer to Chapter 7 for more information on computer storage.

Expanding the USB universe with hubs

There never seem to be enough USB ports. Fortunately, when you need more USB ports, you can quickly add them by plugging a USB hub into your PC.

The eSATA port

A relatively new port on the port scene is eSATA. SATA is the standard for connecting disk drives inside the console to the PC's motherboard. eSATA is basically an external version of that port standard, allowing you to connect eSATA hard drives and optical drives to your computer.

Not every PC comes with eSATA ports, and most external disk drives that use eSATA can also be connected using the USB port. For now, eSATA is an option, one that may either become more popular in the future or join a long line of once-upon-a-time port standards for the PC.

To properly pronounce eSATA, say "ee-SAY-tuh."

A USB *hub* allows you to greatly expand your PC's USB universe. A typical expansion hub, shown in Figure 10-2, connects to the console's USB port. By plugging in the USB hub, you increase the number of USB gizmos you can attach to your computer system.

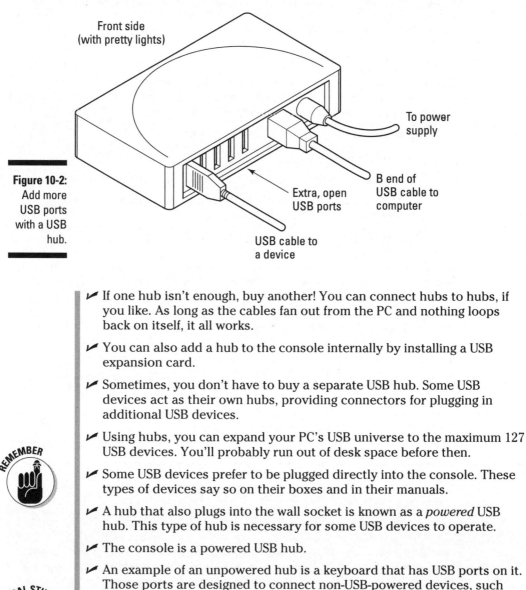

Front side
(with pretty lights)

To power
supply

B end of
USB cable to
computer

Extra, open
USB ports

USB cable to
a device

Figure 10-2:
Add more
USB ports
with a USB
hub.

- ✔ If one hub isn't enough, buy another! You can connect hubs to hubs, if you like. As long as the cables fan out from the PC and nothing loops back on itself, it all works.

- ✔ You can also add a hub to the console internally by installing a USB expansion card.

- ✔ Sometimes, you don't have to buy a separate USB hub. Some USB devices act as their own hubs, providing connectors for plugging in additional USB devices.

- ✔ Using hubs, you can expand your PC's USB universe to the maximum 127 USB devices. You'll probably run out of desk space before then.

- ✔ Some USB devices prefer to be plugged directly into the console. These types of devices say so on their boxes and in their manuals.

- ✔ A hub that also plugs into the wall socket is known as a *powered* USB hub. This type of hub is necessary for some USB devices to operate.

- ✔ The console is a powered USB hub.

- ✔ An example of an unpowered hub is a keyboard that has USB ports on it. Those ports are designed to connect non-USB-powered devices, such as mice.

- ✔ The first hub (your PC) is the *root* hub.

Legacy Ports

When the PC was first designed, external gizmos were attached to the console by using ports named after the gizmos. If you wanted to attach a keyboard, mouse, or printer, for example, you would use a specific keyboard, mouse, or printer port.

As more and more peripherals became available to computers, it became obvious that you couldn't have a unique port for every gizmo. So, eventually, standards such as USB were developed, which handle a variety of devices.

Despite the USB standard, your PC may still support a handful of these older ports, or *legacy ports.* Here's the round-up:

Mouse port: The computer's mouse plugs into the mouse port.

Keyboard port: The computer's keyboard plugs into the keyboard port.

Printer port: The printer plugged into the printer port — though, because of the printer port's technical nature, people commonly added other devices to the printer port, including external scanners and hard drives.

COM port: The old COM port was the most versatile of the legacy ports. Into the COM port you could plug an external modem, a computer mouse, or a serial printer. Some PCs came with two or more of these ports.

Other legacy ports exist, standards from the rubble and detritus that follow in the computer industry's wake. One of my favorites was the old SCSI port standard. The funnest thing about SCSI was its pronunciation: "skuzzy." Otherwise, the standard was clunky and difficult to configure. Living through such things reminds me how nice the computing world is now, with its pleasant and flexible USB port.

Connect Bluetooth gizmos

Bluetooth is the name of a wireless standard used to connect devices to your computer. You can use Bluetooth to add a variety of wireless gizmos. As long as the console supports Bluetooth, or has a Bluetooth adapter installed (usually stuck into a USB port), you can connect devices such as a keyboard, a mouse, a printer, or even a monitor. You can also use Bluetooth to connect to mobile devices, such as tablets and smartphones, for exchanging files.

Because Bluetooth is a wireless communications standard, it's covered in Part III. Check out Chapter 22.

✔ The printer port was also known as the parallel port. In IBM lingo, it was the LPT port, where LPT was an IBM acronym-thing for line printer. PRN port was also used; PRN is how the word *printer* looks when the keyboard is broken.

✔ The serial port is also known as the COM or COM1 port. Some grizzled veterans of the Commodore 64 Wars call it the RS-232C port.

Expansion Slots

The internal way to expand your PC is by adding new circuitry directly to the motherboard. Believe it or not, it's possible for you to do such a thing without wielding a soldering iron.

To internally expand your PC, you can take advantage of the motherboard's *expansion slots.* Into those slots, you plug *expansion cards.* Although people don't often expand their computer systems this way, it's a good method for adding hardware options not included with the basic PC configuration.

I could prattle on about the history of PC expansion cards and riff the names of all the standards, but I won't. Today pretty much one standard exists: PCIe, which stands for PCI Express.

Oh, and PCI stands for *Peripheral Component Interconnect,* which is useful to know in case you're being mugged and you want to befuddle your assailant with technojargon.

✔ A common type of PCI Express card to add to a PC is a high-end graphics card. See Chapter 8 for more information on graphics.

✔ Older expansion slot types might also be found on the PC's motherboard. They exist primarily for compatibility with antique PC hardware.

✔ The number and type of slots available in your computer depend on the size of the console's case as well as on the motherboard's design. Small-footprint PCs have the fewest expansion slots. Mini-desktop systems, all-in-one PCs, and nearly all laptops lack expansion slots. Tower computer models have the most — sometimes up to eight!

✔ Most expansion cards come squirming with cables. This mess of cables makes the seemingly sleek motherboard look more like an electronic pasta dish. Some cables are threaded inside the PC; others are left hanging limply out the back. These cables make the internal upgrading and installation process difficult.

✔ The backsides of most expansion cards stick out the rear of the consoles; the card's back replaces the metallic slot cover to reveal special connectors or attachments for the expansion card.

Chapter 11

P Is for Printer

In This Chapter

▶ Understanding computer printers

▶ Finding things on the printer

▶ Feeding the printer ink

▶ Choosing the right paper

▶ Installing a printer

▶ Controlling the printer

▶ Printing in reverse order

▶ Stopping a document from printing

This chapter is brought to you by the letter *P*. *P* stands for *PC*. It also stands for *peripheral*. One of the PC's preferred peripherals is the printer. *Printer* starts with *P*. PCs prefer printers, specifically for producing output on paper. The printer makes all that possible.

The Printer, the Paper, the Document Maker

Printers are a necessary peripheral in any computer system. That's because dragging the PC around and showing everyone what's on the screen is just too much of a chore. No, it's much better to *print* your stuff on paper, to create a *hard copy* of your data, documents, and doodles.

Surveying the printer landscape

Computer printers come in all shapes and sizes, some with just the bare bones and others with features galore. When you strip that all away, you'll find only two types of printers, categorized by how the ink gets thrown on the paper. Those two types are inkjet and laser.

Inkjet: The inkjet printer creates its image by spewing tiny balls of ink directly on the paper. That jet-of-ink action gives this printer category its name. The inkjet printer is the most common type of computer printer.

Laser: Laser printers are found primarily in the office environment, where they deftly handle high workloads. The printer uses a laser beam to create the image, which somehow helps fuse toner powder (ink) onto the paper. The result is crisp and fast output, but at a premium price over standard inkjet printers.

All inkjet printers are color printers, though I suppose there may still be some monochrome (black only) models available. Laser printers come in both monochrome and color varieties.

A special type of inkjet printer is the *photo printer.* This type of printer uses a wider variety of inks for better-quality color printing. For example, a typical inkjet printer uses four ink colors: black, cyan, magenta, and yellow. A photo printer may add two additional colors, light cyan and light magenta, for more vivid output.

All-in-one printers combine a basic inkjet printer with a fax machine, scanner, and copier. This type of printer is popular in home and small offices because it replaces four devices.

- ✔ You can print a color image or document on a monochrome printer; the printout will just be in black and white.

- ✔ Inkjet printers are by no means messy. The ink is dry on the paper by the time the paper comes flopping out of the printer.

- ✔ Higher-priced printers offer a higher-quality output, faster speed, more printing options, the capability to print on larger sheets of paper, and other super-hero features. Low-priced printers are good but print more slowly. And besides, the manufacturer makes up the cost difference on the prices they charge you for the ink.

Touring the typical printer

Take a moment to examine the PC's printer to look for some specific items. Use Figure 11-1 as your guide.

Paper feed: The paper feed is where you store the paper on which the printer eventually prints. For more information, see the section "Eating paper," later in this chapter.

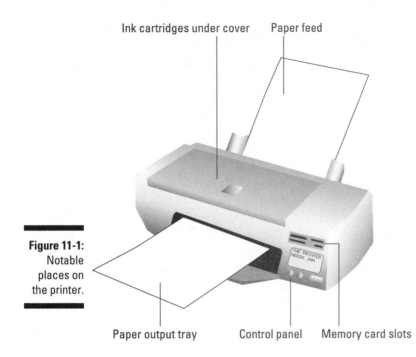

Ink cartridges under cover   Paper feed

Figure 11-1:
Notable
places on
the printer.

Paper output tray   Control panel   Memory card slots

Manual/envelope feeder: The printer may have a special slot, tray, or foldout-thing used to manually feed special papers or envelopes. It may be hidden on your printer, and it's not shown in Figure 11-1, so rummage around a bit to see whether your printer has such a deal.

Ink/toner replacement: Printers don't go on printing forever. At some point, you need to feed the thing more ink. Be sure that you know how to open the printer to find where the ink goes. See the section "Drinking ink," later in this chapter.

Control panel: Refer to the next section for the details.

Memory card reader: Many photo printers have a place where you can directly plug in your digital camera's memory card. This area could be a media card slot or even a USB port into which you could plug a thumb drive.

Paper output tray: The printed paper comes out and is stacked in the output tray. If the paper comes out face up, be sure to see the section "Printing in reverse order," later in this chapter.

Using the printer's control panel

Every printer has a control panel somewhere on its body. The fancy models have LCD screens that display text and allow you to select photos from a media card for printing. Less fancy printers may have only a couple of buttons or lights.

Besides choosing options, ejecting paper, clearing jams, and other mundane duties, the most important thing to look for on the printer's control panel is the Cancel button. That button's purpose is to stop printing. See the section "Stopping a printer run amok," later in this chapter.

- ✔ If your printer seems to lack a control panel, it's probably controlled by using a software control panel in Windows.

- ✔ All-in-one printers have the most complex control panels. You use the control panel to set the printer's mood, whether it's working as a copier, scanner, or fax. A software program in Windows also helps make those decisions, though the advantage of the printer's control panel is that you can make copies or print when the computer is turned off.

- ✔ Keep your printer's manual handy, somewhere near the printer where you can easily find it. You may never read the manual, but if your printer suddenly pops up and displays Error 34, you can look up Error 34 and read how to fix it.

Drinking ink

The Chinese invented ink over 3,000 years ago, but it's still basically the same stuff you use to print stuff on paper with your computer printer. The type of ink and how it's stored depend on which type of printer you're using.

Inkjet printers use *ink cartridges.* Laser printers use *toner,* a powdery ink substance that also comes in a cartridge.

All printers use black ink or toner. Color printers also use black ink plus color inks.

Replacing the ink in your printer works differently for each printer manufacturer. Instructions are usually found on the inside of the lid or compartment where the ink cartridges reside. Overall advice: Be careful! Spill the ink and you've got a serious mess.

✔ The printer has a drinking problem. Printer manufacturers take advantage of that dependency by selling ink at a very high price. It's the old "Give away the razor and sell them the blade" concept all over again.

✔ Some manufacturers sell their cartridges with return envelopes so that you can send the old cartridge back to the factory for recycling or proper disposal.

✔ Make sure that you don't breathe in the dust from a laser toner cartridge or else you'll die.

✔ Sometimes, the colors in an inkjet printer come three to a cartridge. Yes, it's true: If only one color of ink goes dry, you must replace the entire cartridge even though the other two colors are still available. So is it more economical to buy the cheaper three-in-one ink cartridges or the more expensive cartridges individually? Mathematicians are still working on the problem.

✔ Make a note of which type of inkjet cartridges your printer uses. Keep the catalog number somewhere handy, such as taped to your printer's case, so that you can re-order the proper cartridge.

✔ Always follow carefully the instructions for changing cartridges. Old cartridges can leak and spread messy ink all over. Buy rubber gloves (or those cheap plastic gloves that make you look like Batman) and use them when changing the ink or toner cartridge. I also suggest having a paper towel handy.

✔ When the laser printer first warns you that `Toner [is] low`, you can squeeze a few more pages from it by gently rocking the toner cartridge: Remove the cartridge and rock it back and forth the short way (not from end to end), which helps redistribute the toner dust.

✔ Rather than buy new cartridges, consider getting ink cartridge refills or recharged toner cartridges. Be sure that you deal with a reputable company; not every type of ink or toner cartridge can be reused successfully.

✔ Never let your printer cartridges go dry. You may think that squeezing every last drop of ink saves you money, but it's not good for the printer.

Eating paper

Next to drinking ink, printers eat paper. Fortunately, paper isn't as expensive as ink, so it doesn't bankrupt you to churn through a ream or two. The only issue is where to feed in the paper. Like feeding a baby, there's a right end and a wrong end.

The paper goes into a feeder tray either near the printer's bottom or sticking out the top.

Some laser printers require you to fill a cartridge with paper, similar to the way a copy machine works. Slide the cartridge all the way into the printer after it's loaded.

Confirm that you're putting the paper in the proper way, either face down or face up. Note which side is the top. Most printers have little pictures on them that tell you how the paper goes into the printer. Here's how those symbols translate into English:

✔ The paper goes in face down, top side up.

✔ The paper goes in face down, top side down.

✔ The paper goes in face up, top side up.

✔ The paper goes in face up, top side down.

Knowing the proper paper orientation helps when you're printing on both sides of a sheet of paper or loading items such as checks for use with personal finance software. If the printer doesn't tell you which way is up, write *Top* on a sheet of paper and run it through the printer. Then draw your own icon, similar to those just shown, to help orient the pages you manually insert into the printer.

Always make sure that you have enough printer paper. Buying too much isn't a sin.

Choosing the proper paper

There's really no such thing as a typical sheet of paper. Paper comes in different sizes, weights (degrees of thickness), colors, styles, textures, and I assume, flavors.

The best general-purpose paper for computer printing is standard photocopier paper. If you want better results from your inkjet printer, getting specific inkjet paper works best, although you pay more for that paper. The higher-quality (and spendy) inkjet paper is good for printing colors because it is designed to absorb the ink.

At the high end of the spectrum are specialty papers, such as photographic papers that come in smooth or glossy finishes, transparencies, and iron-on T-shirt transfers. Just ensure that the paper you get is made for your type of printer, inkjet or laser.

✔ Some printers are capable of handling larger-size paper, such as legal or tabloid size. If so, make sure that you load the paper properly and tell your application that you're using a sheet of paper that's a different size. See the later section "Basic Printer Operation" for more information.

✔ Avoid thick papers because they get jammed inside the printer. Thicker paper stock can't turn corners well.

✔ Avoid using erasable bond and other fancy dusted papers in your printer. The powder coating on these papers gums up the works.

✔ Don't let the ads for expensive paper fool you: Your inkjet printer can print on just about any type of paper. Even so, the pricey paper *does* produce a better image.

Where the Printer Meets the PC

As with all other computer peripherals, the PC-printer relationship has a courting phase. It involves an introduction, some dating, and finally, a full-on-marriage. You'll be grateful that the entire operation is much faster and far more successful than in human relationships.

Connecting the printer

Printers are really their own computers, containing a processor, memory, networking, and sometimes mass storage. Getting the printer and computer connected is too routine to be considered a miracle, yet I'm constantly surprised when the operation meets with success.

Number one concern: Printers don't come with cables. You will need to get a standard, USB, A-to-B cable to connect the printer directly to your computer.

Another concern: Often you have to install the printer software *before* you connect the printer. Check the setup guide to ensure that you're performing the proper steps in the correct order. In most cases, thankfully, printer software is automatically installed by Windows after the printer is attached.

Keep in mind that the printer need not be connected directly to the computer. Especially in an office situation, or where you have multiple computers that need to use a single printer, you can connect the printer to the computer network for equal access and sharing. See Chapter 21 for information on connecting a network printer.

✔ Some printers demand to be directly connected to the computer, not plugged into a USB hub.

✔ You can connect a number of printers to a single computer. In fact, networked PCs have access to multiple network printers.

✔ It's okay to leave the printer on all the time. The printer automatically slips into a low-power mode when it's no longer needed. However, if you don't print often (at least every day), it's perfectly fine to turn off the printer.

Finding the printer in Windows

You'll find the various printers available to your PC in a central spot in Windows. For Windows 8 and Windows 7, that location is the Devices and Printers window, shown in Figure 11-2. For earlier versions of Windows, the logically named Printers window is the location.

Windows 8   Windows 7

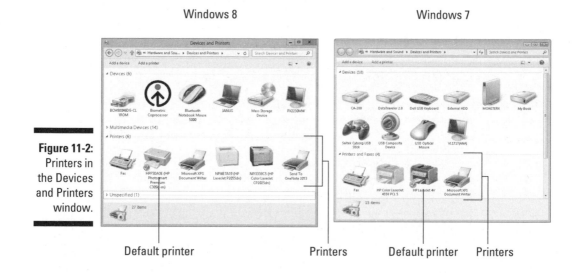

Figure 11-2: Printers in the Devices and Printers window.

Default printer   Printers   Default printer   Printers

To visit the window where the printers lurk, obey these steps:

1. **Summon the Control Panel.**

   Refer to Chapter 14 if the way to the Windows Control Panel is unfamiliar.

2. **In Windows 8 and Windows Vista, click the View Devices and Printers link, found below the Hardware and Sound heading.**

   In Windows Vista, the link is named Printer.

Icons shown in the Devices and Printers window represent various gizmos connected to your PC, including the monitor, the keyboard, external storage, webcams, and gamepads (refer to Figure 11-2). You'll find a Printers category, under which all printers available are listed, including network printers.

One printer in the list is known as the *default* printer, shown by the green check mark (refer to Figure 11-2). The default printer is identified as your computer's primary printer. and is the printer used most of the time. A default printer is handy, especially when your PC has multiple printers and you don't want to waste time choosing one each time you print.

Setting the default printer

To ensure that Windows uses your favorite printer whenever you do a quick print, choose that favorite by making it the default. Follow these steps:

1. **Open the Devices and Printers window.**

   Refer to the preceding section for specific directions.

2. **Right-click the printer you plan to use most often.**

3. **Choose Set As Default Printer from the pop-up menu.**

   The green check mark on the printer's icon confirms that you've speci-fied the default printer.

4. **Close the Devices and Printers window.**

You can change the default printer at any time by repeating these steps. To choose any printer for a particular print job, you can use the Print dialog box, as described in the next section.

Basic Printer Operation

The least effective yet most satisfying way to use a printer is to yell at it. Try as I may, that technique doesn't work. Instead, rustle up the Print command — the best, and only, way to get your computer efforts down on paper.

Printing something

The key to printing in any Windows program is to summon the Print screen or the traditional Print dialog box. You'll find a Print command nestled on the File menu. For newer Windows 8 programs and apps, a Print screen is used. Both locations are shown in Figure 11-3. The best way to get there is to use the Ctrl+P keyboard shortcut.

Print buton

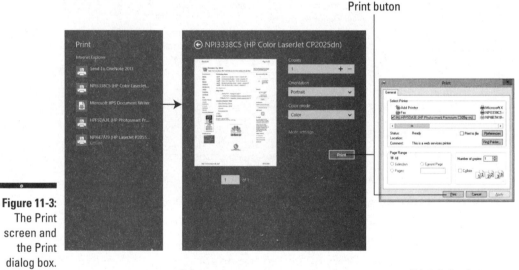

Figure 11-3:
The Print
screen and
the Print
dialog box.

Print screen   Print dialog box

To print the entire document, just click the Print button. In Windows 8, you may need to first choose a printer; then you can set options or just click or touch the Print button (refer to Figure 11-3).

If you want to print on a specific printer, such as that nice color laser printer that Edward hogs in his office, choose it from the list.

Place a value other than 1 by the Copies or Number of Copies field to print several copies of your work.

Set the number of pages to print (Page Range) to print specific pages from the document. For example, type **2** to print only page 2, or type **3-9** to print pages 3 through 9.

Click the Print button after making your choices to print your document. Or you can click Cancel or press the Esc key to not print anything.

✔ Some printer options, such as paper size and orientation, might be set in the Page Setup dialog box. To get there, you must choose the Page Setup command from the File menu.

✔ Use the Print command only *once.* When the printer seems unbearably slow, just wait a while before thinking that you goofed up and choosing the Print command again. Otherwise, you print one copy of the document for every time you use the Print command.

✔ Rather than waste paper, use the preview window (refer to Figure 11-3). If you don't see it, look for a File➪Print Preview command. Review the document before it's printed.

Printing in reverse order

Some printers cough out pages face up. What that means is that everything you print is in reverse order, with the last page printed on top. You can fix that problem by directing the program to print your stuff in reverse order, last page first. That's a job for the Printer's Properties dialog box.

To see the printer's Properties dialog box, right-click the printer's icon in the Devices and Printers (or Printers) window. Choose the Printer Properties command.

The printer's Properties dialog box can be used to set various advanced printer options, one of which can be reverse printing. I'd love to tell you specifically where to find that option, but it varies from printer to printer. If the printer has the capability to print in reverse order, a command will be found somewhere in that dialog box. After making the proper setting, click the OK button to confirm and close the dialog box.

If you don't find the reverse printing option in the printer's Properties dialog box, look to the specific software you're using. Hunt down a Page Setup command on the File menu. The reverse printing command may be located there instead.

Stopping a printer run amok

The most frustrating printer experience you can have is wanting the dumb thing to stop printing. It happens. Often.

The fastest, bestest way to stop printing is to look on the printer's control panel for a Cancel button. Press that button, and all printing stops. Oh, a few more pages may pop out of the printer, but that's it.

Another, more technical way to stop printing involves opening the printer's window and manually canceling the print job. The problem with that technique is that the printer is just too fast; by the time you find and open the printer's window, the document has finished printing.

Chapter 12

PC Audio Abilities

In This Chapter

▶ Understanding sound hardware

▶ Configuring speakers

▶ Setting up sound in Windows

▶ Changing the volume

▶ Playing sounds for certain events

▶ Recording sounds

▶ Using Windows dictation

*O*riginally, a computer's audio was a simple bell. *Ding!* When the first microcomputers came out in the 1970s, they had small, tinny speakers to emulate the bell. *Beep.* Your computer's audio system has moved far beyond that primitive beep. Built into the chipset on the PC's motherboard is specialized sound circuitry, including a complete music synthesizer. [*Insert symphony sound here.*] The computer can talk, sing, and even ding like a bell. It can also listen to you.

Also see Chapter 26, which covers playing music on your PC.

The Noisy PC

All PCs include sound-generation hardware on the motherboard. This hardware can process and play digitally recorded sounds, play music from external media (such as a CD), generate music using the onboard synthesizer, and record sounds. That's a lot of capability, yet it's so common on a PC that the manufacturers seldom boast about it.

 ✔ When you're really into audio, you can add more advanced sound hardware to your PC by using an expansion card. This type of upgrade is necessary only for diehard audiophiles, people who are composing their own music, or professionals who use their PCs as the heart of an audio studio.

✔ If your PC lacks expansion slots or you have a laptop with limited audio, you can upgrade by adding an external USB sound device, such as the Sound Blaster Audigy system.

Speakers hither and thither

The PC console has always come with a pitiful, internal speaker. It still does, but in addition, your PC most likely came with a standard set of stereo (left-right) speakers. That's fine for basic sound, but the PC is capable of so much more.

The next step up from the basic speaker set is to add a *subwoofer*. It's a speaker box designed for low-frequency sounds, which gives oomph to the bass in music or adds emphasis to the sounds in games.

Typically, the subwoofer sits on the floor beneath your PC. It plugs directly into the PC's speakers jack (see Chapter 2), and the stereo speakers plug into the subwoofer.

The final step up the audio ladder is to go with surround sound, similar to the sound setup for a home theater. In that configuration, you can have multiple speakers located around the computer, depending on the implementation of surround sound hardware you're using.

Figure 12-1 illustrates all possible locations for speakers in a surround sound setup. You'd be nuts to have *all* those speakers connected at one time, but it's possible. Table 12-1 lists the options for surround sound.

Table 12-1	Surround Sound Speaker Options
Surround Sound Version	*Speakers Used*
3.0	Left, right, back surround
4.0	Left, right, surround left, surround right
4.1	Left, right, surround left, surround right, subwoofer
5.1	Left, right, center, surround left, surround right, subwoofer
6.1	Left, right, center, side left, side right, back surround, subwoofer
7.1	Left, right, center, side left, side right, surround left, surround right, subwoofer

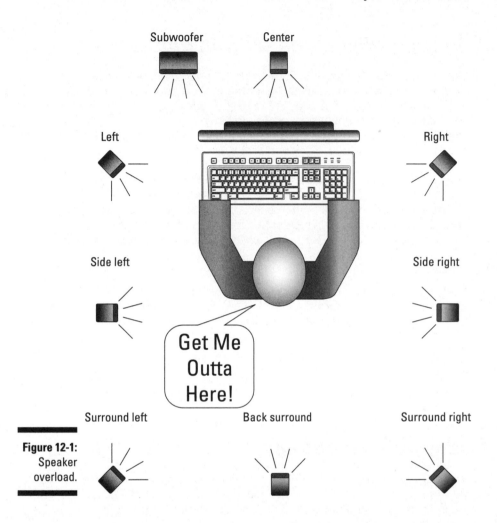

Figure 12-1:
Speaker
overload.

✔ Some monitors come with built-in speakers, though they're generally terrible.

✔ I recommend getting speakers that have a volume control, either on the left or right speaker. A bonus is a mute button on the speaker. Note that some high-end speaker systems have the volume and mute buttons on a control (wired or remote).

✔ The *.x* part of a surround sound specification refers to the presence of a subwoofer: .0 means no subwoofer; .1 means one subwoofer; .2 means two subwoofers.

✔ If you have an audio expansion card on your PC, be sure to plug the speakers into that card.

✔ Refer to my book *Troubleshooting & Maintaining Your PC All-in-One For Dummies,* 2nd Edition (Wiley) if you're having trouble hearing sounds from your PC.

In your own world with headphones

Rather than startle everyone in the room when you launch artillery in a computer game, consider using headphones with your PC instead of an external sound system. A good set of headphones can truly emulate a sound environment beyond what the traditional stereo speakers offer. In fact, some high-end gaming headphones can cost more than the standard home-theater surround sound system. They're worth it.

Good headphones come with a volume control and maybe even a mute button on the same wire that connects the headphones to the PC. Better headphones come with a built-in microphone for online communications as well as game playing. This type of headphone is often referred to as a *headset.* Headphones (or headsets) plug into the console's headphone jack.

✔ Plug a headphone or headset into the jacks on the front of the console.

✔ Headsets have two audio jacks: One goes into the speaker jack; the other, into the microphone jack. They're color-coded to help you plug them into the proper holes: pink for the microphone, lime green for the speakers.

✔ Look for headphones that are comfy on your ears, with big, puffy "cans."

✔ I don't recommend a nonstereo headset. It has only one earpiece, which is okay for online communications but lousy for game-playing.

Microphone options

Any cheesy microphone works on a PC. If sound quality is important to you and you're using your PC as a digital audio studio, you have to spend money on microphones and mixers and all that. But if that's not you, any old microphone does the trick.

✔ Two popular types of microphones are used on a PC: condenser and dynamic. Either one works with a PC, though if your PC's sound equipment isn't up to snuff, I recommend getting a sound mixer to use as a preamp.

✔ If you plan to use voice over the Internet or dictation, get a headset. See the preceding section.

Sound Control in Windows

Being a hardware thing, the computer's audio system serves subject to the PC's potentate, the operating system. Windows exercises its dictatorial control in a place called the Sound dialog box, beautifully illustrated in Figure 12-2.

Figure 12-2:
Sound
control
happens
here.

To display the Sound dialog box, follow these steps:

1. **Open the Control Panel.**

   Refer to Chapter 14 for information on finding the Control Panel.

2. **Choose Hardware and Sound.**

3. **Click the main Sound heading.**

   The Sound dialog box appears.

Later sections in this chapter discuss various things you can do with the Sound dialog box.

Windows also features a second location for controlling PC audio. In the notification area on the taskbar, you find a tiny volume control. Using that control is covered later in this chapter, in the section "Adjusting the volume."

Configuring the speakers

To adjust the PC's speakers in Windows, follow these steps:

1. **Summon the Sounds dialog box.**

   Refer to the steps in the preceding section.

2. **If necessary, click the Playback tab in the Sounds dialog box.**

3. **Choose the playback device.**

   For example, click Speakers (refer to Figure 12-2).

4. **Click the Configure button.**

   If the Configure button is unavailable (dimmed), there's nothing to configure; you're done.

5. **Work through the Speaker Setup Wizard to ensure that your speakers are set up properly and that everything is working.**

6. **Close the Sounds dialog box, and then click OK.**

Configuring the microphone

To set up your PC's microphone, follow these steps:

1. **Open the Control Panel window.**

2. **Choose Ease of Access.**

3. **Choose Set Up a Microphone, below the Speech Recognition heading.**

4. **Work through the Microphone Setup Wizard to properly configure the microphone attached to your PC.**

Adjusting the volume

To make the PC louder or quieter or to just shut it up, you can use the Volume Control icon in the notification area. Click that icon once to display the volume control slider, as shown in Figure 12-3. Use the mouse to slide the gizmo up for louder or down for quieter, or click the Mute button to turn off the sound.

Switch between headphones and speakers

Your PC can have both speakers and headphones attached, but you can hear sounds from only one of those devices at a time. To switch between them, right-click the Volume icon in the notification area and choose Playback Devices from the pop-up menu. In the Sound dialog box, on the Playback tab, choose the device you want to use: speakers or headphones. Click the Set Default button to confirm your choice, and then click OK.

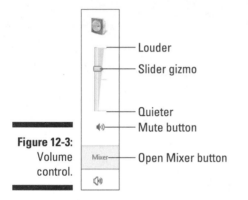

Louder

Slider gizmo

Quieter

Mute button

Figure 12-3:
Volume
control.

Open Mixer button

In Windows 8, the volume can be set by choosing the Settings charm from the charms bar. The volume control is the top-center icon at the bottom of the charms bar. See Chapter 14 for more information on the charms bar.

✔ Don't forget that your speakers may contain volume settings. You can use those settings in addition to the volume control in Windows, though I recommend adjusting the Windows volume control first.

✔ Choosing Mixer from the volume control pop-up (refer to Figure 12-3) displays a more complex volume setting window, where you can set the volume for various noise-producing gizmos and activities in Windows.

Windows Goes Bleep

That old bell from the early computers wasn't used purely for entertainment value. It was an alert, an alarm. *Ding!* That meant you had to pay attention. The computer was angry. Well, maybe not angry, but the bell wasn't to be ignored.

Your PC still uses sound to alert you to various situations serious and trivial. Windows again proves to be the master of selecting and setting those audio alerts. To see how the alert sounds are set, follow these steps:

1. **Right-click the speaker icon in the notification area.**

   In Windows 8, you can view the notification area from the desktop. Press Win+D.

2. **Choose the Sounds command from the pop-up menu.**

   The Sounds dialog box appears with the Sounds tab front and center. The scrolling Program Events list highlights various things going on in Windows. The speaker icon next to an event means that a sound is associated with that event.

3. **Select an event to assign a sound to it.**

   For example, select New Mail Notification, which is the sound that plays when Windows Mail picks up new e-mail.

4. **Click the Test button to hear the current sound.**

   Not every event has a sound, so the Test button is disabled when there's no sound to preview.

5. **Choose a new sound from the Sounds menu.**

6. **Click the Test button to preview the sound you selected.**

7. **Click the OK button when you've finished assigning sounds.**

You can use any sound found on your computer for an event. To do so, choose the event (Step 3) and click the Browse button. You can then use the Browse dialog box to search for sound files on your PC.

✔ To remove a sound from an event, choose (None) from the top of the Sounds drop-down list.

✔ The best source for sounds is the Internet, where you can find web page libraries full of sound samples. To find them, search for *Windows WAV file sounds.*

✔ You can also use sounds that you record yourself, assigning them to specific events in Windows. See the later section, "Recording your own sounds."

✔ Windows is also capable of speaking, using an accessibility tool called the Narrator. I'd go into more detail, but the Narrator can get very annoying after a while because it reads *everything* on the screen, not just alert messages.

It Listens

Don't get your hopes up. The days of talking casually to the computer are still *far* in the future. In fact, I doubt that we'll ever just bark orders at a PC, mostly because the Windows interface isn't designed for vocal interaction. Still, it's possible, in a crude way. Also possible is the art of recording your own sounds, including the sound of your voice.

Recording your own sounds

For simple sound recording, you can use the Sound Recorder program that comes with Windows. The program sports a straightforward interface, as shown in Figure 12-4.

Figure 12-4:
The Sound
Recorder.

Assuming that a microphone is already connected to your PC and set up for use in Windows (see the earlier section "Configuring the microphone"), sound recording works like this:

1. **Press the Win+R keyboard shortcut to summon the Run dialog box.**
2. **Type** Soundrecorder **(all one word) and press the Enter key.**

   Just type **Soundrecorder** with no space between *Sound* and *recorder.*

   Upon success, the Sound Recorder app starts.
3. **Click the Start Recording button.**
4. **Talk: "blah blah blah."**
5. **Click the Stop Recording button when you're done.**
6. **Use the Save As dialog box to save your audio recording.**
7. **Close the Sound Recorder window.**

You can use the Sound Recorder to capture audio from any sound-producing gizmo attached to your PC, such as a turntable or VCR. Simply connect the gizmo to the proper line in audio jack on the console, and then follow the same steps for recording your voice.

✔ If you need something better than the Sound Recorder program, I recommend Audacity, which is free and available on the Internet at `http://audacity.sourceforge.net`.

✔ The Windows Media Player is used to play the sounds you record. See Chapter 26 for more information.

Dictating to the PC

Blabbing to your PC isn't perfect, but it has come a long way from the days when you had to spend hours (up to 20) to train the computer to understand your voice. Man, that was tiring, not to mention the cottonmouth you'd get from talking for such long stretches! Things are better today.

To get started with speech recognition in Windows, you need a microphone or, preferably, a headset. The next stop is the Control Panel to set up the microphone. Follow these steps:

1. **Open the Control Panel.**

   See Chapter 14 for information on accessing the Control Panel.

2. **Click the Ease of Access heading.**

3. **Choose the link Start Speech Recognition.**

   The Setup Speech Recognition Wizard starts.

4. **Work your way through the wizard.**

   The wizard helps you set up a microphone; you review some options and settings. Just keep saying "Next" and you'll be fine. Or do as I did and bail out of the thing once you tire of training.

 When speech recognition is turned on, the Speech Recognition microphone window appears on the desktop, as shown in Figure 12-5. If you don't see the window, double-click the Speech Recognition icon in the notification area (shown in the margin). Right-clicking the Speech Recognition icon displays a handy and helpful pop-up menu of options.

To activate Speech Recognition, say "Listen" or click the big microphone button on the window (refer to Figure 12-5). To turn off Speech Recognition, say, "Stop listening."

Figure 12-5:
The Speech
Recognition
microphone
window.

Many Windows commands can be uttered while Speech Recognition is on, such as Open, Save, Print, Close, and Undo.

To test out speech recognition, activate it as described earlier in this section. Then dictate the following paragraph:

> Open WordPad. Hello, period. I am trying out the dictation feature in Windows period. This is really neat period. I hope the results are not too embarrassing period. Save document no I mean save period. Save this. Save this document. What's the command to save the document? Aw, forget it.

I hope you meet with better success.

✔ People who receive the most benefit from dictation software spend lots of time training their computers to understand them.

✔ Another popular dictation package is Dragon Naturally Speaking, at www.nuance.com.

Chapter 13

Delicious Hardware Leftovers

. . . .

In This Chapter

▶ Understanding power management

▶ Choosing a power management plan

▶ Setting up a dial-up modem

▶ Gauging modem speed

▶ Making the dial-up Internet connection

. . . .

I'm a big fan of leftovers. For some reason, my mom's goulash was much better the second night. And who doesn't live for the remnants of Thanksgiving Day dinner? Well, maybe not after a week, but you have to admit that there's good value in having leftovers.

Computers have lots of hardware guts, most of which you can merrily skip over in your efforts to become comfortable with your own PC. Two items among those digital leftovers are worth a good look. The first is the PC's power management system, and the second is the dial-up modem, still hanging on after all these years.

Manage the PC's Power

Your computer lusts for power. It's not the same power that some megalomaniac or fast-food store manager would want. No, the PC wants power from the wall. Electricity. Juice. As lord of your computer, you have control how much power the PC consumes, managing its thirst so that the system works but your electric bill doesn't go through the roof.

> ✔ *Power management* is a general term used to describe the capability of computers and other appliances, such as television sets and teleportation pods, to become energy-smart.

✔ The power management hardware enables a computer to turn itself off.

✔ Power management also gives your PC the capability to sleep or hibernate. Refer to Chapter 4.

✔ If you're really into saving the planet, be sure to properly dispose of old computer parts. Never just toss out a PC, a monitor, or especially a battery. Try to find a place that recycles old technology. (There be gold in them thar consoles!)

✔ The current power management standard is the Advanced Configuration and Power Interface (ACPI). It specifies various ways the PC can reduce power consumption, including placing the microprocessor in low-power mode, disabling the monitor, halting the hard drives (which normally spin all the time), managing battery power in a laptop, as well as other more technical and trivial methods.

Choosing a power management plan

Windows hides its power management settings in the Power Options window, shown in Figure 13-1. To display that window, obey these steps:

Figure 13-1:
The Power
Options
window.

— Customize a plan

— Show more plans

1. **Open the Control Panel.**

   Refer to Chapter 14 for directions.

2. **Click the Hardware and Sound heading.**

3. **Click the Power Options heading.**

   The Power Options window appears.

The Power Options window features various plans for managing the power in your PC, as listed in Figure 13-1. You can see more plans by clicking the downward-pointing arrow button thing, as illustrated in the figure.

Each plan tames two power-mad items in the computer's hardware inventory: the monitor and the rest of the computer. Specifically, the plans control when to dim or turn off the display and when to sleep the rest of the computer.

The key to invoking the power control is the timeout. The computer observes your activity; when there hasn't been any input for a given amount of time, Windows turns off the display or puts the computer to sleep. That action saves energy.

To choose a plan, select the radio button next to the plan name. Close the Power Options window and you're done.

You can also customize any plan, or create your own plan by clicking the link Create a Power Plan on the left side of the Power Options window (refer to Figure 13-1). Follow the directions on the screen. Be sure to give your power plan a clever name, such as *Dan's Plan,* which is ideal when your name happens to be Dan.

✔ Power management doesn't turn off the monitor; it merely suspends the video signal to the monitor. An energy-smart monitor detects the lack of signal and then automatically enters a low-power state. This state is often indicated by the monitor's power lamp, which dims, glows another color, or blinks while the monitor is in power-saving mode.

✔ See Chapter 4 for more information on Sleep mode.

Adding a hibernation option

Windows has never put the option to hibernate your PC in an obvious place. Because of that, my advice for putting the computer into Hibernation mode is to assign the hibernation command to the console's power button. Here's what to do:

1. **Open the Control Panel.**

2. **Choose Hardware and Sound.**

3. **Below the Power Options heading, choose the link Change What the Power Buttons Do.**

4. **From the menu button by the option titled When I Press the Power Button, choose Hibernate.**

   If two columns of options are available (On Battery and Plugged In), ensure that both menu buttons show the word Hibernate.

5. **Click the Save Changes button.**

6. **Close the Control Panel window.**

After following these steps, pressing the console's power button hibernates the computer.

See Chapter 4 for more information on PC hibernation.

Setting options for battery-powered PCs

It's obvious that a laptop computer is battery-powered. What isn't obvious is that a desktop PC — even some hulking, immobile behemoth — can also be battery-powered. Such a thing happens when you plug your computer into a UPS (Uninterruptible Power Supply) and that UPS is connected to the PC by a USB cable.

For the sake of power management, when you have a battery-powered PC, you'll discover *two* columns of options in the Edit Plan Settings window: The first column is labeled On Battery; the second is labeled Plugged In.

Options for the On Battery column are for when the computer is on battery power: a laptop out free and wild, a desktop powered by a UPS during a power outage, or when Kevin trips over the power strip again.

You set the options for the Plugged In column for when the computer is using power from the wall socket. That's the only power settings column that appears (untitled) when you have a PC that doesn't have a battery or battery power source.

Obviously, you want more power savings when your PC is running on batteries. For a laptop, changing the display and sleep values to something low, but not too low, makes sense. For a PC running on a UPS, my advice is to either hibernate or shut down the computer: Set the timeout value to one minute.

- ✔ Also see Chapter 4 for more information on UPSs.

- ✔ For more information on using your laptop and managing its battery life, see my book *Laptops For Dummies,* 5th Edition (Wiley), available exclusively in this solar system.

Merry Modems

Modem is a combination of two technical and cumbersome words, *mo*dulator and *dem*odulator. Beyond that, what a modem does is way too technical for me to bore you with here. Suffice it to say, modems are all about communications, primarily between your own PC and a remote computer elsewhere.

This section is about the old, clunky, yet still quite common dial-up modem. I express my sincere and deep regrets if you still use one. Yes, I recognize that the faster, cooler, much more desired broadband (fast) modem is what everyone needs. So whether you have a dial-up modem out of choice, or you reside in a district where broadband just isn't available, this section is for you.

- ✔ Even though you can use modems to connect any two computers, the primary purpose of a modem today is to connect your PC to the Internet.

- ✔ Chapter 20 covers broadband modems, which are part of the bigger arena of computer networking.

Adding a dial-up modem

The traditional PC modem is the dial-up modem, which uses the telephone system — the old land-line telephone system — for communications. Essentially, a dial-up modem serves as your computer's phone, though the phone calls are made to other computers (and fax machines), not to people.

Modems come in two types, internal and external. The internal models plug into an expansion slot on the PC's motherboard. The external models dangle outside the PC, tethered to a USB port.

To make the modem useful, it must be connected to the phone system — the old land-line phone system: The modem connects to a standard telephone jack, just like a regular phone. Indeed, with a modem in your computer, you're using the telephone system to place calls, though noisy data is being sent, not the dulcet tones of human communication.

- ✔ There's no extra cost for using a modem on a standard phone line. When the modem makes a long-distance call, you pay the same rates as for a voice call.

- ✔ You can't use your phone while your modem is talking. In fact, if somebody picks up another extension on that line, it garbles the signal and may lose your connection — not to mention that the human hears a horrid screeching sound.

Measuring modem speed

The gauge used to judge a modem is its speed, measured in *kilobits per second* (Kbps), or thousands of bits per second. A typical dial-up modem runs at about 55 Kbps, which is fast enough to transmit a page of text in less than a second.

✔ Modem speed is relative; the advertised speed for a modem doesn't guarantee that all communications take place at that speed.

✔ While getting a page of text in a second seems fast, most of the information on the Internet is graphical. Graphics take much longer to transmit than plain text.

✔ The speed of 55 Kpbs is the top data rate possible using existing telephone technology. That's not fast today, but still pretty impressive: When modems first appeared in the late 1970s, their speed was 300 bps, or about 1/200th of today's dial-up modem speeds.

Configuring a dial-up Internet connection

Unlike the automatic, all-the-time broadband connection, a dial-up Internet connection is something you must configure. If you're lucky, your ISP has provided you with the basic information and perhaps even a Getting Started guide. If not, you can experience the horror of setting things up manually on your own. Or just follow these steps:

1. **Open the Control Panel window.**

   Chapter 14 contains directions on how to open the Control Panel.

2. **Below the heading Network and Internet, choose View Network Status and Tasks.**

   The Network and Sharing Center window appears.

3. **Click the link Set Up a New Connection or Network.**

   In some versions of Windows, the link is titled Set Up a Connection or Network.

4. **Select the item in the list labeled Set Up a Dial-Up Connection; or in Windows 8, choose the Connect to the Internet option.**

5. **In Windows 8, choose the Set Up a New Connection Anyway option, and then on the next screen, choose Dial-Up.**

   In some versions of Windows, you may need to choose the option Broadband (PPPoE) instead of Dial-Up.

6. **If necessary, click the Next button.**

7. **Fill in the information as given to you by your ISP: its phone number, your account name (user name), and your password.**

   The username and password are used here to get into your ISP's account. They may be different from the username and password that you use to access your e-mail inbox, and the logon and password you use for Windows.

8. **Place a check mark by the Remember This Password option.**

9. **Type a name for the connection.**

   If the ISP is named CompuSoft, for example, type *CompuSoft* in the box.

10. **Ensure that the dial-up modem is plugged into a phone cord and that the phone cord is plugged into a telephone jack.**

11. **Click the Connect button.**

    Windows uses your modem to test-dial the phone number you entered.

The best news is that you need to do these steps only once. Well, unless you're using more than one ISP, in which case you need to repeat them. Better news is when your ISP has its own configuration software, in which case you can dispense with these steps and use that software to connect to the Internet.

Connecting to the Internet on dialup

The easiest way to connect to the Internet when you have a dial-up modem is to simply open or use an Internet program. For example, start up a web browser or tell your e-mail program to fetch new mail. Either action forces Windows to look for an Internet connection, by either connecting automatically or presenting a list of connections for you to choose.

To disconnect you have to "hang up" the modem. Rather than unplug the phone line, try right-clicking the little modem icon in the notification area. Choose the Disconnect command from the context menu that pops up.

  ✔ The dial-up modem must be connected to the telephone system before you can make the connection.

  ✔ After the connection is established, a tiny modem connected icon appears in the notification area. It's your clue that the PC is connected to the Internet. You can also right-click that icon to break the connection or check its status.

Part III
Basic Computing

System icons　　　Desktop　　　Shortcut icons　　　Sidebar gadgets

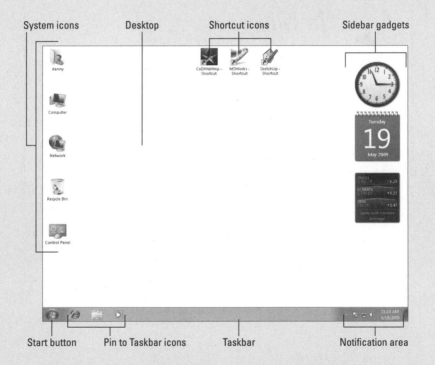

Start button　　Pin to Taskbar icons　　Taskbar　　Notification area

In this part . . .

Computer hardware is interesting technology and not really intimidating once you get to know it. But you don't own a computer merely to have its carcass sit there and impress you. No, owning a computer is about using that hardware, getting something done, having the computer assist you in your 21st-century duties. That job is a software job, with you sitting in the driver's seat. And your task is much easier after you clear the hurdle of basic computing.

Chapter 14

The Windows Tour

In This Chapter

▶ Understanding operating systems

▶ Checking out the Start screen

▶ Using the charms bar

▶ Visiting the desktop

▶ Finding the taskbar

▶ Getting at the Start button menu

▶ Viewing the notification area

▶ Accessing the Control Panel

1 remember that Microsoft originally wanted to call its new PC operating system *Doors* and not Windows. That was because, as a graphical operating system, Doors opened the doors of access to the vast power of the computer. Also, doors are easier to walk through than windows. Sadly, the estate of the late Jim Morrison sued, so Microsoft had to settle on Windows instead.

Yeah, I made up that entire paragraph.

Software controls the hardware, and the primary piece of software that controls the hardware is the operating system, Windows. Although this book is primarily about hardware, you have to use Windows to get things done with PC hardware, such as adjusting the mouse, getting on the network, and using the mass storage system. Rather than scatter that important information about Windows all over this book, I thought I'd put it here, in this chapter. Welcome to the Windows tour.

What's an Operating System?

The most important piece of software in your PC is its *operating system*. It has several duties:

- ✓ **Control the computer's hardware:** Hardware does nothing without software to tell it what to do, and the operating system *is* that software.

- ✓ **Manage all the computer programs:** The operating system isn't the only software in your computer, but it is the software in charge of all the other software.

- ✓ **Organize the storage system:** The operating system is in charge of the computer's memory, both long-term and short-term. For the long-term storage system, the operating system organizes and maintains, in files, the stuff you create on the computer.

- ✓ **Interface with you:** The operating system must also provide a way for you, the human, to use the computer. There is no requirement that this duty be a pleasant one.

On PCs, the most common operating system is Microsoft Windows. Other operating systems are available for the PC, but Windows defeated them all in a bloody battle involving treachery, betrayal, and sweeping romantic drama that only high school computer nerds would appreciate.

- ✓ The operating system is the most important piece of software in your computer. It's in charge.

- ✓ The operating system typically comes with the computer when you buy it. You never need to add a second operating system, although operating systems are updated and improved from time to time.

- ✓ When you buy software, you buy it for an operating system, not for your brand of computer. So, rather than buy software for your Dell, HP, or Crazy Larry's PC, you look in the Windows section of the software store.

- ✓ Often the Windows section is the *only* section in the software store.

Windows and Its Gooey, Glorious Graphical Interface

One of a computer operating system's primary duties is to interface with you, the human. Windows does that by presenting you with a graphical visage, spackled with interesting items given unusual names:

- ✔ Start screen

- ✔ Charms bar

- ✔ Desktop

- ✔ Taskbar

- ✔ Start button menu

- ✔ Notification area

The key to manipulating your computer is to know what those names refer to and how to use each of them to get things done. This section explains the details.

Windows sports a graphical user interface, or GUI. It's pronounced "gooey." Seriously.

Exploring the Start screen

Because Hell already has a vestibule, the folks who designed Windows 8 were forced to make its lobby, its home base, its starting point something called the Start screen. It's is the first thing you see after you sign in to Windows. Figure 14-1 illustrates the Start screen in a quasi-cheerful manner.

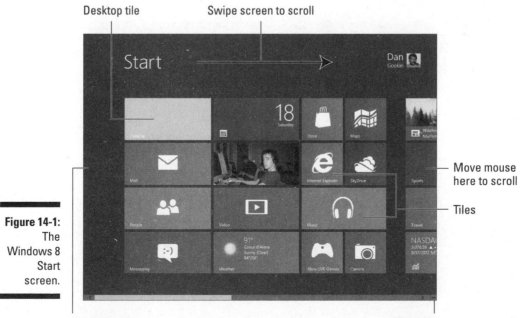

Figure 14-1:
The
Windows 8
Start
screen.

If you're familiar with older versions of Windows, you'll recognize that the Start screen is essentially a full-screen replacement for the Start button. You can start programs or apps by touching or clicking their tiles.

 ✔ *App* is short for *application.* It's a special type of program that runs directly from the Start screen, avoiding the Windows desktop.

 ✔ You can quickly summon the Start screen by pressing the Win key on the keyboard.

 ✔ You can quickly recover from the shock induced by Windows 8 by drinking the whiskey found in the cupboard.

 ✔ My biggest complaint about the Window 8 Start screen is that, unlike the Start menu it replaced, you cannot use it to show *all* the programs on your computer. See Chapter 15 for information on finding all your programs.

Summoning the charms bar

Windows 8 offers some key tasks and duties up on the charms bar, which slides in from the right edge of the screen. To summon the charms bar, move the mouse up to the top-right corner of the display. The charms bar appears, as shown in Figure 14-2.

Point mouse here to see the charms bar

Charms bar

Figure 14-2:
The
Windows 8
charms bar.

Choose a charm by touching or clicking on its icon. Of all the charms, the one referenced most often in this book is the Settings charm, found on the bottom of the list. That charm deals with some hardware items you may see referenced in this book from time to time.

The charms bar appears whenever you move the mouse to the top-right corner of the display, even when you're viewing the desktop or a traditional Windows program.

Working at the desktop

For versions of Windows before Windows 8, the main screen is the desktop, shown in Figure 14-3. Windows 8 also has a desktop, which you can access by clicking or touching the Desktop tile (refer to Figure 14-1) or by pressing the Win+D keyboard shortcut.

The desktop is where the actual windows appear, the windows containing your programs, games, and other fun computer whatnot. Features on the desktop include icons, gadgets, and the taskbar.

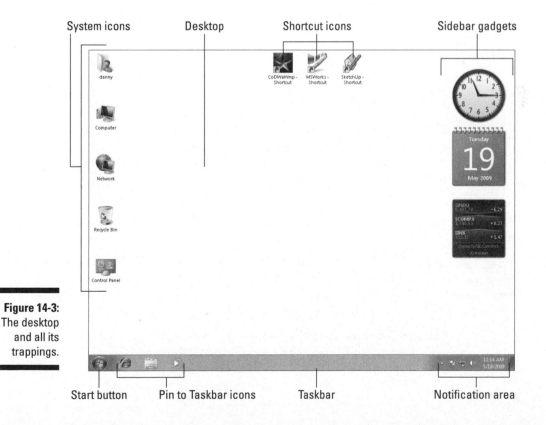

Figure 14-3: The desktop and all its trappings.

Icons are tiny pictures that represent information or programs stored on your computer. System icons represent fun and interesting places to visit in Windows. Shortcut icons are used to start programs, visit websites, and more. See Chapter 15 for more information on icons.

Windows sidebar gadgets display information such as the time or stock quotes or images or games or other diversionary items. The gadgets may appear along the edge of the desktop; they can float anywhere; or they might not even show up.

The taskbar is its own unique gizmo, covered in the next section.

Not shown in Figure 14-1 is the *mouse pointer,* the tiny arrow that manipulates the graphical goodies you see on the screen. The mouse pointer is controlled by the mouse, covered in Chapter 9.

- ✔ The Windows 8 desktop looks identical to the one shown in Figure 14-3, though in Windows 8 there is no Start button.
- ✔ The desktop background, or wallpaper, can be a fancy image or picture, a slide show, or the famous *Snowbank* painting, shown in Figure 14-3.
- ✔ The desktop is called a desktop for traditional reasons. Early graphical operating systems featured a desktop that really did look like a desktop, complete with paper pad, clock, glue, scissors, and other desktop-y things.

Using the taskbar

The action in Windows takes place on the desktop, but that action starts at the taskbar. The taskbar is normally found lurking at the bottom of the display, as shown in Figure 14-4. On the taskbar dwell various interesting and useful items:

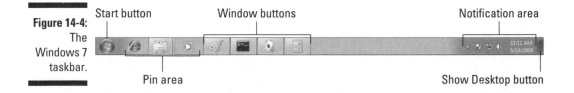

Figure 14-4: The Windows 7 taskbar.

Start button   Window buttons   Notification area

Pin area   Show Desktop button

Start button: From Windows 7 on back to the early Cro-Magnon versions of Windows, this button is where you start programs and control Windows. Window 8 uses the Start screen instead.

Pin area: The icons on this part of the taskbar are used to quickly start programs or perform common tasks in Windows.

Window buttons: A button appears on the taskbar for each window or program running in Windows. Those things are called *tasks,* which is why the taskbar is called the taskbar and not the candy bar.

Notification area: This part of the taskbar contains tiny icons that help you run your computer or alert you to certain things going on.

The taskbar is locked into position, held at the bottom of the desktop by digital bolts made of the strongest bits. Still, the taskbar can be unlocked and moved, so it might not always be at the bottom of the screen. Further, the taskbar can be configured to be hidden, though it pops up automatically if you point the mouse at the edge of the screen where the taskbar was last seen.

Accessing the Start menu

On the left end of the taskbar, you'll find the Start button — assuming that the taskbar is docked at its usual spot on the bottom of the screen. As its name suggests, the Start button is used to start things in Windows. What kinds of things? Trouble!

Seriously, clicking the Start button displays the Start button menu, shown in Figure 14-5. It's from that menu that you can start just about any program or activity in Windows.

Important things to find on the Start button menu are listed in Figure 14-5. The Start button menu can be customized, so it may not appear exactly like what you see in the figure, but it's close.

One of the most important items on the Start button menu is the All Programs menu. When you click the All Programs triangle (refer to Figure 14-5), the left side of the Start button menu is replaced with a list of programs and folders. You can either choose a program from the list to run the program or choose a folder to see additional programs. Chapter 15 offers more information on the Start button menu and your programs.

✔ In Windows XP, the Start button has the word *Start* on it.

✔ A quick way to pop up the Start button menu is to press the Win key on your computer's keyboard. But keep in mind that in Windows 8, pressing the Win key displays the Start screen.

✔ You make the Start button menu go away by pressing the Esc key on the keyboard.

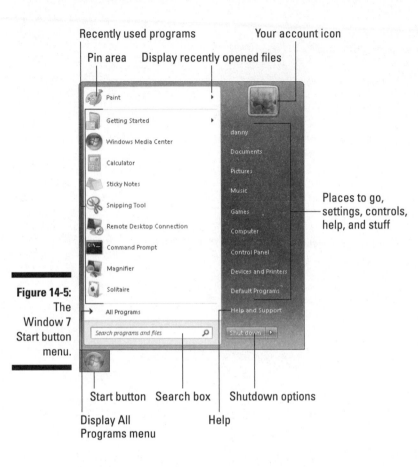

Recently used programs

Pin area   Display recently opened files

Your account icon

Places to go, settings, controls, help, and stuff

Figure 14-5:
The Window 7 Start button menu.

Start button   Search box   Shutdown options

Display All Programs menu   Help

Looking at the notification area

Those teensy icons on the far right side of the taskbar aren't just sitting around waiting for a bus. Nope, they are part of a thing called the *notification area*. The icons, along with the current date and time, allow you to control various things in Windows, check in on running programs, adjust the volume, and perform other miscellaneous chores.

As with just about everything in Windows, the notification area can be customized. You can see a lot of icons there, a few, or none. Also, icons may come or go. Don't let the random nature of the notification area vex you.

✔ You can see more information about the special programs by clicking, right-clicking, or double-clicking the wee icons. Windows is inconsistent on the action required so try all three: click, right-click, and then double-click.

✔ Some icons display pop-up bubbles with messages in them as various things happen in Windows. Click the X in the pop-up bubble to dismiss the message.

✔ To customize the notification area, right-click the time display and then choose the Properties command from the shortcut menu. Use the System Icons window to show or hide notifications from Windows. Click the Customize Notification Icons link to set how other items come and go in the notification area.

The Control Panel

As the top dog, the operating system must have a direct method of control over your PC's hardware. There has to be a special window or panel where that control could take place. Logically enough, it's called the *Control Panel.*

The easiest way to summon the Control Panel in Windows 8 is to obey these steps:

1. **Right-click the lower-left corner of the display.**

2. **Choose the Control Panel command from the shortcut menu.**

In Windows 7 and earlier versions of Windows, display the Control Panel window thusly:

1. **Click the Start button.**

2. **Click the Control Panel menu item on the right side of the Start button menu.**

The Control Panel has two distinct looks, shown in Figure 14-6: category view and icon view. Computer nerds prefer the icon view; cats enjoy the category view.

To switch views, use the View By menu located in the upper-right corner of the Control Panel window (refer to Figure 14-6). Choose Category, Large Icons, or Small Icons.

In Windows Vista, in the upper-left, choose Control Panel Home for category view or choose Classic View for icon view.

Windows XP shows the Control Panel in icon view only.

Change view

Category view

Change view

Icon view

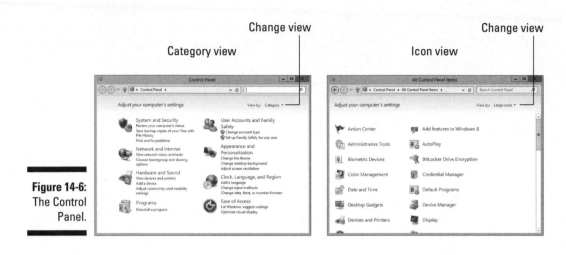

Figure 14-6:
The Control
Panel.

Chapter 15

It's the Software Chapter

In This Chapter

▶ Understanding computer programs

▶ Adding software to your PC

▶ Starting programs

▶ Adding new software

▶ Getting programs from the web

▶ Removing software

▶ Updating and upgrading software

▶ Keeping Windows up-to-date

*B*eyond the operating system, you use software in your PC to get something done. Computer software is available to do all sorts of things, be it work, be it play, or be it something you claim is important but really isn't, such as social networking. All that activity is the reason why you bought a computer, and the software makes it happen.

Software Cavalcade

The operating system isn't the only software you use on your computer. The typical computer features lots of software. Some of it lurks in deep, dark places, controlling specific pieces of hardware. Most software, however, is productivity software, designed for the human operator to get work done. Oh, and some of it is entertainment software, which is the fun stuff.

Computer software is known by several different names. In addition to the general term *software,* you find:

App: An abbreviation for application (see below), although the term technically describes smaller, specific software found on a smartphone or tablet. In Windows 8, you'll find apps on the Start screen.

Application: A category of software used for productivity or to create things. Applications are the software that does the work.

Driver: A special type of software that allows specific hardware to work. For example, a specific *video driver* is required for the operating system to use the PC's graphics hardware.

Game: Software for fun, of course.

Malware: This term refers to nasty software, the viruses, Trojans, spyware, and other creeps that are designed to cause you angst. No one installs this software on purpose.

Program: A general term for all software. Whether it be an app, a game, or a driver, it's a computer program.

Utility or tool: Software designed to help you manage the computer or diagnose or fix problems. For example, you may use a tool to optimize the performance of your computer's storage system.

Programs on Your PC

Your computer day involves more than just staring blankly at the monitor. Of course, I'm assuming that your supervisor is watching while you use the computer. When you work by yourself, or are at home, please feel free to stare blankly at the monitor. When you want to get work done, you'll need to rustle up some programs, as described in this section.

Hunting down programs in Windows

The software on your computer doesn't just jump up and beg to be run. Well, some of it does. Some programs start automatically, but the rest of the time you must venture out and fetch a program to run. The method for locating these programs was pretty uniform until Windows 8 sauntered into town.

Start a program in Windows 8

Software that is geared toward Windows 8 appears on the Start screen as a tile. To visit the Start screen, press the Windows (Win) key on the keyboard. Touch or click a tile to start a program.

For example, to start the Mail program, touch or click the Mail tile found on the Start screen. The program or app opens on the screen, ready for action.

- ✔ Some tiles on the Windows 8 Start screen are apps, or miniprograms that run full screen. Other tiles represent traditional Windows programs that run in windows on the desktop. Still more tiles could be web page bookmarks, which open a browser app so that you can view that page.

- ✔ To see a list of all the programs on your computer, right-click the Start screen and choose the command All Apps, which is in the lower-right corner. You'll see the Apps screen, which shows buttons (or tiles) for all the apps on your PC.

- ✔ The Apps screen doesn't show *all* the programs on your PC, but rather all the most useful ones. Your computer has thousands of programs but you'll use only a handful regularly.

Start a program in Windows versions before Windows 8

Before version 8, Windows users found programs on the Start button menu, tucked away in the All Programs submenu. Clicking the All Programs submenu displayed an organized list — a menu — full of categories, each stuffed with shortcut icons to start just about every program installed on the PC.

For example, to start the Paint program, click the Start button, choose All Programs, then choose Accessories, and then choose Paint. The Paint program's window opens up, ready for action.

- ✔ The All Programs menu is named Programs in Windows XP.

- ✔ The Start button menu lists recently run programs on the left side of the menu. Click one of those programs to start it up again.

- ✔ A quick way to find programs on the Start menu is to use the Search Programs and Files text box, found in the lower-left corner of the pop-up menu. Start typing a program name, and then choose the matching program icons that appear in the list.

- ✔ Newly installed applications appear highlighted on the Start button menu. That way, you can easily find stuff you've just installed. See the later section, "Installing a program from an optical disc."

Running a program from the desktop

A handy way to run programs is to start them from the desktop. In fact, the desktop you see on your PC right now may be decked out with tiny program shortcut icons. To start a program, double-click its desktop icon.

The taskbar, which you'll find clinging to the bottom of the desktop, can also sport shortcut icons used to start programs. Those icons appear in the Pin area on the left end of the taskbar. To run a program pinned to the taskbar, click its icon button once.

✔ It's handy to have program shortcut icons stuck to the desktop or pinned to the taskbar. I highly recommend that you pin your most frequently used programs to the taskbar. Copy other programs to the desktop as shortcut icons.

✔ To pin an icon to the taskbar, right-click the icon found on the Start screen or Start button menu. Choose the command Pin to Taskbar.

✔ Not every tile on the Windows 8 Start screen or on the Windows 8 Apps screen can be pinned to the taskbar.

✔ To pin an icon to the Start menu, right-click the program's icon on the All Programs menu, and then choose the Pin to Start Menu command. Having icons pinned to the Start menu is another way to keep those programs handy.

✔ To stick an icon on the desktop, right-click the program's icon, such as one you'd find on the All Programs menu, and then choose the command Send To⇨Desktop (Create Shortcut).

Running a program manually

Here's something scary: You can run programs in Windows just like your grandfather did on his ancient DOS computer. That is, you can actually type in the text command that runs a program. Sometimes such a thing is necessary — and often faster — than hunting down an icon.

The secret is to use the Win+R keyboard shortcut. When you press Win+R you summon the Run dialog box. In the Open text box that appears, you can type a command to run any program in Windows — providing that you know the program's super-secret text name.

For example, to run the Paint program, type **mspaint** into the Run dialog box and click the OK button. The Paint program instantly starts because *mspaint* is the super-secret name for the Paint program.

More Software, Less Software

Computer programs don't magically spawn on your computer, growing like mutating fungus in some post-apocalyptic nightmare. Nope, you must invite the programs in. Invitations are extended directly, usually in the form of an optical disc inside a software box, or you can obtain new software from the Internet.

Just as you let them in, you eventually let software back out of your computer. The process is called *uninstalling,* and it rarely involves the use of high explosives.

Installing a program from an optical disc

You have new software. You probably bought it at the store or it arrived bright and shiny from a friendly, sweaty guy driving a delivery truck. Either way, your job is to get the software out of the box and into your computer in a fully functional state. Here's how to do that:

1. **Open the software box and locate the installation disc.**

   When you have more than one disc, note in which order they're used; the discs should be numbered, and you start with the first disc.

2. **Insert the installation disc into the PC's optical drive.**

   Chapter 7 has specific directions for inserting optical discs.

3. **Run the installation program.**

   If you're lucky, the installation program runs automatically after the disk is inserted. Or you see an AutoPlay dialog box, from which you can choose the Install or Setup command. If not, don't despair! Try this:

   a. Press Win+E to open the Computer window.

   b. Right-click the optical drive's icon.

   c. Choose the command Install or Run Program from Your Media. If that command isn't available, choose the AutoPlay command.

4. **Obey the instructions on the screen.**

   Work through the directions on the screen to install, set up, and configure the new software.

Some software lets you run the program right after installation. Other times you may have to hunt down the new program, a task that's described elsewhere in this chapter.

It takes time to learn new software — even computer games. It's natural to be frustrated at first. That's okay; you're only human. Just keep trying and eventually you'll learn the program. Of course, buying a good book about the software is an excellent idea!

- ✔ Generally speaking, few — if any — stores let you return computer software after you open the box.

- ✔ I recommend keeping the box. Use it to store the installation discs as well as the manual or whatever trivial items came in the box.

Finding programs on the Internet

Your quest for free (or not) software on the Internet begins by searching. What are you looking for? Search for the software the same way you would search for information on Estonia, aquatic park restaurants near Cody, Wyoming, or hot pictures of Megan Fox. Use Google or Bing or any available web search engine to find your software.

After you locate the software, the next step is to download it. A *download* is a transfer of information from another computer, or server, to your PC. That operation works like this:

1. **Visit the web page that contains the download link.**

   The link may be text, or it may be a big, fun graphical button. Sometimes, the link takes you to another page. Eventually, you'll find the download link or button.

2. **Click the link or graphical image that begins the download.**

   I recommend clicking the EXE or program file link. Don't click a compressed folder, Zip, or archive file, as doing so involves extra steps before you can actually install and run the program.

3. **Mind the security warning.**

   Most web browsers alert you whenever software attempts to flow into your computer. You must grant permission; otherwise, who-knows-what might be downloaded into your PC.

4. **Click the Save button.**

   When given the choice between opening or saving the file, I recommend Save. That way you'll always have the file should you need it later.

5. **Click the Save button in the Save As dialog box.**

   Generally speaking, the download's filename and its location on your PC's mass storage device are fine. The filename may be cryptic, but it's the name of the program you're downloading, plus perhaps a version number. The file's location is the Downloads folder in your personal account area, which is perfect.

6. **Sit and watch as the file is copied from the Internet to your computer.**

   Doh-dee-doh-doh.

   By the way, what you're downloading is an install or setup program, which will eventually configure and install the software you'll eventually use.

7. **To install the program, click the Open button, or in some web browsers double-click the link or icon representing the downloaded file.**

8. **If you're greeted with a security warning, click the Allow button.**

9. **Obey the directions on the screen to finish the installation.**

   The directions are specific to whatever it is you're installing. If you're installing a program from a compressed folder or Zip file, see Chapter 18.

After installing the program, you can run it or do anything you would normally do with any software installed on your computer. The only difference is that the new software was downloaded from the Internet instead of installed from an optical disc.

- ✔ Get used to obtaining software from the Internet. It's the way most software will be installed on PCs in the future. Well, actually *now*. It's the way software is being installed right now.

- ✔ Avoid visiting web pages that offer free screen savers, desktop backgrounds, or device drivers. Those programs are most likely illegitimate; if you download them, you will regret it.

- ✔ If you search for hacker tools or free movies, music, books, or other illegal material, odds are good that you'll end up at an illegitimate website. The result may be a virus or another infection on your PC, not the software you wanted.

- ✔ The only way to be certain that you're not downloading anything nefarious is to use security software on your PC. See Chapter 24.

- ✔ Downloading a program and installing it works just like installing software you bought from the store. The only difference is that rather than use an optical disc, you use a file you download from the Internet to install.

Uninstalling a program

Nothing makes Windows more irate than when software is rudely and abruptly removed from your computer. Don't use pliers, and especially don't use a periosteal elevator. Instead, follow the proper uninstall procedure. Here's how it works:

1. **Open the Control Panel.**

   Directions to the Control Panel are found in Chapter 14.

2. **Click the Uninstall a Program link, found below the Programs heading.**

   The Programs and Features window appears, listing all software installed on your PC.

3. **Select the program you want to uninstall.**

4. **Click the Uninstall or Uninstall/Change button on the toolbar.**

5. **If prompted by a User Account Control, type the administrator password or click the Continue button.**

6. **Continue reading instructions on the screen to uninstall the program.**

   The uninstall directions vary from program to program, but eventually the program is removed.

Use these steps to uninstall software. Deleting a shortcut icon doesn't uninstall a program. Deleting a program file doesn't uninstall the software either. No, follow the steps in this section to properly, officially, finally remove software.

The Latest Version

It's a common saying in the computer industry that software is never done. In fact, if it weren't for management, programmers would never finish. Even when they do finish, things called bugs need to be fixed and people demand new features, which are added. The result is the *software update* or the more drastic *software upgrade*.

Updating and upgrading

What's the difference between an update and an upgrade? *Updates* are gradual and tiny. They repair, or *patch,* software you've already purchased. For example, an update may fix a bug or problem. An update can fine-tune some features. And updates are usually free.

Upgrades, however, are complete revisions of programs. An upgrade presents a new release of the software, along with a version number. For example, the latest version of Microsoft Office is an upgrade, not an update. Also, upgrades cost money.

My advice: Update frequently. If the manufacturer offers a patch or a fix, install it as recommended. On the other hand, updates are necessary only when you desperately need the new features or modifications or when the upgrade addresses security issues.

✔ Update: A minor fix to some software you own. A patch. No charge.

✔ Upgrade: A new version of the program. You pay for it.

✔ Updates are distributed by the manufacturer. As long as you register your software, you'll be alerted to updates, usually by e-mail. Most of the software updates you receive are downloaded through the Internet, installed just like software you download from the Internet.

✔ Here's something else to keep in mind: If you're still using Doodle Writer 4.2 and everybody else is using DoodleWriter 6.1, you may have difficulty exchanging documents. After a while, newer versions of programs become incompatible with their older models. If so, you need to upgrade.

✔ In an office setting, everybody should be using the same software version. Everybody doesn't have to be using the *latest* version, just the *same* version.

Updating Windows

I highly recommend that you keep your PC's operating system updated. This task requires regular communications between your computer and the Microsoft mothership. No need to fret: The scheduling happens automatically. If any new updates, or patches, are needed, they're automatically installed on your computer. You need to do nothing.

Well, you do need to ensure that you configured your PC to accept automatic updates by using the Windows Update service. Here's how:

1. **Open the Control Panel window.**

2. **Click the System and Security heading.**

3. **Below the Windows Update heading, find the Turn Automatic Updating On or Off link and turn it On.**

   Ensure that updates are being checked regularly, on a schedule.

4. **Click the OK button if you made any changes.**

   You may need to type the administrator's password or click the Continue button to confirm your choice.

5. **Close the window.**

The updates will happen regularly. Depending on how you've directed Windows to keep itself updated, you may be prompted to install an update or the updates may happen automatically. If you're prompted, simply restart your PC and the updates are installed. Or you may discover that your computer restarts automatically, especially if you leave it on all night. Either way, keeping Windows up-to-date is important.

Updating Windows is part of your PC's overall security. See Chapter 24 for more information about PC security.

Upgrading to the latest version of Windows

Microsoft upgrades Windows to a new version about once every few years. The newer version offers better features and a different way of doing things than did the previous version. Even so, you don't have to upgrade to the newer version of Windows. In fact, I strongly recommend against it.

Windows is your PC's operating system. It's closely geared to the hardware in your computer. It has been so customized that replicating that specific customization, especially with a newer version of the operating system, is *very* difficult. That's why upgrading Windows causes lots of people problems, compatibility issues, and unnecessary headaches.

If you really want the new version of Windows, my advice is to buy a new computer with the new version of Windows preinstalled.

Chapter 16

Fun with Files and Folders

● ●

In This Chapter

▶ Understanding the whole file thing

▶ Saving and naming files

▶ Understanding file types

▶ Visiting famous folders

▶ Finding your account folder

▶ Creating new folders

▶ Working in the Open dialog box

● ●

*H*ere's a computer secret: Understand what a *file* is and you and your computer will have a far more productive relationship. That's because the file is the basic unit of computer storage. It's a container, into which all sorts of wonderful, mysterious, and useful things are kept.

Coupled with the file is another digital container, the *folder*. Folders hold files, keeping them organized, which helps you keep your sanity. Just as keeping your sanity may somehow be important to you, understanding files and folders is central to the goal of maintaining a harmonious relationship with your PC.

Behold the File!

All that digital information stored inside your computer doesn't float around, wild and loose like grains of sand in a dust storm. Instead, that information is kept neat and tidy inside little digital jars. Those jars are called files.

A *file* is a chunk of information stored in a computer.

Most likely, the first computer scientists chose the word *file* because of its association with files used in an office setting. In a way, computer files are like paper files, but far more versatile. On your computer, a file can hold a text document, an image, music, a video, ugly raw computer data, or a program.

✔ Unlike the jars Aunt Trudy uses for her pear preserves, the container that holds a file isn't of a fixed size. It can be as big or as small as needed to hold the information inside the file.

✔ Computer programs are used to create files. When you save information in a program, such as a document in a word processor, you're creating a file.

✔ Files are created in computer memory, but they're kept on the mass storage system. See Chapter 7.

Describing a file

If you were ever battered by a computer file, the police would probably ask you to describe your assailant. Files have no height or weight. They lack body odor, scars, or tattoos. So how would you describing one?

The good news is that computer files rarely assault people. If they did, or should the opportunity arise for you to describe a file, you'd use one or more of the following characteristics:

Name: All files have a name, or *filename*. The name is given to the file when it's created and, I hope, describes the file's contents or gives you a clue as to the file's purpose.

Icon: Files are represented visually in the Windows operating system as tiny pictures. The type of picture gives you an idea as to the type of file or which program was used to create the file. The icons are also how the file is manipulated, copied, deleted, and so on.

Figure 16-1 illustrates several files, showing their icons and names. Some files, such as Word documents, use a standard image for the icon. Other files, such as the Picture and Fax examples, show a document or image preview. A generic icon is used for files where the file type is unknown or not recognized.

Other trivial details: Files also have a size, date, and type. The size is the amount of storage required for the file's contents, measured in bytes. The date is applied to the file when it's created, but also whenever it's updated or modified. The file type is set by the file's contents, such as plain text, graphics, or audio.

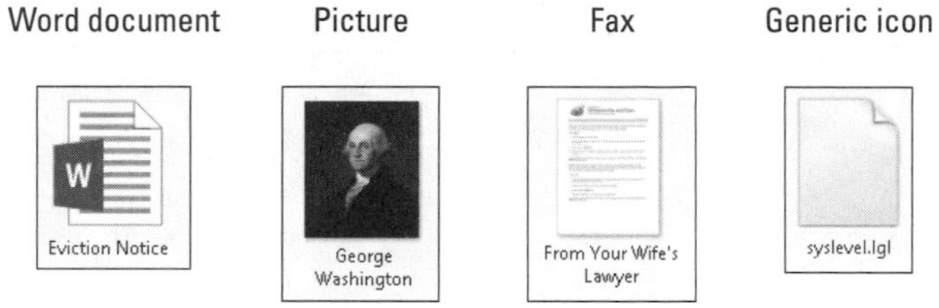

Word document   Picture   Fax   Generic icon

Figure 16-1:
Files with
icons and
names.

Eviction Notice   George Washington   From Your Wife's Lawyer   syslevel.lgl

Another attribute used to describe a file is its location. That's a big deal, so the file's location is covered later in this chapter, in the section "Folder Folderol."

✔ Not every version of Windows displays image previews for an icon.

✔ A file's name and icon both appear in the various folder windows displayed by the Windows Explorer program. Further details about the file can be displayed, but only when the folder is customized to display that information; use the folder's View button or menu to change the way files are displayed.

✔ File type is closely related to the file's icon. All files created by a specific program, for example, are of the same type and sport the same icon.

✔ Files can be named just about anything. Although, like driving a tank through a shopping mall, some rules are involved. See the next section.

✔ A file can be any size, from zero bytes to billions of bytes. Refer to Chapter 6 for more information on bytes.

Creating a new file

Files are born in the programs you use, conceived in the computer's memory. At some point, preferably early and often, you save your work. That's a key word, *save.* When you use a program's Save As command, you're creating a file. Specifically, the Save As dialog box, shown in Figure 16-2, is what makes files on your computer.

Of all the fun potential crammed into the Save As dialog box, only three key things are done with regards to creating a new file:

Give the file a name. Use the File Name text box to type a short, descriptive name for the file. See the next section for information on filenames.

Set the file type. Use the Save As Type button menu to choose which type of file to save. This step is necessary only when a unique file type is required, such as when sharing a document with another computer or saving an image in a specific graphics file format.

Favorite folders and other
locations for saving files

Location where the
file will be saved

File's specific location (address bar)

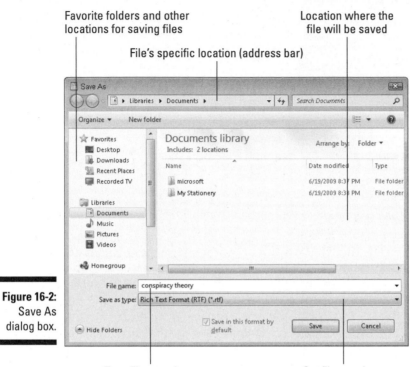

Figure 16-2:
Save As
dialog box.

Type filename here

Set file type here

Choose the file's location. The Save As dialog box features lots of gizmos for choosing the file's location. Files dwell in folders, so choosing the proper folder helps keep your stuff organized. See the later section, "Folder Folderol."

The final thing to do is to click the Save button, which actually creates the file.

- ✔ The Save As dialog box is but one way to make a file. Files can also be created from copies of other files.

- ✔ Windows 8 apps, and some newer Microsoft programs, use a Save screen as opposed to the traditional Save As dialog box. The Save screen features the same basic controls as the Save As dialog box, though in fine Microsoft tradition, everything is moved around randomly for no apparent reason.

- ✔ The Save command works identically to the Save As command when a file is first created. After that, the Save command is used to update or refresh the file. You're not prompted to choose a name, location, and file type when you update a file.

- ✔ The Save command can also be accessed from the Save button on a toolbar or by pressing Ctrl+S on the keyboard.

> ✔ After a file has been saved, the file's name appears on the title bar (at the top of the window). That's your clue that a file has been saved.

Naming files

According to Genesis, Adam named all the animals on the earth. I'm assuming that Adam was more than three years old, because he didn't name every animal he saw "dog." Regardless, unless you discover some new beast, the opportunity to name animals is long past. You do, however, have ample opportunity to name files on your PC.

The best rule for naming files is to be descriptive and brief. Use letters, numbers, and spaces in the name. Here are some examples:

```
Bio
Pool Party
Speech August 8
2013 Vacation to Omaha
How to drive whilst in Canada
```

Each of these examples is a good filename, which properly explains the file's contents. But before you run amok with creativity, here are the official Windows file-naming rules:

Characters: Files can be named using any combination of letters and numbers, plus a smattering of symbols.

Length: Technically, you can give a file a name that's over 200 characters long. Don't. Long filenames may be *very* descriptive, but Windows displays them in a funny way, or not at all, in many situations. Better to keep things short than to abuse long-filename privileges.

Forbidden characters: Windows gets cranky when you use any of these characters to name a file:

```
* / : < > ? \ | "
```

These symbols hold special meaning to Windows. Nothing bad happens if you attempt to use these characters. Windows just refuses to save the file — or a warning dialog box growls at you.

Periods and spaces: You can't name a file using all periods. Spaces are okay, as are most other non-forbidden characters.

You bestow a name on a file when it's created by using the Save As dialog box. You can also rename a file, which is part of file management — something most Windows users avoid, so I barely cover it in Chapter 17.

> ✔ Uppercase or lowercase filenames don't matter to Windows. Internally, Windows sees all files as uppercase.
>
> ✔ Although case doesn't matter in a filename, it *does* matter when you're typing a web page address.

Understanding the filename extension

Beyond the name, Windows identifies files by their file type. The type is used to assign an icon to that file and to associate the file with a program. For example, Word documents are associated with the Microsoft Word program, which is how Windows knows to start Word whenever you open a Word file icon.

The way Windows identifies the file type is by using the secret, last part of a filename, the *extension.* Just as your last name identifies your family, the filename extension in Windows identifies a file's type.

The filename extension is automatically appended to files you create. It's set by the Save as Type button in the Save As dialog box (refer to Figure 16-2). You don't normally see the extension because Windows hides it, but it's there.

You can direct Windows to display that extension for you. Abide by these steps:

1. **Open the Control Panel.**
2. **Click the Appearance and Personalization heading.**
3. **Below the Folder Options heading, click the Show Hidden Files and Folders link.**

   No, you don't see hidden files or folders, but by clicking the link, you quickly see the View tab in the Folder Options dialog box.

4. **Remove the check mark by the item on the list that says Hide Extensions for Known File Types.**

   Or, if the item is already set the way you like, you're just dandy.

5. **Click OK to close the Folder Options dialog box.**
6. **Close the Control Panel window.**

With the extensions visible, you'll see them appended to all the filenames in Windows. Well, all the filenames that have extensions; not every file has an extension.

✔ When you elect to show filename extensions, be careful never to change or delete the extension when you rename a file. Also, there is no need to type the extension when you use the Save As dialog box to save a file; the program adds the extension for you automatically.

 ✔ The filename extension starts with a period and is followed by one to four characters. For example, the `.txt` filename extension is used to identify text files. Web page files use the `.htm` or `.html` filename extension. Graphics files have a number of filename extensions, depending on the graphics file type: `gif`, `jpg`, `png`, and `tiff`, for example.

 ✔ Gazillions of filename extensions are out there, too many to list here. If you're curious, you can visit the website `www.filext.com` to review or look up a filename extension.

Folder Folderol

A *folder* is a container for files, designed to help keep your files organized. It was chosen over the earlier file container, the rubber band, which was too constricting on the larger files.

 ✔ A *folder* is a storage place for files. All files dwell in folders.

 ✔ Folders keep like files grouped together — the way barbed wire keeps prisoners, vicious animals, and toddlers from wandering off.

 ✔ Without folders, your PC's mass storage would contain tens of thousands of files, all listed one after the other. It would take you months to find anything.

 ✔ Folders appear in Windows using the folder icon. When the folder is empty, it appears as shown in the margin. A folder with contents appears full, sometimes even previewing the contents in the folder icon itself.

 ✔ To open the folder, double-click it with the mouse. Folders open into a window that displays the folder's contents. The program that displays folder windows is called Windows Explorer.

 ✔ Folders may also be referred to as *directories*. This term is merely a throwback to the early days of computing and the Unix operating system, which was used by Julius Caesar.

Understanding subfolders and parent folders

Folders can contain both files and other folders. When one folder exists inside another, it's a *subfolder*. This term has nothing to do with underwater naval vessels or hoagie-like sandwiches.

Subfolders add to the concept of file organization. After all, if you have a folder named Vacations, having a subfolder named Disneyland would make sense. Into the Disneyland folder you would put files associated with your Disney vacation. Figure 16-3 illustrates the concept.

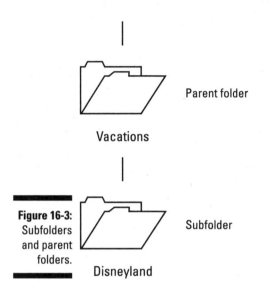

Figure 16-3: Subfolders and parent folders.

Parent folder

Vacations

Subfolder

Disneyland

The Disneyland folder is a subfolder of the Vacations folder. Likewise, the Vacations folder is the parent folder of the Disneyland folder. You could also say that the Vacations folder is one level up from the Disneyland folder.

 ✔ Creating subfolders is part of organizing your files. See the section "Making a new folder," later in this chapter, for the details.

 ✔ No limit exists on the number of subfolders you can have. A folder can be inside a folder inside a folder, and so on. If you name the folders well, it all makes sense.

Reviewing famous folders

Folders are a necessary part of file organization, and they're used all over your computer: When Windows first configures your PC, it creates a slew of folders, some for it and some for you. Software you install on your computer also creates folders. It's folder madness!

Here are some folders common to all Windows computers:

Desktop: The top folder in Windows is the Desktop, the same desktop you see when you're using older versions of Windows or trying to avoid the Start screen in Windows 8. Icons you store on the desktop appear in the Desktop folder, as do the Control Panel icon and the Computer folder, the Recycle Bin folder, and other legendary folders.

Computer: This folder contains all the mass storage devices available to your computer. These devices include disk drives, optical drives, media storage, as well as any network drives you're using.

The root folder: The first, or only, folder on a mass storage device is called the *root* folder. In the same way a tree trunk has many limbs branching out from it, all other folders on your hard drive branch out from the main, or root, folder. All storage media attached to your PC have a root folder.

Recycle Bin: This special folder represents the place where files go after they're deleted. No, it's more like Purgatory than Hell. An icon for this folder usually squats on the desktop.

Network: This folder represents available network connections, which include computer, printers, and media-sharing gizmos. Networking is covered in Part IV.

User Profile: The main folder for your stuff is named after your account and referred to as the User Profile folder. Within this folder, you find various sub-folders to help you organize your stuff. See the next section.

Similar to the concept of the folder is the *library,* which is unique to Windows 8 and Windows 7. A library is not a folder but rather a collection of folders. You'll find libraries for your documents, music, videos, and pictures. You can also create libraries to store computer games, specific projects, or your col-lection of racy salt shaker photos, for example.

Beyond your User Profile folder and the desktop, you should never add, delete, or change any files or folders in any other folder. Only files in your User Profile folder, which includes the Desktop folder, belong to you.

Finding a place for your stuff

The *User Profile* folder — a dog-ugly name for the thing — is the main folder for storing your stuff in Windows. It's named after your account on the com-puter. So, if your account is named Danny, the User Profile folder is named Danny. That name was chosen when Windows was first configured.

To see the contents of your User Profile folder, press Win+E to summon the My Computer window, and then choose your account name from the left side of the window. You can also choose your account name from the menu button, as illustrated in Figure 16-4. Click the triangle to display the menu, and then choose your account name.

Choose your account name here

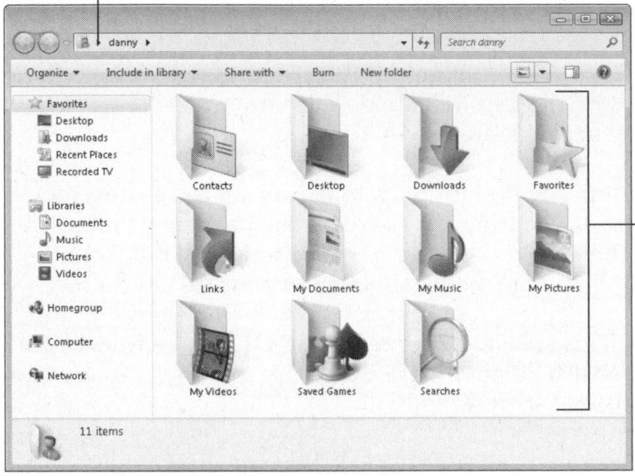

Contents of your
User Account folder

Figure 16-4:
The User
Account
folder
window.

Inside your User Account Folder window, you find about a dozen folders precreated for you, each of which helps you organize the stuff you collect or create on your computer. Table 16-1 lists the folders commonly found.

Table 16-1	Subfolders in the User Profile Folder
Folder Name	*Contains*
Contacts	A database of people's names used by e-mail, list-making, or personal-information programs
Desktop	A duplicate of files and shortcuts placed on the desktop
Downloads	Files retrieved from the Internet
Favorites	Bookmarks set and used by Internet Explorer
Links	Shortcuts to popular files and folders, displayed in the Windows Explorer window
My Documents	Text documents and similar files
My Music	Audio and music files, used by Windows Media Player and other musical programs
My Pictures	Digital images, photographs, drawings, and artwork
My Videos	Films, movies, and animations
Saved Games	Information retained by games so that you can remember your spot or high score from a previously played game
Searches	A set of predefined or saved file searches

Additional subfolders may be found in your User Profile folder — folders you created yourself or folders added by programs you installed. That's all okay; the User Profile folder is your own, and it's where you're supposed to create folders to help organize your stuff.

- ✔ All applications automatically choose the User Account folder or one of its subfolders when you use the Save As dialog box to save a file.

- ✔ You might also see files saved or opened from the various libraries in Windows. See the later section "Working with libraries."

- ✔ In Windows Vista, the My Documents, My Pictures, My Music, and My Video folders are named without the *My* prefix.

Making a new folder

It's up to you to keep your files organized, and the User Account folder is the fertile ground in which you plant those folder seeds.

Yeah, that was corny.

To create a new folder, obey these steps:

1. Open a folder window.

Folders dwell within folders, so open a folder icon to display a folder window. In that window you'll be creating the new folder.

2. Click the New Folder icon on the toolbar.

In Windows Vista, you need to click the Organize button to display its menu, and then choose the New Folder command.

The New Folder icon appears in the window, ready to be given a new name.

3. Type the new folder's name.

Make it short and descriptive; the same rules for naming files also apply to folders.

4. Pressing the Enter key locks in the new folder's name.

You can use the folder immediately after creating it.

You can also create a new folder when saving a file; a New Folder button appears in the Save As dialog box (refer to Figure 16-2).

- ✔ Sometimes, the New Folder button gets pushed off the Windows Explorer toolbar. It's still there; you just need to click the "show more" chevron at the end of the toolbar to display the New Folder button.

✔ The program that displays folder windows is Windows Explorer. When you open a folder window, you're opening a new Windows Explorer window.

Working with libraries

A *library* is a special feature in Windows 8 and Windows 7. It contains a selection of files from multiple folders. I suppose it's a handy thing to have, especially when working with large projects or collections of files that may exist in several folders. I've never really used it that way. Still, libraries pop up often when you use the Save As or Open dialog boxes to locate files.

To display the list of libraries available on your PC, or shared between computers on the network HomeGroup, choose the Libraries heading from the left side of any Windows Explorer window; press Win+E to summon a Windows Explorer window. Libraries appear in their own window, as shown in Figure 16-5.

Choose libraries   Click to create   Library
from here   a new library   icons

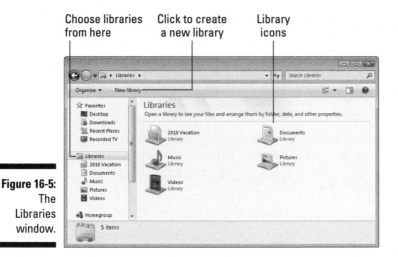

Figure 16-5:
The
Libraries
window.

To view the contents of a library, double-click to open its icon. Libraries contain files and folders. Yet the files and folders you see are culled from various folders located throughout your PC's storage system, as well as from, possibly, the computer network.

✔ You can work with files in a library the same as you can work with files in a folder.

✔ To see which folders are included in a library, click the link located by the word *Includes* below the library name in the Windows Explorer window.

✔ If you create or save any files (or folders) in a library, they're created in your own account's area on your computer. Even so, they're still available from the Library window.

✔ To create a new library, click the New Library button (refer to Figure 16-5). Name the library, and then use the Include Folder button to browse for folders and files to add to the library. In Figure 16-5, you see the 2010 Vacation library, which contains folders for pictures, videos, and other items related to that disastrous trip.

Using folders in the Open dialog box

As you use your computer, you often find yourself digging through folders with the Open or Browse dialog box, to fetch a file somewhere. For example, you want to open that document you worked on yesterday, the one that contains your plans for winning the Junior Miss Avocado pageant.

The Open dialog box, depicted in Figure 16-6, is summoned by using the Open command (or Ctrl+O). Similarly, its sister, the Browse dialog box, appears whenever you issue a Browse command. Either way, the dialog box lets you hunt down a specific file somewhere on the PC's mass storage system.

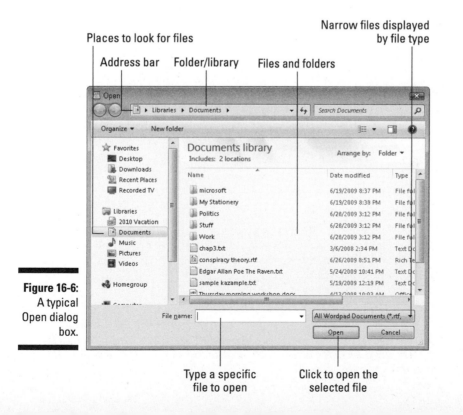

Places to look for files

Address bar   Folder/library   Files and folders

Narrow files displayed by file type

Figure 16-6:
A typical Open dialog box.

Type a specific file to open

Click to open the selected file

Yes, the Open dialog box looks and works a lot like a Windows Explorer window. It has the same panes, toolbar, and file list. The bonus information specific to opening files, however, is found near the bottom of the dialog box (refer to Figure 16-6).

The File Name text box allows you to manually enter a filename — which is a typically silly and nerdy thing to do, so I don't recommend it.

The File Type button is used to help narrow the list of files in the Open dialog box. By showing only files of a certain type, you can more easily scope out the file you want.

Finally, you click the Open button to open the selected file. Note that the Open button often has a menu button next to it. Clicking that button displays options for opening a file.

- ✔ Not every program can open every type of file. Programs work best with the files they create themselves.

- ✔ The Open dialog box's look varies subtly from program to program, but it works the same way in all of them.

- ✔ When you're really stuck finding a file, use the Windows Search command. See Chapter 17.

Chapter 17

The Grim Topic of File Management

In This Chapter

▶ Selecting groups of files

▶ Moving or copying files and folders

▶ Copying files to removable media

▶ Making a file shortcut

▶ Deleting and undeleting files

▶ Renaming files and folders

▶ Finding lost files

*F*or so long, I've wanted to write a chapter in one of my books that no one would read. So I thought, "What could I do to guarantee that the topic would be avoided?" This chapter's title is carefully crafted so that the subject sounds as boring as possible. The topic descriptions are dull and technical. And the section headings have all the spice and verve of a 1970s Fortran programming manual. There! I've done it. Feel free to skip all the information in this chapter. Don't read it!

Organized File Torture

Really? You're still reading? Man, are you gullible. I figured that you'd be completely disinterested in doing anything with the files you create on your computer. I mean, wouldn't a good *For Dummies* philosophy be "leave everything alone and pray that nothing bad happens"? Can't the damn files manage themselves?

Managing files because they can't manage themselves

You'll be delighted to discover the copious ways to torture files. Beyond taunting them verbally, you can use various file management commands to copy, move, or rename the files. You can also delete a file, which is the ultimate form of invalidation. None of that sinister activity can take place, however, until you *select* a file for abuse.

- ✔ File management is the process of organizing files and folders on your computer's mass storage system. If it were a class at Hogwarts, it would be taught by Professor Snape.

- ✔ The operating system provides the tools necessary to manage files.

- ✔ If you did everything properly with files and folders the first time, file management wouldn't be necessary. But, no, you did things wrong. See? This is all your fault.

Selecting files for torment

Files (and folders) must be *selected* before you can abuse them. As with any pogrom, you can select files individually or in groups.

Select a single file

To select a single file, click its icon once with the mouse. Click. A selected file appears highlighted onscreen, similar to the one shown in Figure 17-1. The file named REUNION is ready for action.

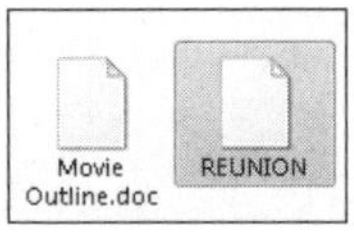

Figure 17-1:
The icon (file) on the right is selected.

Select all files in a folder

To select all files inside a folder, press the Ctrl+A keyboard shortcut. This command highlights all files in the window — including any folders (and all their contents). The A in Ctrl+A probably stands for "All the guilty ones."

Select a random smattering of files

Suppose that in a folder brimming with files you need to select four icons, the four ugliest icons, similar to the ones shown in Figure 17-2.

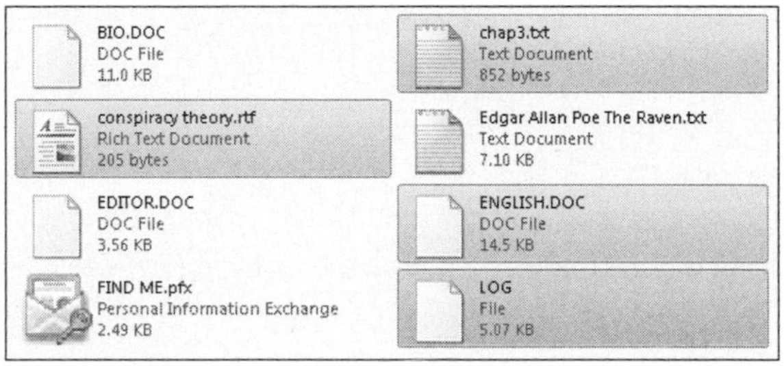

Figure 17-2:
A random smattering of files is selected.

BIO.DOC — DOC File — 11.0 KB	chap3.txt — Text Document — 852 bytes
conspiracy theory.rtf — Rich Text Document — 205 bytes	Edgar Allan Poe The Raven.txt — Text Document — 7.10 KB
EDITOR.DOC — DOC File — 3.56 KB	ENGLISH.DOC — DOC File — 14.5 KB
FIND ME.pfx — Personal Information Exchange — 2.49 KB	LOG — File — 5.07 KB

Here's how:

1. **Click to select the first file.**

2. **Press and hold down the Ctrl key.**

3. **Click to select the next file.**

4. **Repeat Step 3 to select additional files.**

5. **Release the Ctrl key when you're done selecting files.**

Now you're ready to manipulate the selected files as a single, guilty group.

To deselect a file from the group, just Ctrl+click it again.

Select a swath of files in a row

To select a queue of files, such as those shown in Figure 17-3, pursue these steps:

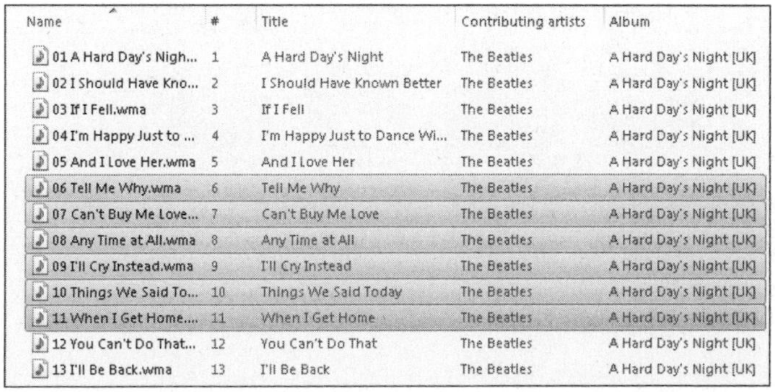

Name	#	Title	Contributing artists	Album
01 A Hard Day's Nigh...	1	A Hard Day's Night	The Beatles	A Hard Day's Night [UK]
02 I Should Have Kno...	2	I Should Have Known Better	The Beatles	A Hard Day's Night [UK]
03 If I Fell.wma	3	If I Fell	The Beatles	A Hard Day's Night [UK]
04 I'm Happy Just to ...	4	I'm Happy Just to Dance Wi...	The Beatles	A Hard Day's Night [UK]
05 And I Love Her.wma	5	And I Love Her	The Beatles	A Hard Day's Night [UK]
06 Tell Me Why.wma	6	Tell Me Why	The Beatles	A Hard Day's Night [UK]
07 Can't Buy Me Love...	7	Can't Buy Me Love	The Beatles	A Hard Day's Night [UK]
08 Any Time at All.wma	8	Any Time at All	The Beatles	A Hard Day's Night [UK]
09 I'll Cry Instead.wma	9	I'll Cry Instead	The Beatles	A Hard Day's Night [UK]
10 Things We Said To...	10	Things We Said Today	The Beatles	A Hard Day's Night [UK]
11 When I Get Home....	11	When I Get Home	The Beatles	A Hard Day's Night [UK]
12 You Can't Do That...	12	You Can't Do That	The Beatles	A Hard Day's Night [UK]
13 I'll Be Back.wma	13	I'll Be Back	The Beatles	A Hard Day's Night [UK]

Figure 17-3:
A queue of files is selected.

1. **Line up the files in the window.**

   In Windows 8, click the View tab and choose List from the Layout area. In older, better versions of Windows, choose List from the View menu button on the toolbar.

2. **Click to select the first file in your group.**

3. **Press and hold down the Shift key.**

4. **Click to select the last file in your group.**

5. **Release the Shift key.**

The files are now ready for abuse. Well, maybe not "ready" for it, but it's coming.

Lasso a group of files

If you want to treat your files like the bovine vermin that they are, use the mouse to lasso them into a group. Figure 17-4 illustrates how it's done.

To lasso the files, start by pointing the mouse above and to the left of the icon herd you want to rope. Holding down the mouse button, drag down and to the right to create a rectangle surrounding ("lassoing") the file icons (refer to Figure 17-4). Release the mouse button, and all the files you have lassoed are selected as a group. A vocal "Yee-ha!" is considered appropriate — and intimidating — in this circumstance.

Figure 17-4:
Lasso a
group of
files with
the mouse.

Releasing files from selection

To unselect a file, simply click anywhere in the folder (but not on an icon). Or you can close the folder window, in which case Windows immediately forgets about any selected files.

To answer your question: No, the files don't feel any sense of relief from being de-selected. They won't appreciate you any more for it, either. Bastards.

The Actual File Torture Itself

As Shakespeare once famously wrote, "How can I torture my files? Let me count the ways." Sure, I'm paraphrasing the Bard, but in all seriousness, you'll find an infinite number of ways to oppress files on your PC. Of the myriad methods, a few stand out. You'll find them described in this section.

If you make a mistake when performing any file torture action, you can immediately undo the procedure by pressing Ctrl+Z, the Undo command shortcut.

Copying a file

The easiest way to increase the pleasure of torturing files is to make more of them. In Windows, you duplicate files and folders by using the Copy command. It's the same command used to copy chunks of text or graphics. In this instance, you can copy files or folders to an external storage device or to another folder. It works like this:

1. **Select the files or folders you want to move or copy.**

2. **Press Ctrl+C.**

   Ctrl+C is the keyboard shortcut for the Copy command.

3. **Open the folder where you want the files to be copied.**

   The folder can be another folder in your User Account area, a subfolder, a parent folder, or even a folder on some removable media you just stuck into the PC.

4. **Press Ctrl+V to paste the files into the folder window.**

   The copied files appear in the window.

Copying files makes duplicates; after you copy the files, you have the original as well as the copy you just made.

- ✔ When you copy a folder, you're copying all files in that folder plus all files in any subfolders.

- ✔ Copying files makes duplicates. As an alternative, you might consider creating a *shortcut file* instead. See the later section "Creating a shortcut" for more information.

- ✔ The Cylons were created by using the Copy command.

- ✔ You can also copy a file by dragging its icon from one folder window to another. It's technical, however, because you need to open both folder windows at one time and arrange them on the desktop so that you can see what you're dragging with the mouse. Also, you must press and hold down the Ctrl key to ensure that the file is *copied* between folders, not moved.

Moving a file

To move a file, you perform the same steps as outlined for copying a file in the preceding section. The difference is that the moving operation is a *cut-and-paste*, not a copy-and-paste; in Step 2 in the preceding section, press Ctrl+X for cut rather than Ctrl+C for copy.

- ✔ After you paste the file, the original is deleted. Any remaining files don't mourn the moved file because they have no souls.

- ✔ If you elect to move a file by dragging it between two folders, you must remember to press the Shift key when dragging to ensure that the files are moved, not copied.

Creating a shortcut

I can understand the need to copy a file to removable media. In that case, the whole file is required, even if it's big and fat and full of nonsense. But in your own PC's storage system, there is no need to make full-on duplicates of your files — especially when they're big and fat and full of nonsense. In that case, you can just make a file shortcut.

A file shortcut is a copy of the original file, but without all the bulk. It's merely a signpost that says, "The real file is over there somewhere." When you open a shortcut, Windows is smart enough to find the original and open it instead. I know that sounds unbelievable, but in fact it's true: Windows can be smart sometimes.

To create a shortcut, start out as if you're copying the file. Refer to Steps 1 through 3 in the earlier section "Copying a file." The difference comes when you paste: Rather than press Ctrl+V to paste the file copy, you right-click in the folder. Choose the Paste Shortcut command from the pop-up menu.

 File shortcuts sport a tiny arrow nestled in the lower-left corner, as shown in the margin. That's your clue that the file is a shortcut and not a full-blown copy.

✔ Shortcuts are most commonly used to reference programs installed on your computer. For example, you can create a shortcut to the Microsoft Word program and put it on the desktop for easy access. Such is the essence of the file shortcut.

✔ To quickly create a shortcut on the desktop, right-click an icon and choose Send To⇨Desktop (Create Shortcut) from the pop-up menu.

✔ Shortcuts are often named with the suffix Shortcut. You can edit out the Shortcut to part, if you like. Refer to the next section.

✔ Shortcuts work only on your computer. Do not e-mail them to your friends, because they receive only the stubby shortcut and not the original file.

 ✔ Have no fear when you're deleting shortcuts: Removing a shortcut icon doesn't remove the original file. In fact, the original file couldn't care less.

Renaming files

Nothing sends a file into a depressive funk like giving the pitiful thing a ridiculous name. Gleefully obey these steps:

1. **Click the file's icon once to select it.**

2. **Press the F2 key, the keyboard shortcut for the Rename command.**

   Just to let you know, the person who thought that the F2 key would make an excellent keyboard shortcut for the Rename command has been killed in a prolonged and cruel manner.

3. **Type a new name or edit the current name.**

4. **Press the Enter key to lock in the new name.**

The only time this operation fails is when you abuse the file-naming rules (laid down in Chapter 16), or you attempt to use the name of an already existing file in the same folder.

✔ The goal of renaming a file is to be descriptive and clever. If you can't muster that, it's safe to forget that F2 is the keyboard shortcut for the Rename command.

✔ Windows lets you rename a group of icons all at once. The process is the same as renaming a single icon, except that when the operation is completed, all selected icons have the same new name plus a number suffix. For example, you select a group of icons and press the F2 key. When you type `Picture` as the group filename, each file in the group is given the name `Picture (2)`, `Picture (3)`, and so on, to the last file in the group — `Picture (274,369)`, for instance.

Deleting files

Ah, the fun part. Even if you harbor no evil intent, it makes sense to go on a file-purging binge every so often. The task involves cleaning out the dead-wood — removing files and folders you no longer want or need, or which have postured themselves in a condescending manner.

To obliterate a file, select it and press the Delete key on your keyboard. You may see a confirmation prompt; click Yes. The file is gone.

Well, not really. The files you delete aren't killed off. They're banished to a digital purgatory called the Recycle Bin; see the next section.

✔ You can delete a file also by dragging its icon from the folder window to the Recycle Bin icon on the desktop (if the Recycle Bin icon is visible).

✔ You can delete folders just like you delete files, but keep in mind that you delete the folder's contents — which can consist of dozens of icons, files, folders, jewelry, small children, widows, and refugees.

✔ Never delete any file or folder unless you created it yourself.

✔ Programs aren't deleted in Windows; they're uninstalled. See Chapter 15.

Bringing dead files back to life

Because you may be reading this section during a time of urgency, I shall waste no time: If you just deleted a file — and I mean *just* deleted it — you can use the Undo command to get it back: Press Ctrl+Z on the keyboard. There. It's back.

If you've deleted a file any time before "just now," you can safely revive it. Rather than occupy a hilltop castle and wait for a thunderstorm, follow these steps:

1. **Open the Recycle Bin on the desktop.**

   If the Recycle Bin icon isn't visible on the desktop, press Win+E to summon a Windows Explorer window. Then in the address bar, click the triangle to the left of the word *Computer* to display a menu, and choose Recycle Bin from that menu.

2. **Select the file you want recovered.**

3. **Click the Restore the Selected Items button on the toolbar. (In some versions of Windows, the button is named Restore This Item.)**

   The file is magically removed from Recycle Bin limbo and restored afresh to the folder from which it was so brutally seized.

4. **Close the Recycle Bin window.**

These steps may not work when too much time has passed since the file was deleted. Windows keeps its victims in Recycle Bin purgatory for months — or longer — depending on how frequently you purge files. After a longer period of time, you'll have to resurrect long-dead files from a backup copy. See Chapter 18.

Find Escaped Files

Files get lost every day. Either they run off and hide in some bizarre, unknown folder, or some midnight demon picks them up and moves them. The reason for their absence varies, but the method used to hunt them down and bring them to justice is consistent.

You'll find Search text boxes available in every folder window. Look in the upper-right corner of the window. In the text box, type the file's name or text that might be found in the file. Press the Enter key, and Windows begins a fanatical search for matching files.

To muster the official Search command in Windows, press the Win+F keyboard shortcut. Use the window that appears to type more information about lost or missing files.

✔ Start the search in a parent folder, such as your User Account folder or the Computer folder window. The search progresses downward through the folders.

✔ To drag the file back into a proper folder, follow the steps from the section "Moving a file." Cut the file from the Search Results window, open the folder window where you'd expect the file to be, and paste.

✔ When you find yourself searching for the same stuff over and over, you can save the search. Click the Save Search button in the Search Results window. You can then redo the search by opening the saved search icon in the Saved Searches folder, found in your User Profile folder.

✔ Just to be difficult, the Search command in Windows 8 uses not a folder window but rather a Search screen. Results appear full-screen. You can't save a search or customize the search for specific file attributes. If you're making a list of reasons to despise Windows 8, add the Search command to it.

Chapter 18

Save Your Butt When You Really Screw Up

In This Chapter

▶ Restoring modified files

▶ Creating a backup copy

▶ Understanding compressed folders

▶ Extracting files from a compressed folder

▶ Installing software from a Zip file

*Q*uiz time! Which is more important in a computer system, hardware or software? The answer is the software, which controls the hardware. What's the most important part of software? Why, it's the stuff you create, the files stored on your computer's mass storage system. What happens when files gets damaged, deleted, or demented? Why, you have to use that backup safety copy to save your butt. What happens when you don't have a backup safety copy? Why, you read this chapter.

For general butt-saving advice, consider my book *Troubleshooting & Maintaining Your PC All-in-One For Dummies,* 2nd Edition (Wiley). All the cool kids read it.

The File You Had Yesterday

If a file is lost, you can find it. When a file has been deleted, you can recover it from the Recycle Bin. But when a file has been changed or overwritten with new information, getting it back requires some sorcery.

✔ Refer to Chapter 17 for information on finding lost files or lifting them from the electronic purgatory that is the Windows Recycle Bin.

✔ Windows warns you when a file is about to be overwritten. But if you're working on the file and you save a new version, you cannot get the old version back unless you heed my advice in this section.

Recovering with File History

Windows 8 features its own, unique method of file recovery. It's called File History, and it's similar to the Previous Versions function found in older, better versions of Windows (and covered in the next section).

Before getting all excited about using the File History feature, confirm that it's set up properly. Obey these steps:

1. **Ensure that your computer has an external hard drive.**

   The PC needs an external hard drive to best use File History. Connect such a device to your PC immediately if you want to enjoy this feature. See Chapter 7.

   Oh, and this isn't the last time in this chapter that I bemoan the necessity of an external hard drive. Just do it now. Put down the book. Get an external hard drive.

2. **Summon the Control Panel.**

3. **Below the System and Security heading, click the Save Backup Copies of Your Files with File History link.**

4. **Click the Turn On button.**

   If you see the Turn Off button, File History is already on. You're set. And if you can't click the Turn On button, then go back and reread Step 1.

Once active, the File History function monitors your files. Every so often, it duplicates the files, keeping copies hidden away on that external hard drive. During times of anguish, you can recover one of those historical copies. To do so, summon the File History window.

The quick and easy way to summon the File History window is to follow these steps:

1. **Press the Win+R keyboard shortcut.**

   The Run dialog box appears.

2. **Type** filehistory **in the text box.**

   That's one word, **filehistory**. Don't type a space between _file_ and _history_.

3. **Click OK.**

   The File History window appears, similar to what's shown in Figure 18-1.

Date files were backed up   Select an icon to restore

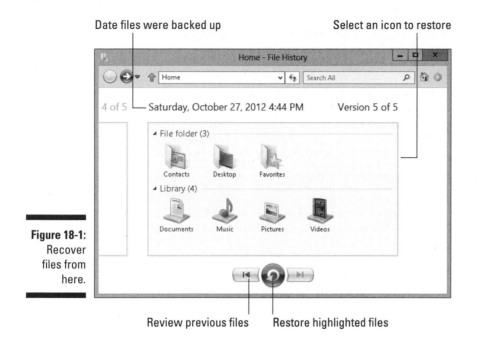

Figure 18-1:
Recover
files from
here.

Review previous files   Restore highlighted files

4. **Browse the folders to locate the file you want to recover.**

   You can go left or right, as illustrated in Figure 18-1, to browse for older versions of the same file.

5. **Click to select the file, and then click the Restore button.**

   The historic version of the file is about to be copied to the same folder as the original, but before the file is restored:

6. **Choose the option Replace the File in the Destination.**

   The historic file replaces the current version.

You can select multiple files or even folders to restore. As long as the File History feature is turned on, you should — in theory — never lose a file.

   ✔ The File History feature works only when it's enabled.

   ✔ If files lack historical versions, or you just activated the File History feature, there will be nothing to recover.

   ✔ You can use a network location as well as an external drive for the File History feature.

   ✔ File History is the only form of backup included with Windows 8.

Restoring previous versions

Windows 7 and Windows Vista sport a feature I call Previous Versions. It lets you recover older versions of a file that may have been overwritten with new data or where you've saved an update and then changed your mind.

To recover the previous version of a file, heed these steps:

1. **Right-click the file or folder you want to recover.**

2. **Choose the command Restore Previous Versions.**

   The icon's Properties dialog box appears, with the Previous Versions tab up front, similar to what's shown in Figure 18-2. It may take a few moments for Windows to locate the various previous versions.

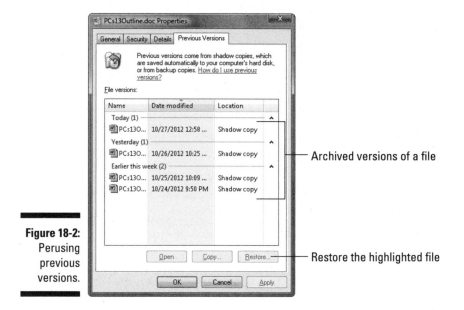

Figure 18-2: Perusing previous versions.

Archived versions of a file

Restore the highlighted file

3. **Click the highlight the version of the file you desire to recover.**

   It could be the most recent version or an antique.

4. **Click the Restore button.**

   A special warning dialog box may appear, telling you that the restored, previous version replaces the existing version you have. If so, click the Restore button again.

When you'd rather keep both the historical as well as current version of the file, click the Copy button in Step 4. The restored, previous version then becomes a duplicate file located in the same folder.

The Previous Versions feature may not be available on all releases of Windows, such as the Home or Student version. See? You thought you were saving money by getting that version of Windows when you were just being cheap.

The Previous Versions feature might also be disabled when mass storage space is running low.

The OMG Safety Copy

Perhaps the best way to secure the data on your computer is to do a full, serious, swear-to-your-favorite-deity, computer backup. Such a thing involves either an external storage device or a special Internet service.

The easiest way to configure a backup program for your PC is to buy an external hard drive that comes with a backup utility. The one I recommend is the Seagate hard drive with Replica software installed. It works like a dream, which means it works far more efficiently than any version of the Backup software included with Windows.

Another way to configure backup is to use one of the Internet backup services. The service regularly copies files from your PC to storage somewhere on the Internet. Beyond being automatic, the advantage of the Internet copy is that if your home or office is crushed by a flaming meteor, your files survive.

Well, I suppose a meteor could smash into the Internet backup company's headquarters, but I think they probably have more than one location for storing your data.

Here is a smattering of Internet backup services to peruse:

- Backblaze: www.backblaze.com
- Carbonite: www.carbonite.com
- MozyHome: www.mozy.com

Most of these services charge a nominal monthly fee, though you might also find a discounted annual rate. Additional fees apply when you plan on backing up more than one computer, as well as if you go over a certain amount of storage. Well, and you need Internet access too, which is kind of another fee. Fees, fees, fees.

OMG stands for "Oh, my goodness!" and other similar sayings.

Zip-a-dee-do Folders

Doesn't everyone have their favorite medieval torture devices? There's the rack, the iron maiden, and myriad things you can do with hot, molten lead. For a file, the preferred form of torment is *compression*. It's possible to take multiple files and squeeze out the juice, compacting them into a single unit. That unit, or archive, can then be sent quickly over the Internet or stored long-term as an archive.

Because files are digital, they can be decompressed back to their original forms with no loss of data, integrity, or self-esteem. Such is the beauty of the file archive.

Whether files enjoy compression or not, archiving is yet another way you can store files for later retrieval. Or you can be traditional and send the archive as an e-mail attachment or somehow fling it out on the Internet.

The archives are officially known as *compressed folders* in Windows. They're also called *Zip* files.

- ✔ Zip files, or compressed file archives, feature their own, unique icon, shown in the margin. See the zipper? Cute.

- ✔ Like a traditional folder, a compressed folder contains files and folders. It's not really a folder, however; it's merely a special type of file.

- ✔ Compressed folders are called *Zip files* because Windows uses the Zip file compression algorithm, and also because the filename extension is *zip*. Zip doesn't stand for anything; the developer chose the name because zippy means *speedy*.

Compressing files

Say you have this group of rowdy files. You want to pack them all up on a media card and send them to a military academy. That could happen one at a time, or you could lasso each file into a group. Better still, you can compress them all into a compact form and copy them as a single unit. Here's how to compress one or more files:

1. **Select the files you want to compress.**

   You can compress files in a group, or you can compress one single, large, bloated file.

2. **Right-click the group of files.**

3. **Choose the command Send To⇨Compressed (Zipped) Folder.**

   A new compressed folder is created. Its name, which is preset and stupid, is selected.

4. **Type a new name for the compressed folder.**

   Be short, sweet, and descriptive.

The new compressed folder contains an archive, or duplicate copy, of the files you selected in Step 1. You can now copy that compressed folder, e-mail it, or store it on external media. The files remain compressed into that single unit until you extract them. Extracting files is covered in the next section.

✔ You can also create an empty compressed folder: Right-click a blank part of a folder window or the desktop, and then choose New⇨Compressed (Zipped) Folder. Rename the icon and you're in business.

✔ After a compressed folder has been created, you can add new files to it simply by dragging and dropping the file icons to the compressed folder's icon. This action copies the file into the compressed folder; it does not move the file.

✔ Files stored in a compressed folder occupy less storage space than the original files. That was the idea behind compressed folders, back in the early days of computer telecommunications: It takes less time to transmit a smaller file, which is important over slow dial-up modem connections.

✔ Some types of files compress well, such as text files. Other file types don't compress at all. Certain audio and movie file types don't compress. Some graphics file types, such as TIFF, don't compress. That's because the file's contents are already compressed. You can still archive those files into a compressed folder, but you're not saving any storage space.

Examining a compressed folder archive

To see which files are hiding inside a compressed folder, open the folder. On the screen, it appears as if you've merely opened any old, boring folder — but you haven't. What you're looking at is a compressed file archive, similar to what's shown in Figure 18-3.

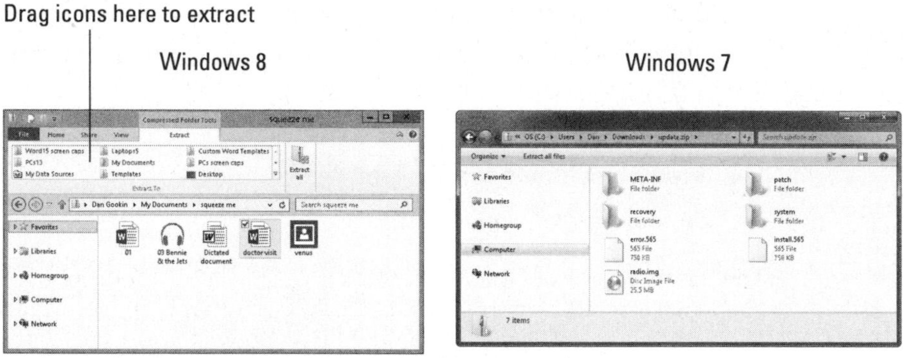

Drag icons here to extract

Windows 8

Windows 7

Figure 18-3: Browsing insides of a compressed folder.

Despite a potential for aggression, you can really do only three things when looking at files imprisoned in a compressed folder:

✔ You can just snoop around. You can see what files and folders are inside the archive. Open folders inside the compressed folder to check their contents. You can even open compressed folders inside of compressed folders. If that concept blows your mind, watch the 2010 film *Inception*.

✔ You can preview some types of files. Double-click an icon inside the compressed folder window to have a peek. Some files open in programs that let you preview their contents — but you cannot change the file unless you first extract it.

✔ You can extract one or more files. To extract an individual file, drag it out of the archive. In Windows 8, you can select the file and then click a folder from the list to extract it to a specific location (refer to Figure 18-3).

Most commonly, you'll probably want to extract all the files from the compressed folder archive. To do that, follow these steps:

1. **Open the compressed folder.**

2. **Click the Extract All or Extract All Files toolbar button.**

   The Extract Compressed (Zipped) Folders window appears.

3. **Click the Extract button.**

   Windows creates a folder with the same name as the compressed folder and extracts (copies) all files from the compressed folder into the new folder. That new folder then opens on the screen.

4. **Close the compressed folder window.**

Extracting files from a compressed folder does not remove the files from the archive. The files remain in the compressed folder until you delete them individually or simply delete the compressed folder.

To remove a file individually from a compressed folder, right-click its icon and choose the Delete command. Click the Yes button to confirm.

Installing software from a compressed folder

Although I recommended against it in Chapter 15, occasionally you'll download new software to your computer from the Internet, and that software is in the compressed folder (Zip) format. Committing this sin isn't damning, but it requires that you perform a few extra steps to install the software.

Specifically, after you extract all the files from the compressed folder, as described in the preceding section, you need to locate the Install or Setup program in the new folder created. Run that program. Follow the steps on the screen to continue installing the software.

✔ When the Install or Setup program doesn't appear in the window, open the only folder in the window, or open the BIN folder.

✔ If the whole compressed folder download thing bothers you, search for a version of the download that uses a self-extracting format rather than Zip. Those files end with the *exe* filename extension. If such an option is available, choose it. See Chapter 15.

Chapter 19

The Optical Disc Factory

In This Chapter

▶ Understanding the disc-burning thing

▶ Inserting the disc

▶ Choosing a proper format

▶ Working with the disc in Windows

▶ Wiping out an RW disc

▶ Labeling discs

▶ Throwing away a disc

*L*ong ago in computer land — the fairy tale place, not the retail outfit — the optical disc was king. It was the removable media of choice, handy, portable, and nearly indestructible by anyone over the age of five. New software arrived in the kingdom on optical discs. And the kingdom's citizens could even create their own optical disks, both CDs and DVDs. The process was called *burning,* and it didn't involve a stout wooden pole, rope, or immolation of any royalty.

Disc Creation Overview

I must confess that the halcyon days of the optical disc are well behind us. As a technology, optical discs have been replaced by high-capacity thumb drives and media cards. Still, PCs come with optical drives, and cheap, writeable optical discs are plentiful. Therefore, creating your own optical discs is something computer owners still do, but probably not for much longer.

Oh, don't feel bad: No one today weeps for the loss of the floppy disk, despite the fact that floppy disks were once the most popular form of removable computer storage. In fact, back when the first PC was introduced, floppy disks were the *only* form of storage media available to the PC. Things change.

What to put on the disc?

The burning burning-question is "What kind of data should I put on an optical disc?" Unlike all other storage media, optical discs work most efficiently when information is written sequentially — like an archive — because recordable discs are not truly interactive media. Although you can use them that way, a lot of storage space is wasted in the process.

These days, the best use of an optical disc is to archive information for long-term storage. You can use the discs also to send digital information through the good old post office or mail service, though that practice isn't common with the advent of high-speed Internet.

Finally, how much information can be stored on an optical disc is limited. For a CD, it's about 80MB — which isn't a lot. On a dual-sided DVD, you can store up to 8GB of your digital junk, but that's still not a whopping amount of information. Again, the storage limitation is yet another reason why I believe PCs of the future won't come with optical drives.

If your PC has an optical drive, it can read optical disks, both CDs and DVDs. If your PC has a recordable optical drive, it can also write to those discs. How can you tell? Look at the front of the optical drive for tattoos on the faceplate. Refer to Table 19-1 for definitions of what that cryptic text could mean.

Table 19-1	Recordable Optical Disc Formats
Format	*What It Means*
CD-R	The standard recordable CD format
CD-RW	A format in which the disc can be recorded just like a CD-R, although it can be completely erased and used again
DVD-R	The most popular DVD recordable format, compatible with computers and home movie DVD players
DVD+R	A DVD recordable format that records much faster than DVD-R but isn't as compatible with home movie DVD players
DVD-RW	The erasable version of the DVD-R format, where the disc can be erased and used again
DVD+RW	The erasable version of the DVD+R format
DVD R DL	A dual-layer version of the DVD-R format that holds twice as much data but can be read only in dual-layer optical drives
DVD RAM	Also known as RAM2; can be recorded to and erased similarly to the RW format but is way, way out of fashion

The optical drive is the hardware part of the equation. The software side is supplied by Windows. Blank optical media is recognized by Windows once you insert the disc into the drive. Later sections in this chapter dwell on what to do when Windows identifies a recordable optical disc.

Your PC may have also come with a third-party disc creation tool, such as the popular Nero program. You can use that program instead of Windows (it's easier to use), but this book covers only the Windows method of burning a disc.

Beyond the hardware and software, media is required in the form of a recordable optical disc. As long as you get the kind of discs the PC's optical drive can eat (refer to Table 19-1), you're set.

- ✔ An optical drive with the Multi label on it can pretty much record *all* the various optical disc formats.

- ✔ Discs are cheap! I recommend buying them in 25-, 50-, or 100-disc packs.

- ✔ You may not think that the discs are cheap, but when CD-Rs first came out in the 1990s, they were about $5 a pop. Recordable DVDs were originally $15 each!

- ✔ Some CD-Rs are labeled specifically for music. These music CD-Rs are of a lower quality than data CD-Rs because music doesn't have the same accuracy demands as data storage.

- ✔ The RW format discs are more expensive than the other, write-once disc formats.

Birth of a Disc

As long as you have a recordable optical drive in your PC, a stack of recordable discs handy, plus your favorite beverage, you and Windows can make data discs like rabbits make bunnies. Although you probably won't make the discs as enthusiastically as the rabbits make the bunnies.

Burning a disc

Brace yourself for disc-creation action. After you've obtained a recordable disc of a format compatible with your computer's optical drive, shove that disc into the PC's optical drive.

In Windows 8, a pop-up box appears that says Tap to Choose What Happens with Blank CDs. Tap that box with your finger, or click it using the mouse. In older versions of Windows, an AutoPlay dialog box appears, similar to what's shown in Figure 19-1.

Windows 8   Windows 7

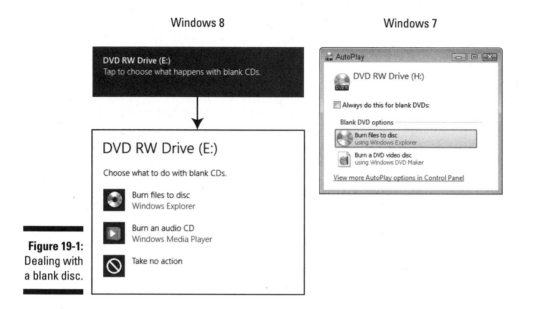

Figure 19-1:
Dealing with
a blank disc.

After tapping or clicking the box (Windows 8), or viewing the AutoPlay dialog box (Windows everything else), follow these steps:

1. **Choose the Burn Files to Disc option.**

   The Burn a Disc dialog box shows up.

   If you don't see the Burn Files to Disc option, the disc has already been prepared for use. You're done. Start using the disc.

2. **Type a name for the disc.**

   Name the disc based on its contents. Or you can just accept the current date, which is already shown in the dialog box.

3. **Choose a formatting option.**

   In Windows Vista, you'll need to first click the Show Formatting Options button to reveal the formatting option choices. Two formats are available, both of which are equally confusing:

   • *Like a USB Flash Drive* or *Live File System:* In these formats, information is written to the disc immediately. You can eject the disc, use it in another computer, and then reinsert the disc and keep adding files to it. You can use the disc until it's full.

- *With A CD/DVD Player* or *Mastered:* These formats collect files to be written to the disc, storing them on the PC's mass storage system (the hard drive). All waiting files are written to the disc at one time. Then the disc is *closed,* and further writing to the disc is prevented.

Of the two formats, the mastered format is more compatible with other optical drives, and it makes the most efficient use of disc space. The USB flash drive and live file system formats, however, work more like traditional removable media in a PC.

4. Click the Next button.

For the USB flash drive and live file system, Windows formats the disc, preparing it for use. Click the Yes button if you're prompted by the "This will take a long time" warning. It's a realistic warning, too; it does take a *long* time to format the disc.

The CD/DVD player and mastered formats don't require preparation at this time; the disc isn't officially prepared for use until you eject it.

5. Start using the disc.

The disc is *mounted* into your PC's mass storage system. Windows may display an additional AutoPlay dialog box for the disc, or it might automatically open the disc's folder window. The optical drive's icon shows up in the Computer window. The disc is ready for abuse.

- ✔ Not seeing anything displayed after inserting a recordable optical disc could mean that the disc is defective. Try another.

- ✔ If you don't see anything displayed after repeatedly inserting recordable optical discs, the PC may not have a recordable optical drive.

- ✔ You can summon the AutoPlay dialog box for any disc by right-clicking that disc's icon in the Computer window. From the shortcut menu, choose the command Open AutoPlay.

Working with a USB flash drive or live file format disc

After setting up a USB flash drive or live file format recordable disc, discussed in the preceding section, you can work with it just like you work with any removable storage media: Copy files to the disc's window, create folders, and manage files as you normally do. Information is written to the disc as soon as you copy it over. That's why it's the *live* file system — your interaction with the disc is pretty much real-time.

Time is not on the optical disc's side

Optical disc storage is not permanent. It's long-term, sure, but scientists in white lab coats have determined that information stored on an optical disc does degrade over time. Plenty of variables are involved, and I won't mention the variables because it's been years since I read the article and I've completely forgotten what they are. But they are variables nonetheless.

Another consideration when storing information long term is a concept known as the *digital desert*. There's only one *s* in *desert* so it means

the sandy, dry place and not something sweet you want to eat, but shouldn't.

The digital desert refers to file formats that are abandoned or forgotten over time. For example, when I was writing computer books in the 1990s, images were stored in the PCX (PC Paintbrush) file format. That file format is now obsolete and is not readable by any of today's software. So, effectively, those files I dutifully archived at that time are today pretty much useless.

When you're ready, you can eject the disc. You can then use the disc on another PC or reinsert it into your computer. You can continue to burn files to the disc until it's full or it catches fire.

You can erase, rename, or move a file after it has been burned to a USB flash drive or live file system disc, but doing so wastes disc space. If possible, try to do your file manipulations *before* you copy the files to the disc.

Working with a CD/DVD player or mastered disc

You work with a CD/DVD player or mastered disc just as you would work with any media in Windows. Files can be copied, folders can be created, and so on. The only difference you see is that the files you put on the disc appear with a download flag on their icon, as shown in the margin. The icon also appears ghostly, or dimmed.

The reason for the faint download icon is that nothing is actually written until the disc is ejected. Feel free to manage the icons at any time with no fear of affecting anything on the disc. And please, don't hold your breath while you're managing the files.

When you're ready to burn the disc, follow these steps:

1. **Open the Computer window.**

2. **Open the optical drive's icon.**

    You see the files and folders waiting to be burned to the disc.

3. **In Windows 8, click the Finish Burning button, found on the Disk Tools Manage tab; in Windows 7 and Windows Vista, click the Burn to Disc toolbar button.**

   The Burn to Disc dialog box appears.

4. **Enter a name for the disc.**

5. **Set a recording speed.**

   The recording speed preselected for you is, doubtless, okay — though one school of thought says that choosing the *slowest* recording speed ensures a reliable disc-writing session. Who knows?

6. **Click the Next button.**

   The files are burned to the disc. The disc is ejected automatically when it's done.

7. **Remove the disc from the drive.**

8. **Click the Finish button to close the Burn to Disc dialog box.**

You cannot write any additional information to a mastered disc after it's been burned.

Using the Burn button

Folder windows sport a toolbar button that can be used to quickly copy, or burn, one or more files or folders to a recordable optical disc. In Windows 8, the button is titled Burn to Disc and is found on the Share tab. In older versions of Windows, the button is called Burn and is found on the toolbar.

After clicking the Burn to Disc or Burn button, any selected files are copied to the disc. If a disc isn't in the drive, the PC pops open the optical drive and a dialog box prompts you to insert a writable disc into the drive. Do so.

Erasing an RW disc

RW discs are prepared and worked with just like regular recordable discs — the ones without the *W*. All information in this chapter applies to both formats. The main difference is the addition of a toolbar button that lets you reformat the RW disc and start over.

To reformat the RW disc, comply with these steps:

1. **Open the Computer window.**

   The keyboard shortcut is Win+E.

2. **Click to select the optical drive.**

3. **Click the Erase This Disc toolbar button.**

   In Windows 8, the button is found in the Drive Tools Manage tab.

4. **Follow the directions on the screen to completely erase the disc and start over.**

   Basically, you click the Next button, wait, and then click the Finish button.

When you're done, you can use the disc over again. In fact, double-click its icon in the Computer window and you're off to format the disc, as described in the earlier section "Burning a disc."

- ✔ RW discs are different from other recordable discs. It says *RW* on the label, and the disc is more expensive, which is most obvious when you try to taste it.

- ✔ RW discs may not be readable in all optical drives. If you want to create a CD with the widest possible use, burn a CD-R rather than a CD-RW disc. For a DVD, use the DVD-R format.

- ✔ It's often said that RW discs are best used for backing up data because they can be reused over and over. However, on a disc-per-disc basis, it's cheaper to use non-RW discs instead. And, for the sake of convenience, I recommend using an external hard drive rather than optical discs to back up your stuff. See Chapter 18.

Labeling the disc

I highly recommend labeling all removable media, from recordable discs to memory cards. Even if you name things only A or B, that's fine because it helps you keep track of the discs.

- ✔ Label your disc *after* it's been written to. That way, you don't waste time labeling what could potentially be a bad disc (one that you would throw away).

- ✔ I use a Sharpie to write on the disc. Write on the label side; the other side is the one containing your important data. You don't want to write on that.

- ✔ Only if the label specifically says that it's chemically safe for a recordable disc should you use it. Otherwise, the chemicals in the sticky label may damage the disc and render the information that's written to it unreadable after only a few months.

Disposing of a disc

Sure, you can just toss a disc into the trash. That's okay — in most places. Some communities, however, classify an optical disc as hazardous, and it must be properly disposed of or sent off for recycling.

If you don't want anyone else to read the disc, you probably don't want to throw it away intact. The best solution is to destroy the disc by getting a paper shredder that can also handle crunching optical discs.

Some folks say that you can effectively erase a disc by putting it in a microwave oven for a few seconds. I don't know whether I trust or recommend that method. And don't burn a disc; its fumes are toxic.

Part IV
Networking Nonsense

The 5th Wave   By Rich Tennant

"Good news! I found a place where the router works with the PC upstairs and the one in the basement."

In this part . . .

1t would be an utter joy for me to tell you that you never need to bother with computer networking. A bespectacled, charming geek named Melvin will do the job for you. He will set up the network, troubleshoot problems, and provide insightful solutions without offending you with his poor hygiene. Sadly, neither of us will ever see that scenario.

Today's PC is a networked PC. Even when your PC is the only one around, a broadband modem is probably loitering nearby. Such a gizmo requires a network hose whether you like it or not. I could go on about wireless networking, computer viruses, and more, but I don't have the space on this page, so all that nonsense happens in the chapters garnishing this part of the book.

Chapter 20

The Non-TV Kind of Network

In This Chapter

▶ Understanding networking

▶ Reviewing wired network hardware

▶ Connecting the network

▶ Choosing a wireless network

▶ Getting a wireless gateway

▶ Making the broadband connection

When I grew up — way back in the last century, kids — *network* meant ABC, CBS, or NBC. Those are the Big Three television networks. Sorry PBS — you don't count. So when the *computer* network came about, I figured it would be some dull TV channel where nerds talked about parity bits, paper tape storage, and avoiding the GOTO instruction. But I was wrong.

Nearly everyone who has PC today also has a computer network. It's crazy! The network is simply another basic part of owning a computer, like having a printer or a sore neck. This chapter explores the hardware half of networking. The software side is shoved into Chapter 21.

The Whole Network Enchilada

A computer network can be vast, uncharted, dangerous ground on which you tread. Better bone up on some basics before you do something foolish.

Understanding the network

A computer network is simply two connected devices. They talk. They laugh. They fight over shared resources like Captain Kirk and Mr. Spock dueling out the *pon farr* on planet Vulcan. To understand that last sentence, you can watch Episode 30 from the classic TV series *Star Trek*. Instead, you might want to read this handy list of various resources that are shared over a computer network:

Mass storage: You can access information stored on other network computers.

Printers: All computers on a network can use one or more printers connected to or shared on the network.

Internet access: Although each computer secretly wants its own broadband modem, you can force all PCs on a network to share a single modem and its prized high-speed Internet connection.

Media player: Windows lets you share media files (video, audio, and pictures) among computers, as well as with any Xbox game consoles or Internet-ready TVs attached to the computer network.

None of these fun and marginally interesting activities takes place until you connect, set up, and configure a computer network for your home or small office. That's the bad news. The good news is that after you've connected everything, you don't need to mess with the network hardware ever again.

Well, *rarely*. You rarely need to mess with the network hardware ever again. I suppose my job is to encourage you to read this entire chapter despite the harsh realities of something completely dweebish like computer networking.

Going wired or wireless

Network goodness enters your computer in one of two ways. The traditional way is over a wire or, as I prefer to call it, a network hose. The newer way is wirelessly, which involves fewer wires than the traditional, wired type of computer network.

Both forms of computer network, wired and wireless, use the same terminology and pretty much the same gizmos. More setup and configuration is involved with a wireless network, and that type of network is more prone to attack, but most people still favor it. I don't know why.

In my office, I use both wired and wireless networking. The computers are wired, but my phone and various tablets connect wirelessly to the network. You can set up a similar system in your domicile. This chapter explains the basics.

Avoidable network jargon

Here are definitions of some network terms that may frequent your eyes or ears. Please don't memorize any of this geek slang! Refer to the explanations only in times of dire woe.

Ad hoc: On this type of network, wireless computers are connected to each other but not necessarily through a router or central access point. It's kind of the swingers type of network.

Client-server: A network setup where one main computer is accessed by other computers. That computer would be the server; the other computers are clients. The server runs special server software, which the other network computers access to handle e-mail, run programs, and share files. This book doesn't specifically cover the client-server type of network.

Ethernet: This term refers to the standards and protocols used for networking. Ethernet is the most popular personal networking standard, and it's a standard for communications on the Internet as well. That's how computer networking is closely tied to the Internet. The specifics of Ethernet aren't important to understanding

the whole networking ball of wax. Just be sure that you say it properly: "EETH-er-net."

LAN: When you connect a group of computers to form a network, you make a *local area network,* or LAN. You pronounce LAN like *land* without the *d* at the end, like how Aunt Minnie pronounced "land sakes!"

Peer-to-peer: A network that simply connects computers is known as a *peer-to-peer network.* In that scheme, no single computer is in charge; each computer is "on the network," just like any other computer. Peer-to-peer contrasts with the client-server type of network.

Server: A computer that runs a program shared by other computers on the network. The server can be local, such as what happens with a client-server network, or it could be on the Internet. When you access a web page, for example, your computer is requesting information from a web server. The server can be a computer or, more commonly, software running on that computer.

The Wired Network

When you enjoy having wires all over your home or small office, you should opt for the wired form of computer networking. Actually, it's just called "computer networking." Only wireless networking sports an adjective.

A basic wired network setup involves four basic pieces of network hardware:

- ✔ The networking adapter, or NIC
- ✔ The cables
- ✔ The gateway or router
- ✔ A broadband modem

Figure 20-1 illustrates a typical network layout using the four basic gizmos, but also some other networking doodads such as a few computers and a printer.

At the center of the network is the gateway, which is often called a *router,* though it's a gateway. See the later section "Putting the gateway, which isn't really a router, at the center of your network."

All the cables branch out from the gateway. The cables connect the computers to the gateway, but also connect other devices, such as the printer and broadband modem shown in Figure 20-1. The broadband modem is connected to the Internet through a convenient hole in the wall.

The network setup illustrated in Figure 20-1 is typical but not standard. The network you create may look similar, though you can cleverly disguise the cables, run them through walls, or drape them across the ceiling. The whole setup can be very flexible.

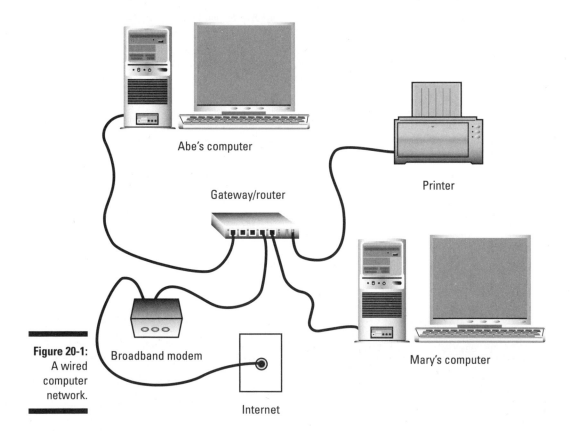

Abe's computer

Gateway/router

Printer

Figure 20-1:
A wired
computer
network.

Broadband modem

Mary's computer

Internet

Connecting to Saint NIC

Your PC can yearn for a network connection, but like the awkward teenager fantasizing about the Hollywood starlet, unless it has networking hardware all that pining goes to waste. The key is for the computer to have a NIC.

You must know two important things about the NIC. First, it's pronounced *nick,* as in "Nick-nack paddywhack, give a dog a bone." Second, it stands for *network information card.* This is the hardware your PC needs to accept the network cable and make the network connection.

Good news: Just about every dang doodle PC sold today comes with a built-in NIC. You can verify that it's there on your PC's rump, clustered into the I/O panel described in Chapter 2.

✔ The wired NIC features an RJ-45 adapter. That's the official name for the hole into which you plug the network cable. (All the items in this list are technical, so just pretend that three of these icons appear in the margin.)

✔ The standard NIC is measured by its speed in Mbps, or megabits per second: 10 Mbps is too slow, 100 Mbps is faster, and 1000 Mbps (1 *gigabit*) is the fastest and bestest.

✔ The NIC may also be known as an Ethernet card or a network adapter.

Wiring the network hoses

The non-wireless computer network demands the presence of wires to connect computers and all other network gizmos. The wire used is a cable known as Cat 5, or Category 5, networking cable. It might also be known as a Cat 6 or even Cat 5e.

One end of the cable plugs into the NIC in your computer. The other end plugs into a central location, such as the gateway illustrated in Figure 20-1.

✔ Computer network cable comes in a variety of lengths and in several bright and cheerful colors.

✔ There is no incorrect way to plug in a network hose; you can plug either end into the computer's NIC. Plug the other end into the gateway.

✔ If you don't want to go through all the networking wire mess, simply opt for a wireless network, discussed later in this chapter.

Putting the gateway, which isn't really a router, at the center of your network

At the center of the computer network is the *gateway*. It's the location where all the network wires connect. Why isn't it called a router? Because it's not a router. It's a gateway. Did the gizmo cost less than $500? Then it's not a router.

The gateway's job is to coordinate local network activity and to communicate with a larger network, the Internet. It may also provide firewall support, which helps prevent bad guys on the Internet from accessing the computers on your local network.

✔ Many gateways feature USB ports for adding a printer or networked hard drive. That's a plus. The printer or hard drive can be accessed by any computer on the network.

✔ Normally, heavy configuration of the gateway is unnecessary; most of them come ready-to-wear right out of the box. Even so, I recommend that you assign the gateway a new password as part of its setup. Refer to the gateway's manual for information on how to access its control panel program and set the new password, or just have someone else do it for you.

✔ There's no need to turn off the gateway after the computer network is set up.

✔ When you need more network connections on your gateway, you buy something called a *switch*. It's basically just a gang of Ethernet ports, which let you add more network computers, printers, and other gizmos to the network. The switch helps you expand your computer network.

The Wireless Life

Q: What's the biggest difference between a wireless network and the traditional, wired computer network?

A: Why do I even need to ask? Everyone knows that the big difference is in the configuration, which involves weirdo acronyms such as SSID and WPA/WPA2 and other stuff you can avoid reading about until Chapter 21. For now, the major hardware difference is, of course, the lack of wires in a wireless network.

Figure 20-2 illustrates a basic wireless network setup. It's pretty much the same as the wired network setup shown back in Figure 20-1. In fact, it's the same illustration, but I just erased the wires, added the little wireless radio things, and changed some of the names. You see, I do all the book's illustrations and they don't pay me extra for it, so that's the best you're going to get.

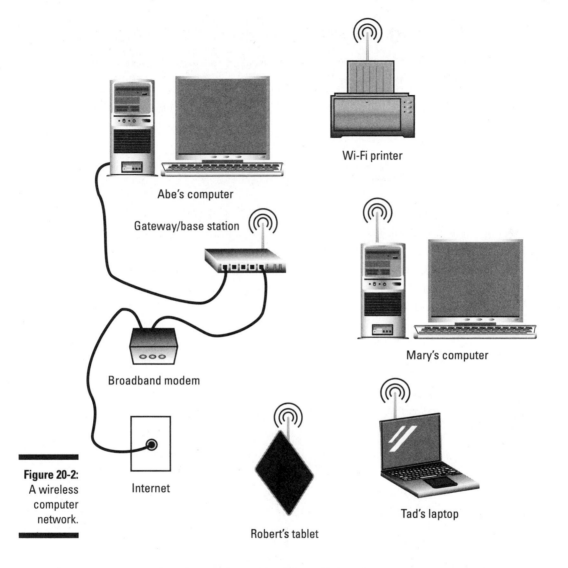

Wi-Fi printer

Abe's computer

Gateway/base station

Mary's computer

Broadband modem

Figure 20-2:
A wireless
computer
network.

Internet

Tad's laptop

Robert's tablet

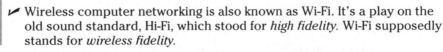

The interesting thing to notice in Figure 20-2 is that not every gizmo is wire-lessly connected to the network. You can mix and match. The only place you can't use a wireless connection is for the broadband modem. That one requires a wire, as shown in the figure.

✔ Just like wired networking, after you get wireless networking configured, you can pretty much leave it alone.

✔ Wireless computer networking is also known as Wi-Fi. It's a play on the old sound standard, Hi-Fi, which stood for *high fidelity*. Wi-Fi supposedly stands for *wireless fidelity*.

Getting used to the 802.11 thing

One additional thing you need to get used to for wireless networking, a thing that wired networking lacks, is the 802.11 number. It's a standard, probably the 802nd standard or the 11th version of the 802nd standard. But all that is unimportant. What is important is the wee little letter that comes after the 802.11.

The wee little letter describes the wireless networking standard. It's important because all the wireless gizmos on the network must use the same standard or communication is kaput. Here's the list:

802.11a: The first standard, which is not really used any longer.

802.11b: The second standard, which was compatible with 802.11a, but not the other way around.

802.11g: A newer standard, faster than 802.11b and quite popular until:

802.11n: The current, fastest, best standard for wireless networking. These devices can communicate with older standards, but not at top speed.

Most wireless networking hardware today adheres to the 802.11n standard. The only thing you need to remember is that all the wireless hardware on the network should be of the same standard.

You pronounce 802.11 as "eight oh two eleven." You can also say, "Eight oh two *dot* eleven" if you're feeling cheeky.

Hooking up the wireless NIC

As with its wired counterpart, the wireless NIC is essentially the gizmo on your PC that connects to the wireless network. It works without a cable, so it uses some kind of dark magic. Contrary to this section's title, there is nothing to hook up.

✔ Not every PC comes with a wireless NIC. You can add one easily, either internally by adding a wireless NIC expansion card or by attaching a wireless USB modem. See Chapter 10 for expansion options.

✔ It's possible to have both a wireless and wired NIC in your computer. They are two different devices, and your PC is capable of having two networking connections at once. Nothing explodes when you create such a setup.

✔ Even devices such as tablets and smartphones can have a wireless NIC. In fact, that method is the cheap way (cheaper than the cellular data service) to connect these gizmos to the Internet.

Obtaining a wireless gateway

Gateways come in both wired and wireless varieties. In fact, the wireless version is far more popular. Both have connections for wired networking, but the wireless gateway broadcasts the wireless network signal, which the wireless NICs on various gizmos can pick up and then connect to the network.

That explanation is the simple one. You'll find more details involved with connecting to a wireless network in Chapter 21.

Another item to consider for the wireless gateway is its broadcast range. In a single room, all devices can pick up the wireless signal. Step outside the room and the signal strength diminishes. Stand behind that lead safe, and the signal disappears entirely. My point is that wireless networking has a distance limitation.

- ✔ When one wireless gateway doesn't work for your home or office, you can buy a second wireless gateway and extend the first. The second gateway acts as a base station, simply rebroadcasting the Wi-Fi signal. This type of setup is called a wireless distribution system, or WDS.

- ✔ A wireless gateway is also known as an *access point*.

- ✔ As with the wireless NICs and other wireless networking stuff, the wireless gateway must be of the same 802.11 flavor as the rest of the wireless network.

The Broadband Modem

High-speed modems are generically referred to as *broadband* modems. These devices are frequently found near the heart of any computer network. In fact, most home computers are networked only to the broadband modem, simply to get that high-speed connection.

Several types of broadband modems are common:

Cable: This type of modem is the fastest you can have. Its only downside is that when more of your neighbors begin using their cable modems, the overall speed decreases. But at 2 a.m., your cable modem *smokes!*

DSL: This type of modem gives you fast access by taking advantage of unused frequencies in existing phone lines. The speed is limited by how far away your location is from the phone company's home office. Also, regular phones used on the same line as the DSL modem require special filters. But otherwise, next to cable, DSL gives you the fastest connection speeds.

Satellite: Combined with an outdoor antenna and a subscription to the satellite service, this modem option is one of the fastest available. Try to get a satellite modem that provides both sending and receiving capabilities. Avoid download-only satellite service.

WiMAX: A broadband wireless standard, WiMAX is like Wi-Fi on steroids. The signal can be broadcast over an entire city, picked up by wireless radios. It's fast. It's convenient. It's often one of the only options available when you live out in the sticks.

In all cases, the modem connects directly with the gateway in the computer network setup (refer to Figures 20-1 and 20-2). The gateway has a special hole for the modem; the hole might be labeled Modem or WAN, for wide-area network. That's the Internet.

✔ You should leave the broadband modem on all the time.

✔ By having a broadband modem attached to your computer network, you allow all computers on the network to share that fast Internet access.

✔ You can buy your own broadband modem or rent one from your Internet provider. I recommend buying the modem, especially when you know that you'll be in the same location and using the same service for at least a year.

✔ DSL stands for Digital Subscriber Line. It has variations, such as ADSL and other *something*-DSL options. Your phone company knows more about this matter than I do. Basically, everyone calls it DSL, no matter what.

Chapter 21

Network Abuse

. . . .

In This Chapter

▶ Checking the network connection

▶ Accessing a Wi-Fi network

▶ Finding network places in Windows

▶ Configuring network sharing

▶ Sharing folders and printers

▶ Accessing shared folders and printers

. . . .

The point of having a computer network is to use it. Beyond some initial anguish, the network behaves about as well as other computer components, causing trouble only at the worst times. But for the most part, the network sits there and does its job. Those few times you need to interact with the network require some avuncular words of advice, which you'll find in this chapter.

"Am I On the Network?"

Of course you're not on the network, although your computer might be. Before getting all panicked, you first need to confirm the hardware connection. Then you can pull a few tricks to see if the PC is talking to other gizmos on the network.

Connecting to a wired network

Windows automatically finds any network into which the PC is plugged. So, by turning on your computer and having that network hose connected, you're more or less done with network configuration. Enjoy a snack.

Connecting to a wireless network

Accessing a wireless, or Wi-Fi, network involves more steps than connecting a wired network. You must choose the connection, often from a full list of available networks.

The wireless network connection works differently whether you're cursed with Windows 8 or are blessed with an older, better version of Windows.

Connect in Windows 8

If you are using Windows 8, follow these steps to hook up to an available wireless network:

1. **Summon the charms bar, and then choose Settings.**

   The quickest way to summon the charms bar is to press the Win+C key combination.

2. **Click or touch the Available icon.**

   The icon is shown in the margin. If you don't see the icon, the computer might already be connected to a wireless network or there may be no networks in range.

3. **Choose a wireless network from the list.**

   Additional information about the network is displayed.

4. **Place a check mark in the box by Connect Automatically if you want to always connect with the wireless network when it's in range.**

5. **Click the Connect button.**

6. **If prompted, type the network's password.**

   The computer is now connected to the wireless network.

Skip up to the section "After the connection is made" to read some vital information about a new wireless connection.

Connect with older, better versions of Windows

If you are using a version of Windows before version 8, obey these steps to hunt down and connect to a wireless network:

1. **Click the wireless networking icon, found in the notification area.**

   When you click the wireless networking icon, a list of available wireless networks appears, as shown in Figure 21-1.

In Windows Vista, you choose the Connect To⇨Wireless Network item, found on the Start button menu.

In Windows XP, you choose Connect To from the Start button menu.

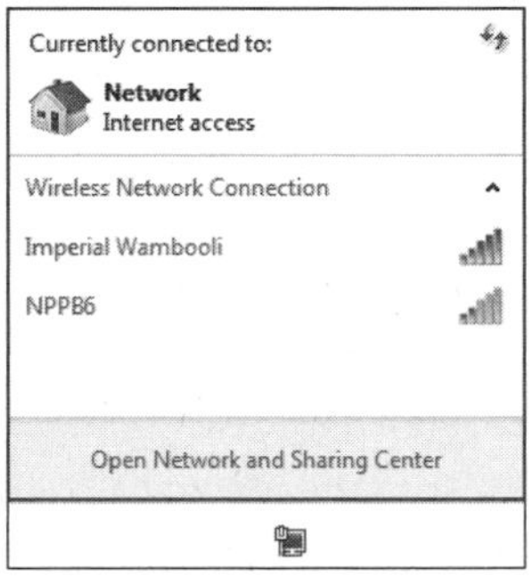

Figure 21-1:
Available
wireless
networks.

Currently connected to:

Network
Internet access

Wireless Network Connection ▲

Imperial Wambooli

NPPB6

Open Network and Sharing Center

2. **Choose a network from the list.**

   The list shows the network name and its signal strength.

3. **Place a check mark by the option Automatically Connect if you plan to use the same wireless network in the future.**

   The Automatically Connect option doesn't appear for every network.

4. **Click the Connect button.**

   Windows attempts to "make friendly" with the wireless network.

5. **If you see a warning telling you that the network is unsecured, click the Connect Anyway option.**

   This message is common for certain free wireless networks that don't require a password for connection. Click the Connect Anyway option to proceed.

6. **Enter the network's password, if you're prompted to do so.**

At this point, you could be connected and ready to use the network, especially if the network is one you commonly use. Keep reading the next section.

After the connection is made

At some point after connecting to the wireless network, Windows may ask you to tell it whether the network is public or private. This question is vital. A *public* network is one that's out in public, one that random and strange people can also use. In that situation, you want to ensure that your PC is locked down and not open to snooping. A home or office network is one in your home or office, available only to safe computers or folks you know. This type of network is more open than the public network.

Some public networks require that you log in or pay to complete the connection process. If you're unsure, open a web browser window; start the Internet Explorer program. Try to connect to a web page. If you're successful, you're okay. Otherwise, heed the directions on that web page to complete the connection.

- When given a choice, pick the wireless network with the strongest signal. The signal graphic appears just to the right of the wireless network's name.

- Avoid connecting to unknown networks in a public location. You're taking a security risk when you don't know exactly which network you're using.

- A few wireless Internet locations offer their password-and-setup information on a USB flash drive. Simply insert the flash drive to connect to the network, or use the drive as indicated by the directions or when you're prompted to insert the drive when you connect to the network. Needless to say, a USB flash drive is a handy thing to have — much better than retyping those long password keys!

Connecting to an unknown wireless network

Some Wi-Fi networks don't broadcast their SSID, which is an acronym that somehow stands for The Network's Name. In that case you need to discover the network's name and then manually connect to the network. Heed these steps:

1. **Open the Network and Sharing Center window.**

   Directions are found in the later section, "Windows Network Central."

2. **Click the link Set Up a New Connection or Network.**

   The Set Up a Connection or Network window appears.

3. **Choose the item Manually Connect to a Wireless Network, and then click the Next button.**

   A screen with a bunch of fill-in-the-blanks items appears. You'll need information about the wireless network to fill in all the blanks.

4. **Fill in all the blanks.**

   Most important, you need the network name (SSID), what type of security is offered (if any), and the password.

5. **Click the Next button.**

   If all goes well, the network is added.

Confirming the network connection

Your best clue to tell that the computer is connected to the network is to check the notification area on the taskbar. If the network icon shows a connection — and doesn't show a warning bubble, exclamation point, or yellow flag —you're connected.

Another way to tell is to fire up a web browser, such as Internet Explorer. If you can get on the Internet and view a web page, the network is up and running.

Finally, you can confirm that your PC is talking to other PCs on the network by opening the Network window: Press the Win+E keyboard shortcut, and then choose Network from the list on the left side of the screen. When you see icons for other computers connected to the network in that window, the network is connected.

Disconnecting from a network

There's no need to disconnect from a wired network. Just leave the cable plugged in all the time and Mr. PC will be fine.

You can manually disconnect from a wireless network by turning off the PC or simply moving out of range.

To manually disconnect from a wireless network in Windows 7, click the Network icon in the notification area and choose the wireless network from the pop-up window. Click the Disconnect button.

In Windows Vista, you manually disconnect from a wireless network by using the Network and Sharing Center; click the link titled Disconnect to the left of the wireless network name.

Windows Network Central

The main location for nearly all networking items in Windows is the Network and Sharing Center, shown in Figure 21-2. That window displays your PC's current network status as well as the Internet connection status.

Windows 8   Windows 7

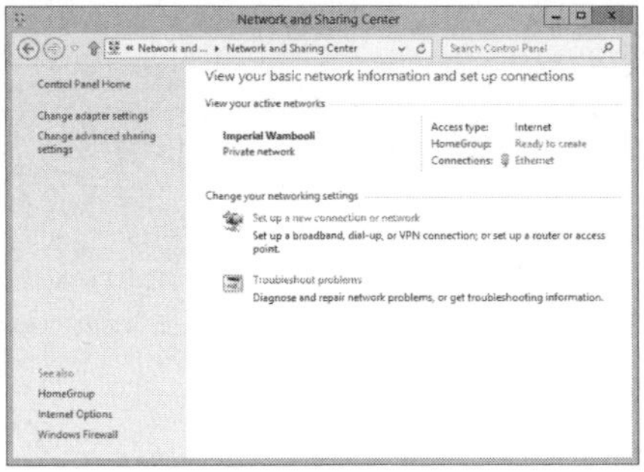

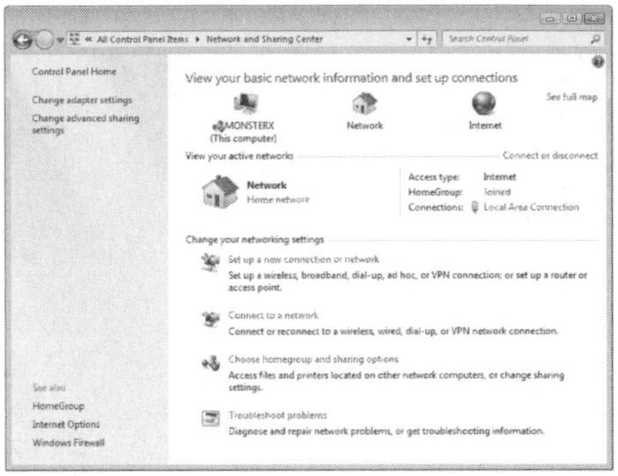

Figure 21-2:
The
Network
and Sharing
Center.

To display the Network and Sharing Center, heed these steps:

1. **Open the Control Panel window.**

2. **Below the Network and Internet heading, choose View Network Status and Tasks.**

    The Network and Sharing Center window appears.

In addition to displaying information about the network and Internet connection, the Network and Sharing Center features links and options where various networking stuff is controlled. It's okay if you want to ignore all those options.

Another network location is the Network window, shown in Figure 21-3. That window lists all the network resources available to your computer. To visit that window, press Win+E to summon a Windows Explorer window, and then choose the Network item from the window's left side.

The Network window organizes available network resources by category. In Figure 21-3 you'll find icons for computers, media-sharing devices, storage devices, and network printers.

✔ To diagnose a problem identified in the Network and Sharing Center window, click the red X to run a network troubleshooter.

✔ Windows XP lacks a Network and Sharing Center. Instead, a Network Connections window is used, which is accessed through the Network Connections icon in the Control Panel.

✔ A media-sharing device is a computer that makes available its photos, videos, and music or something non-traditional such as a game console or an Internet-ready TV.

Figure 21-3:
The
Network
window.

Network Sharing

Computers are not tribal. Your PC won't attach itself to a computer network just because it enjoys being one of the gang. The network must be useful to the computer, as well as its operator. To be the most useful, and fulfill the purpose of having a computer network, resources are shared.

- ✔ Common network resources include mass storage, printers, Internet access, and media players. Review Chapter 20 for the specifics.

- ✔ Internet access is available to all computers on the network without the need for further configuration. Providing that the hardware is set up properly, any computer on the network is on the Internet.

Demanding that Windows share resources

To confirm that your computer is set up to play nice and share stuff on the Internet, follow these steps:

1. Open the Network and Sharing Center window.

Directions loiter earlier in this chapter.

2. **From the left side of the window, choose Change Advanced Sharing Settings.**

   In Windows Vista, the settings are found at the bottom of the Network and Sharing Center window.

3. **Review my recommended settings from Table 21-1.**

   Turn each option on or off by choosing the appropriate button below the option's heading and description.

   In Windows 8 and Windows Vista, you may need to click the Show More (down-pointing chevron) button to display some of the on–off settings.

4. **Click the Save Changes button when you're done.**

   In Windows Vista, you must click the Apply button after making each individual setting change.

Table 21-1 **Settings That Control Sharing on the Network**

Option	Recommended Setting	Effect of Enabling
Network Discovery	On	Your PC can see other computers on the network and other computers can see your PC. It's the "No hiding" option.
File and Printer Sharing	On	Other computers on the network can access shared folders on your PC as well as any printers attached to your PC.
Public Folder Sharing	On	You control access to the Public folder on your PC.
Media Streaming/ Media Sharing	On	Other network users can access your PC's music and media files by using Windows Media Center across the network.
File Sharing Connections	128-bits	You can set the level of encryption for file sharing.
Password Protected Sharing	Off for home offices; On at work	You control who has access to shared files and printers on your PC.
HomeGroup Connections	On (Allow)	You specify whether Windows manages shared files as a HomeGroup or whether you do so manually by logging into each PC on the network.

In case you doubt my suggestions in Table 21-1, here are some clarifications and other items worthy of note:

✔ File and printer sharing are two separate categories in Windows Vista.

✔ The File Sharing Connections and HomeGroups Connections categories are available only in Windows 8 and Windows 7.

✔ The *Public folder* is a location in Windows where you can share files between multiple users on a single PC. You can also share files with folks on the network if you allow Public folder sharing as described in this section.

✔ The Password Protected Sharing option limits access to your PC and its files to only those who have a password-protected account on your PC. This option is a bother for home networks and wherever security isn't an issue. I turn off the option in my office but recommend turning it on in just about any situation except for the most secure ones.

✔ Media Sharing allows you to use Windows Media Center to play or access media files — including pictures, videos, and music — on another PC in the network.

✔ The HomeGroup sharing nonsense was introduced with Windows 7. It exists still in Windows 8. It's yet another way to share mass storage, though it works only with those two versions of Windows. It also requires copious amounts of setup and configuration, so feeling rather fatigued at this point in the chapter, it's a topic I'll leave to a book specific to your version of Windows.

Sharing your PC's mass storage

If you want other people on the network to have access to your PC's mass storage system, well, they can't. But they can have access to a folder on your computer. To do so, you must *share* the folder. Sharing makes the folder — and its contents (all files and subfolders) — available to all other computers on the network. Here's how to share a folder:

1. **Ensure that Network Discovery and File Sharing are enabled on your PC.**

   Refer to the preceding section.

2. **Right-click the folder you want to share.**

3. **Choose Properties from the pop-up menu.**

   The folder's Properties dialog box appears.

4. **Click the Sharing tab.**

5. **Click the Advanced Sharing button.**

   In Windows Vista, enter the administrator password or click the Continue button.

6. **Click to put a check mark by the option labeled Share This Folder.**

   You can set a share name, which helps to better identify the folder on the network.

   If you want others to have full access — to add as well as delete files — then click the Permissions button and place a check mark in the Allow column by the Full Control item.

7. **Click OK.**

   The folder is now shared.

8. **Click the Close button to dismiss the folder's Properties dialog box.**

Other PCs can now access the folder on the network. See the next section.

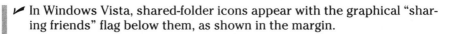

   ✔ In Windows Vista, shared-folder icons appear with the graphical "sharing friends" flag below them, as shown in the margin.

   ✔ To unshare a folder, repeat the steps in this section, but in Step 6 remove the check mark.

   ✔ Don't share an entire storage device, especially drive C. It's a security risk; Windows scolds you when you try to do so.

Accessing a network folder

You access a folder elsewhere on the network just as you would access any folder on your PC's mass storage system. The difference is that you need to browse to the folder from the Network window.

After opening the Network window, as discussed earlier in this chapter, open any computer to see which folders it's sharing. Open a folder icon to reveal its contents, which would be any shared folders on that computer's mass storage system.

You may be required to log in to another computer to access its folders. Logging in, or not, depends on the folder's permissions as set by whoever shared the folder.

Adding a network printer

For most of the newer versions of Windows, any printer on the network is immediately available for use by other network computers. All you need to do is choose that printer from the list displayed in the Printers dialog box.

But, Dan! I don't see the network printer listed!

I'm surprised that by now you wouldn't expect Windows to be completely stupid about finding networked printers. Sometimes it needs a little help. Obey these steps:

1. **Open the Devices and Printers or Printers window.**

   In the Control Panel window, click the View Devices and Printers link, found below the Hardware and Sound heading. The link is called Printer in Windows Vista.

2. **Click the Add a Printer button, found on the toolbar.**

3. **If prompted, choose Add a Network, Wireless, or Bluetooth printer.**

4. **Choose the printer from the list of found printers, and then click the Next button.**

   When the printer you want doesn't appear in the list, you can try clicking the option The Printer That I Want Isn't Listed. Be warned: The screen that follows is technical!

5. **Continue installing the printer.**

   From this point on, installing the printer works like setting up a printer directly connected to your computer.

See Chapter 11 for further scintillating details on printer installation.

You may also be prompted to share the printer on the network. Yeah, that seems dumb, because the printer is already shared on the network. Yet Windows asks anyway. Choose not to share the printer.

Sharing your PC's printer

Any printer directly connected to your computer is available only to your PC and not to other computers on the network. If you want to make the printer available, passed around like the community drinking cup at the town well, follow these steps to share it:

1. **Open the Devices and Printers or Printers window.**

   In the Control Panel window, click the View Devices and Printers link, found below the Hardware and Sound heading. The link is called Printer in Windows Vista.

2. **Right-click a printer directly connected to your computer.**

3. **Choose the Printer Properties command.**

   The printer's Properties dialog box appears.

4. **Click the Sharing tab.**

5. **Place a check mark by the Share This Printer item.**

6. **Click the OK button.**

   You can also close the Device and Printers (or Printer) window.

There you have it. The printer is now shared on the network where anyone — unkempt, unlearned, unwashed — can use it to meet their printing needs.

Chapter 22

Why Does This Book Have a Bluetooth Chapter?

In This Chapter

▶ Using Bluetooth on a PC

▶ Expanding your system wirelessly

▶ Understanding pairing

▶ Connecting to a Bluetooth peripheral

▶ Disconnecting a Bluetooth peripheral

1 could argue that I'm a big fan of technology that's pointless to most people, but I won't. The truth is that most PCs — including laptops — don't come with Bluetooth hardware. They just don't! And if the world contained only PCs running Windows, this chapter would fit on the back of a *For Dummies* matchbook cover and only smokers in bars might read it. There's more to the story though.

The issue you and I face is that lots of other hardware gizmos adore the Bluetooth wireless standard. These gizmos include tablets, smartphones, and even the dratted Macintosh computers. Through their tireless hegemony, Bluetooth is becoming more and more common. Consider perusing this chapter should you ever encounter a Bluetooth device and hold the desire to do Bluetoothy things with it.

That Bluetooth Thing

Bluetooth refers to a wireless standard for connecting computer peripherals and other technological devices. Just as wireless computer networking involves more setup than the wired kind of network, using Bluetooth wireless peripherals involves a bit more than connecting wired peripherals.

✔ As long as the PC is equipped with Bluetooth technology, it can use various Bluetooth devices and gizmos.

✔ Bluetooth peripherals include printers, keyboards, speakers, mice, monitors, robot butlers, various tablets, and cell phones.

✔ Perhaps the greatest advantage of Bluetooth is that it lets you connect wirelessly to a variety of peripherals without having to use a separate wireless adapter for each peripheral.

✔ One disadvantage of Bluetooth is that it's not entirely secure. Although I've not read of any hacking incidents involving Bluetooth (mostly because its range is so short), many large organizations don't allow Bluetooth on their computers because of the security risk.

Understanding Bluetooth

The most-asked question about Bluetooth technology just has to be, "What the hell is up with that name?"

Relax. It's Scandinavian. Or, rather, Ericsson is the Swedish company that developed the Bluetooth standard. The real name is unpronounceable by humans, so the closest we can come is *blue tooth*.

Nerds (who else?) developed the Bluetooth standard to provide a common method for connecting wireless peripherals. Seeing how Swedish computer users were often stranded in their snow lodges, bound with endless wires, the whole thing makes a lot of sense.

Seriously, Bluetooth began its existence as a wireless replacement for the old serial (RS-232) port, popular with PCs in the 1980s and 1990s.

Checking for Bluetooth

All Bluetooth computers and gizmos feature an internal Bluetooth wireless radio. Don't bother looking for it, because it's buried inside the device. That's what the word *internal* means.

 One external clue that a device uses Bluetooth is the Bluetooth logo, shown in the margin. If you find that logo on a printer, for example, you know it's a Bluetooth printer and you could configure your PC to wirelessly print to it.

Not every device sports the Bluetooth logo. For example, a tablet or smartphone doesn't feature the tattoo. Some PC laptops lack the Bluetooth logo, though they may sport an activity lamp that shows when Bluetooth has been activated, similar to the Wi-Fi lamp used to show when wireless networking is enabled.

Adding a Bluetooth adapter

If your PC lacks a Bluetooth wireless radio, you can easily add one: Obtain a Bluetooth adapter. The teensy gizmo, which is small enough to smuggle through customs in your nostril, plugs directly into a USB port.

Even better: USB Bluetooth adapters are cheap!

Best: After you attach a USB Bluetooth adapter, Windows automatically installs Bluetooth software. You don't have to set up a thing.

Controlling Bluetooth in Windows

When Bluetooth is available and configured, you'll see the Bluetooth logo as an icon in the desktop's notification area (on the right end of the taskbar). You use the pop-up menu from that icon to control Bluetooth gizmos from your PC, as shown in Figure 22-1.

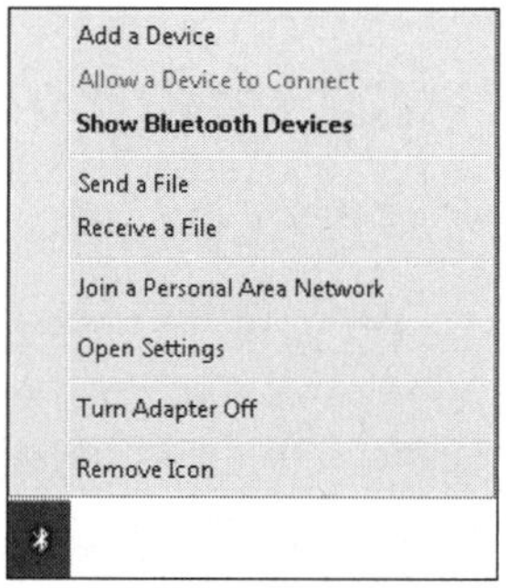

Add a Device
Allow a Device to Connect
Show Bluetooth Devices

Send a File
Receive a File

Join a Personal Area Network

Open Settings

Turn Adapter Off

Remove Icon

Figure 22-1:
Bluetooth
control in
Windows.

The pop-up menu you see on your computer may look slightly different from what's shown in Figure 22-1. Most of the important menu items are there no matter what you see.

An important item in the Bluetooth pop-up menu is Turn Adapter On. Choose that item to turn on the Bluetooth radio.

To turn off the Bluetooth radio, choose the Turn Adapter Off menu item. When you see that item in the menu (refer to Figure 22-1), the Bluetooth wireless radio is on. You're set to go. Otherwise, the menu item reads Turn Adapter On.

✔ There is no need to turn off Bluetooth. I just leave it on all the time.

✔ The Bluetooth adapter may also show up in the bowels of Windows. You may find it in the Devices and Printers window. Even so, most of the control over Bluetooth takes place using the pop-up menu, shown in Figure 22-1.

Bluetooth Pairing

The whole point of Bluetooth is to allow your PC to connect with peripherals and other devices without the burden of wires. Unlike the TV remote, however, you can't just point-and-click to get the job done. Instead, the devices must be paired.

The *pairing* process involves a gentle introduction between the PC and the other Bluetooth device. That's followed by a brief courtship, and then a marriage. Unlike humans, the connection is pretty much the lifespan of the devices, irreconcilable differences be damned.

Walking through the pairing operation

Here is an overview of how the Bluetooth pairing process works:

1. **Ensure that Bluetooth wireless radio is turned on for each gizmo.**

   It takes two Bluetooth gizmos to tango. One is your PC; the other is the peripheral device, such as a keyboard, printer, or smartphone.

2. **Make the gizmo you're trying to connect to discoverable.**

   A discoverable device says, "Yoo-hoo! I'm over here!" It's the Bluetooth mating call.

   Technically, when a device is discoverable, a special Bluetooth signal is broadcast, listing the device as available for pairing with another Bluetooth device. Sure, that explanation isn't at racy, but it's more accurate.

3. **On your PC, scan for available Bluetooth devices.**

   This step may take place automatically or you may have to initiate the scan.

4. **Choose the device from the list of available Bluetooth devices.**

   For example, if you're pairing the PC with a wireless mouse, you'd choose the wireless mouse from the list.

5. Optionally, confirm the connection on the peripheral device.

For example, you may be asked to input a code or press a button. For a wireless keyboard, you may have a type a sequence of numbers. If the code doesn't appear on the screen, look for it in the documentation of the device you're attempting to pair.

6. Use the device.

What you can do with the device depends on what it's designed to do.

The good news is that after you initially pair the device, there's no need to pair it again. Any time the computer is on and Bluetooth device is on, they automatically reconnect.

✔ The reason for pairing the devices is so that some other Bluetooth device doesn't steal away the peripheral. That can happen only if you un-pair the devices, which is covered in the later section "Un-pairing a Bluetooth device."

✔ Bluetooth devices are discoverable for only a brief amount of time, usually two minutes. If the connection fails during that time, you'll need to make the device discoverable again.

✔ If you have trouble connecting the device, ensure that your PC is open to the connection: Click the Bluetooth icon in the notification area and choose the Open Settings command. In the Bluetooth Settings dialog box, ensure that a check mark is next to the option Allow Bluetooth Devices to Find This Computer. Click OK.

Pairing with a device

Here's an example of how to pair with a Bluetooth printer. These steps are more specific than those found in the preceding section:

1. Use the printer's control panel to make the device discoverable.

Look for a Bluetooth menu and choose the item that makes the printer discoverable or that initiates the pairing process.

2. On your PC, click the Bluetooth icon in the notification area.

3. Choose the command Add a Device.

A window or screen appears, listing any available Bluetooth devices. If you're lucky, the one you want to pair appears in that list.

4. Choose the device from the list.

5. In Windows 8, choose the device from the list; in Windows 7, click the Next button.

Now comes the coordination part.

6. **Obey the directions on your computer screen or on the Bluetooth device.**

   There is a time limit, so be quick!

   For my printer, the direction was to type the printer's code on the computer's keyboard. I've also seen the prompt on the printer's screen, where I had to type the code there. For other devices, the pairing may take place instantly. Regardless, obey the directions for *both* devices to complete the pairing.

7. **After the device is paired, click the Next button in Windows 8. In Windows 7, click the Close button.**

You can now use the device as a wireless peripheral on your PC.

   ✔ You can confirm that the device is paired by checking the list of paired devices. See the next section.

   ✔ As with a wired peripheral, there is a limit on the distance between your computer and the peripheral. For Bluetooth, that distance is about 20 feet. In Europe, the distance is far less, just over 6 meters.

Reviewing paired devices

You review and manage the PC's Bluetooth connections by clicking the Bluetooth icon in the notification area and choosing the Show Bluetooth Devices command.

In Windows 8 you see the Devices portion of the PC Settings screen. Paired Bluetooth devices appear in the list along with all the other devices attached to your PC. A clue as to which are Bluetooth gizmos is often the word *Bluetooth* in the device name, such as Bluetooth Mouse 5000.

In Windows 7 and Windows Vista, the Bluetooth Devices window appears after you choose the Show Bluetooth Devices command. Figure 22-2 shows an example. In the window, you see all Bluetooth devices that have ever been paired with the PC. Active connections appear solid; disconnected devices appear dimmed.

You'll find two things worthy of your attention in the screen or window that displays Bluetooth devices. The first is the weirdo names. Bluetooth recognizes the device's internal code name, not the friendly name you probably call the gizmo. An exception is the Nexus 7 tablet, shown in Figure 22-2.

The second thing to notice is that not all paired devices are connected. With some devices, you must direct the gizmo to connect before you can interact with it. The methods of connection vary, but most devices feature a Bluetooth app or menu in which you can activate the connection.

Paired device, disconnected   Paired device, connected

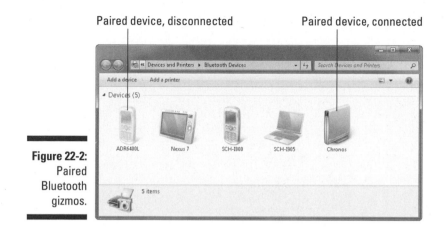

Figure 22-2:
Paired
Bluetooth
gizmos.

Un-pairing a Bluetooth device

Normally there's no need to un-pair a device. If you want to stop using the device, simply turn it off. The connection is broken once the device is off.

Oh. You're being insistent? Well then: The only time you truly need to un-pair a Bluetooth device is if you want to use the device with another Bluetooth computer at the same location. In that case, follow these steps:

1. **Click the Bluetooth icon in the notification area.**

2. **Choose the command Show Bluetooth Devices.**

3. **Click to select the paired Bluetooth device.**

4. **In Windows 8, click the minus button that appears; in Windows 7 and Windows Vista, click the Remove Device toolbar button.**

5. **Click the Remove button (Windows 8) or the Yes button (Windows 7) to confirm.**

After the device is un-paired, you're free to pair it with another Bluetooth computer. Or you can re-pair the device with your PC again. Bluetooth devices have low standards and loose morals and really don't care what they're paired with, as long as they're paired with something.

Chapter 23

As Little of the Internet as Possible

In This Chapter

▶ Understanding the Internet

▶ Obtaining an ISP

▶ Visiting web pages

▶ Searching the web

▶ Saving a web page image

▶ Sharing web pages

I've yet to encounter someone who doesn't understand the Internet or its two main components, the web and e-mail. In fact, most people tell me that they don't understand their PC, but they know how to do the Internet. Given that some 20 years ago the book *Internet For Dummies* was a huge best-seller, mankind has obviously come a long way.

What's left for the Internet? Plenty! Rather than provide yet another useless chapter in a computer book about opening web browsers and going back and forth, I thought I'd drill down and describe only those necessary portions of the Internet, place them in this chapter, and leave it at that. My goal is to make this the shortest chapter in the book without incensing my editor.

What Is the Internet?

I feel compelled to explain how the *Internet* is composed of hundreds of thousands of computers all over the world. Those computers send information, they receive information, and — most important — they store information. That's the Internet in a nutshell.

✔ The Internet consists of all the computers connected to the Internet. Whenever your computer is *on* the Internet, it's part of the Internet.

✔ No one owns the Internet, just as no one owns the oceans. The company you pay for Internet access is merely providing you with the access, not with the Internet's content.

How to Access the Internet

Windows loves the Internet. The affection is so deep that Windows prefers that you have a broadband Internet connection. That means not only that you have a fast connection but also that your PC is *always* connected to the Internet.

See Chapter 20 for information on broadband Internet connections.

Choosing an ISP

You need the following items to access the Internet:

- A computer
- A modem
- Internet software
- Money
- An Internet Service Provider, or ISP
- More money

The first three items you should already have. Money is needed to pay for the fifth item, which is the outfit that provides you with Internet access.

Your ISP can be your telephone company, cable company, wireless provider, or satellite outfit, all of which compete to provide you with broadband Internet access.

Beyond Internet access, a good ISP provides you with some or all of the following items:

- For a dial-up modem, the phone number to call
- Your Internet login ID and password
- Your Internet e-mail name, address, and password (if they're different from your login ID and password)
- The name of your ISP's e-mail server, which involves the acronyms POP3 and SMTP, plus other technical information required to set up various Internet programs
- A phone number to call for help (very important)

Finally, the ISP bills you for Internet access. The prices can be cheap, some-times less than $10 per month for dial-up access. You pay more for faster connections, with some high-speed broadband connections costing upward of $50 per month. Be sure to compare prices when choosing an ISP.

The *S* in *ISP* stands for service. You pay a fee, and the ISP provides you with Internet access *and* service. Service means technical support: someone you can phone for help, classes, software — you name it.

Configuring Windows for the Internet

Windows is automatically set up to use the Internet. By connecting a broad-band modem to your PC or to the PC's network, you suddenly and instantly have Internet access. Windows sees it. You're all set.

Things work differently when you have dial-up access. In that case, you must create a network connection for the modem to use. Directions for this task should come from your ISP, which gives you a phone number to dial, plus perhaps other options to set, such as configuring your e-mail program.

Connecting to the Internet

There's no need to fuss over connecting to the Internet when you use a broadband modem; the connection is always on. Internet programs start up quickly and access the Internet just as fast.

Dial-up connections are active only when you use the Internet. When you run an Internet program, or when any software attempts to access the Internet, Windows directs the PC's modem to dial into your ISP. After making the con-nection, you're on the Internet and can use Internet software.

✔ To test the Internet connection, run the Internet Explorer program or any web browser. By running an Internet program such as a web browser, your computer attempts to make an Internet connection. When the connection works, you see a web page. Otherwise, you see an error message. If so, contact your ISP for assistance.

✔ You should hang up, or *disconnect,* from the dial-up connection when you're done using the Internet. The directions that came from your dial-up ISP explain how to do that.

✔ To cancel a dial-up connection, click the Cancel button when you see it dialing.

✔ Sometimes your dial-up modem may seem like it's randomly connecting to the Internet because some program or Windows itself is requesting information. Canceling that request isn't a problem, nor does it mess things up. Programs can wait until *you* want to connect to the Internet to conduct their business.

It's a World Wide Web We Weave

Yeah, you probably know how to use a web browser fairly well. Most people do. But I'll bet lots of people could still use some of the information held in this section.

Browsing tips

Here are my collected web-browsing tips, honed and polished over the past two centuries:

✔ If you prefer to see a real live menu bar in a web browser that doesn't sport the traditional menu bar, press the F10 key on the keyboard.

✔ Use the Zoom control to make web pages with small text more visible. The control may be found at the bottom of the screen, or you may find it on the View menu. (Press F10 to see the menu.)

✔ Some web browsers use the Ctrl+. (period) to zoom out and Ctrl+, (comma) to zoom in. The period and comma keys are also the < and > keys, which are the less-than and greater-than symbols. That's how I remember these shortcuts.

✔ If a web page doesn't load, try again! The web can be busy, and often when it is, you see an error message. Reload a web page by pressing Ctrl+R on the keyboard.

✔ Refreshing a page is one quick way to fix the "missing picture" problem.

✔ When a web page isn't found, you probably didn't type its address properly. Try again.

✔ Not all web links are text. Quite a few links are graphical. The only way to know for certain is to point the mouse pointer at what you believe may be a link. If the pointer changes to a pointing hand, you know that it's a link you can click to see something else.

✔ When you accidentally click a link and change your mind, click the Stop button, which appears on the address bar with an X symbol. The Internet then stops sending you information.

 ✔ Press Ctrl+D to add any web page you're viewing to bookmark that page or add it your favorites. Don't be shy about it! It's better to add it now and delete it later than to regret not adding it in the first place.

Printing web pages

To print any web page, click the Printer button on the toolbar. That's pretty much it. Well, unless there is no Printer button, in which case you can press Ctrl+P to summon the Print dialog box and print from there.

Sadly, some web pages don't print right. Some are too wide. Some show white text on a black background, which doesn't print well. My advice is to use the Print Preview command to look at what will print before you print it. Press the F10 key to summon the menu bar, and then choose File➪Print Preview.

If you still have trouble printing the web page, try one of these solutions:

 ✔ Consider saving the web page to disk; press the Ctrl+S keyboard combination. After the page is saved, you can open the web page file in Microsoft Word or Excel or any web page editing program and edit or print it from there.

 ✔ Print wide web pages using landscape orientation for printing wider-than-normal web pages: Press the F10 key to summon the menu bar, and then choose File➪Page Setup to change the orientation.

 ✔ Use the Properties button in the Print dialog box to adjust the printer. Press Ctrl+P to see the Print dialog box. The Properties settings depend on the printer itself, but I have seen printers that can reduce the output to 75 or 50 percent, which ensures that the entire web page prints on a single sheet of paper. Other options may let you print in shades of gray (*grayscale*) or black and white.

Searching-the-web tips

The web is full of information, and some of it accurate. The issue is getting to the information you want. Here are my web-page-searching tips:

 ✔ My main search engine these days is Google, at www.google.com, but I can also recommend the Microsoft search engine Bing, at www.bing.com.

✔ Web search engines ignore the smaller words in the English language. Words such as *is, to, the, for, are,* and others aren't included in the search. Therefore:

✔ Use only key words when searching. For example, to look for *The Declaration of Independence,* typing *declaration independence* is good enough.

✔ Word order matters. If you want to find out the name of that red bug with six legs, try all combinations: *bug red six legs, red bug six legs,* or even *six legs red bug.* Each variation yields different results.

✔ When words *must* be found together, enclose them in double quotes, such as *"Green Acres" theme* or *"electric chair" setup.* A quoted search finds only web pages that list the words *electric chair* together in that order.

✔ If the results — the matching or found web pages — are too numerous, click the link (near the bottom of the page) that says Search within results. That way, you can further refine your search. For example, if you found several hundred pages on Transylvania but are specifically looking for Dracula's castle, you can search for *"Dracula Castle"* in the results you found for Transylvania.

Get Stuff from a Web Page

The text and pictures you see on a web page can easily be copied and saved on your own computer. Well, actually, the information you see on the display *is* already on your computer: The text, images, and other stuff you see are sent from the Internet and stored temporarily while you're viewing that web page. This section explains how to save some of that information permanently.

Saving an image from a web page

To save an image from a web page to your PC, right-click the image and choose Save Picture As from the pop-up menu. That command may be worded differently, depending on which web browser you use. Regardless, use the dialog box that appears to find a happy home for the picture on your hard drive.

✔ Nearly all images on the web are copyrighted. Although you can save a copy to your hard drive, you're not free to duplicate, sell, or distribute the image without the consent of the copyright holder.

✔ To set the image as the Windows desktop wallpaper, choose Set As Background from the pop-up menu after right-clicking the image, if that command is available.

Grabbing text from a web page

You can copy text from a web page and save it for later or paste that text into another document or e-mail message. Here's how:

1. **Select the text you want to copy.**

   Drag the mouse over the text, which highlights the text on the web page. The text is now selected.

2. **Press Ctrl+C on the keyboard to copy the text.**

3. **Start your word processor, e-mail program, or what-have-you.**

4. **Paste the text into a document or an e-mail message.**

   Press Ctrl+V on the keyboard or choose Edit⇨Paste from the menu.

5. **Print. Save. Whatever.**

   Use the proper commands to save or print or edit the text.

If you can't paste the text, you need to choose a program into which text can be pasted.

Sharing a web page

When you love a web page so much that you must share it with everyone you know, follow my friendly-yet-threatening words of advice: Share only the web page address.

There is no need to copy and paste the entire web page into an e-mail message or on Facebook. Instead, just copy the web page's address from the address text box. Select the entire text, all of it. Press Ctrl+C. Then move on to whichever program you're using to share that address. Press Ctrl+V to paste the web page address. There. Simple.

Chapter 24

PC Nightmares

In This Chapter

▶ Understanding the computer nasties

▶ Visiting the Action Center

▶ Using a firewall

▶ Stopping spyware

▶ Inoculating against viruses

▶ Coping with the UAC warnings

*D*oes your computer dream? Does it frolic naked through sunlit meadows with nary a cycle spinning in its CPU? Maybe the PC dreams it can fly or that it somehow has magical powers. "Watch me log in without a user present," it boasts, a smile cracking its slumbering visage. Merry, merry thoughts — until you wake up the thing. Maybe that's why the system is so cranky?

If the PC can dream, it's most certainly capable of nightmares. The problem is that the nightmares are the reality. Nasty programs prowl the ether, looking for humble, innocent electronics to infect. Worse, naive users welcome vile software into the computer, despite the system's digital protestations. What follows is unbound woe — unless you leaf gently through this chapter's pages, and uncover the solutions for PC nightmares.

Fight the Bad Guys

Computer bad guys have a host of names as rich and colorful as any comic book (see the sidebar, "PC super-villain roundup"). Knowing the names is important only when you also know the names of the superheroes who help you thwart the plans of the evil ones. Windows has many such superheroes:

The web browser: Microsoft's web browser, Internet Explorer, comes with a rich set of features for keeping your computer safe. These features include ample warnings when software tries to install itself in your PC from the Internet as well as ways to protect you from visiting phony websites. Other browsers also include such tools, but because Internet Explorer comes with Windows, I discuss it in this chapter.

PC supervillain roundup

As with most things about computers, malicious software, or *malware,* is named in either a highly technical or extremely silly manner. Neither name helps: The technical name is confusing, and the silly name is clever for only people who would otherwise understand the technical names. Regardless, here's your handy guide:

✔ **Phishing:** Pronounced "fishing," this term applies to a web page or an e-mail designed to fool you into thinking that it's something else, such as your bank's web page. The idea is to *fish* for information, such as account numbers and passwords. The web page or e-mail tricks you into providing that information because it looks legitimate. It isn't.

✔ **Pop-up:** A pop-up isn't a nasty program, but it can be annoying — especially when you're assaulted by several pop-ups at once. How any legitimate marketing person would believe that multiple, annoying pop-up windows would entice anyone to buy something is beyond me, but it happens and you can stop it.

✔ **Spyware:** A rather broad category, *spyware* refers to a program that monitors, or spies on, what you do on the Internet. The reasoning is advertising: By knowing where you go and what you do on the Internet, information obtained about you can be sold to advertisers who then target ads your way.

✔ **Trojan:** A program is labeled a *Trojan* (horse) whenever it claims to do one thing but does another. For example, a common Trojan is a special screen saver that saves the screen but also uses your PC on the Internet to relay pornographic images.

✔ **Virus:** A *virus* is a nasty program that resides in your PC without your knowledge. The program may be triggered at any time, taking over the computer, redirecting Internet traffic, sending a flood of spam messages, or doing any of a number of nasty and inconvenient things.

✔ **Worm:** A *worm* is simply a virus that replicates itself, by sending out copies to other folks on your e-mail list, for example.

Windows Defender: The Windows Defender program helps you scan for and remove a clutch of bad guys, especially insidious start-up programs and spyware.

Windows Firewall: The firewall helps to close the windows and bar the doors that bad guys use to infect PCs.

Windows Update: Keeping your PC's software up-to-date is important because the bad guys like a target that stands still.

Backup: To keep your stuff safe, I recommend that you back it up. The backup procedure creates a safety copy of all files on your PC so that if disaster strikes — naturally created or motivated by evil — you can recover your stuff.

Antivirus: Your PC needs a good antivirus program to fight infections that fly in from the Internet or arrive on rogue media. Windows 8 comes with anti-virus protection, but older versions of Windows might not. See the section "Using antivirus protection," later in this chapter.

Bottom line: Use these tools to help keep your PC safe and its owner happy.

- ✔ See Chapter 15 for information on using Windows Update.
- ✔ See Chapter 18 for information on backing up your PC's files.
- ✔ You can avoid many nasty programs by simply using common sense. In fact, the most successful computer viruses have propagated simply because of human nature. It's that *human engineering* the bad guys count on, or your ability to be tricked into doing something you wouldn't do otherwise, such as opening a questionable e-mail attachment or clicking a web page link because you're fooled into thinking, "Your PC is at risk!"
- ✔ Your ISP can be of great help in dealing with nasty programs on the Internet. Don't forget to use their assistance, especially when you try fixing things on your own and it doesn't help.

The Action Center

The headquarters for security issues in Windows 8 and Windows 7 is the Action Center, illustrated in Figure 24-1. The Action Center window provides a quick summary of your PC's current security state and lists any pending problems or issues with links or buttons that help you resolve those issues.

Windows 8 | Windows 7

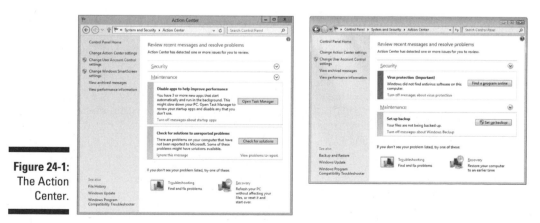

Figure 24-1:
The Action
Center.

To open the Action Center, click the link Review Your Computer's Status, found below the System and Security heading in the Control Panel window. High-priority items are flagged in red in the window, and lower-priority items are flagged in orange. None of the items are flagged in grape.

Click the Show More button in the window to view all the details for your PC's security and maintenance conditions. When an area is expanded, you see lots of status information and updates plus links that take you to specific locations in Windows where you can change settings or deal with issues.

- Generally speaking, follow the advice in the window.

- In Figure 24-1, the Windows 8 Action Center is offering suggestions to improve PC performance.

- The Windows 7 PC (refer to Figure 24-1) is lacking antivirus protection. To solve that issue, click the button Find a Program Online; see the section "Using antivirus protection," later in this chapter.

- Also in Figure 24-1, the Windows 7 PC hasn't yet had its important files backed up. See Chapter 18 for information on PC backup.

- In Windows Vista, the Action Center is named Windows Security Center. It serves the same purpose but lacks a lot of the detail of the Action Center.

Setting up the Windows Firewall

In construction, a *firewall* is used to slow the advance of a fire. It's created from special slow-burning material and rated in *hours*. For example, a three-hour firewall takes, theoretically, three hours to burn through — and that helps protect a building from burning down before the fire department shows up.

On a computer with an Internet connection, a *firewall* is designed to restrict Internet access, primarily to keep unwanted guests from getting in — or out — of the computer. The firewall effectively plugs holes left open when the Internet was originally designed.

Windows comes with a firewall named, coincidentally, Windows Firewall. You start it from the Control Panel: Click the heading System and Security, and then click the heading Windows Firewall. The Windows Firewall window appears, shown in Figure 24-2.

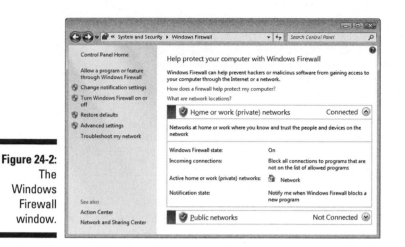

Figure 24-2:
The
Windows
Firewall
window.

As far as you're concerned, Windows Firewall has only two settings: on and off. To change the setting, click the Turn Windows Firewall On or Off link on the left side of the Windows Firewall window (refer to Figure 24-2).

When the firewall detects unwanted access, either to or from the Internet, you see a pop-up window alerting you to the intrusion, such as the one shown in Figure 24-3. At that point, you can choose to allow access by the named program by clicking the Allow Access button. If you want to continue blocking the program, just click Cancel.

Figure 24-3:
Windows
Firewall in
action.

If you're in doubt about your PC's firewall or just want to ensure that it's doing its job, I recommend that you give it a test. Many programs available on the Internet probe your PC's firewall and look for weaknesses. One such program is ShieldsUP!, which can be found on the Gibson Research website at http://grc.com.

Protecting the PC with Windows Defender

Windows Defender is a single name given to a slate of tools used to protect your PC from snooping programs, irritating start-up programs, nasty programs known as spyware, and even viruses. Therefore the *defender* name is apt.

Windows Defender program runs automatically. You're alerted to any problems in the Action Center window (refer to Figure 24-1). To specifically visit the Windows Defender program window, you follow a set of tricky steps:

1. **Press Win+R to display the Run dialog box.**

2. **In the Open text box, type** c:\program files\Windows Defender\ msascui

   Yeah, that's a long complex thing to type. And those are backslashes, not forward slashes.

3. **Click the OK button.**

The Windows Defender main window is rather boring — with a quick summary saying that your PC is running normally — unless you have a problem.

To perform a quick check for any Bad Guys in your PC, click the Scan Now button. Simply heed the directions on the screen to proceed.

Also peruse the next section, which discusses antivirus protection.

- Other antispyware programs are available, and most often they can be found in the various security suite programs.

- It's okay to run more than one antispyware program in your computer at a time. Well, I'd run two, if you have them: another program plus Windows Defender. There's no need to load up on antispyware programs.

Using antivirus protection

Windows Defender offers pretty decent antivirus protection, along with many of the other things it does. Better antivirus protection comes from third-party programs. The best antivirus software you can buy is subscription-based, meaning you pay annually for updates.

Popular antivirus software includes the Norton AntiVirus, McAfee VirusScan, and the AVG program. All of them work. You need to use one. I recommend any of them in addition to the protection offered by Windows Defender.

The run-o-the-mill antivirus program works by scanning your computer for signs of infection. Most programs feature two modes of operation:

Active Scan: In Active Scan mode, your antivirus software takes a look at every dang-doodle file and program on your computer, sniffing out the viral presence. Antivirus programs scan all the files on your PC regularly, if not daily.

Interception: In Interception mode, the antivirus program works to scan incoming e-mail and files you transfer from other computers as well as stuff that floats in from the Internet. If an infection tries to walk into your PC, it's stopped; the program's feet are nailed to the floor and you're alerted to the break-in.

These names, Active Scan and Interception, are my own. The antivirus program you choose probably has its own pet names but still carries out those actions. For example, in Windows Defender, *Active Scan* is referred to as *Read-Time Protection.*

✔ When the antivirus program alerts you to an infection, deal with it! Quarantine or delete the infection immediately.

✔ Antivirus programs use quarantine as a way to isolate potentially infected files, preventing them from attacking your PC. Although the file has been quarantined, it hasn't been deleted, but your system is still safe. (You can delete the quarantined files later.)

✔ You can run two antivirus programs on your PC, though not at the same time. You use only one antivirus program in Interception mode, but you can scan your PC using two antivirus programs, one after the other, to ensure that whatever one misses, the other might catch.

✔ You can access the antivirus program by clicking its little icon, which appears in the taskbar's notification area.

✔ Viruses spread because of simple human engineering. Most folks know not to open strange or unexpected e-mail attachments. Yet viruses continue to be spread by these types of techniques. Perhaps the best antivirus tool you have is your own brain: Being thoughtful and not careless prevents viruses from being installed in the first place, making antivirus programs necessary but not vital.

Paying attention to the UAC warnings

In its efforts to make Windows a more secure operating system, Microsoft has presented you (the human) with something called the UAC, or *User Account Control.* It displays various warning dialog boxes and pop-up windows whenever you attempt to change something in Windows, such as a computer setting or option, or when you try to download software from the Internet. A typical UAC is shown in Figure 24-4.

Figure 24-4:
A typical
UAC.

The UACs are to be expected whenever you see a link or button flagged with the UAC shield icon, shown in the margin. It's your clue that you should expect a UAC warning to appear. If the action is expected, click the Continue button or, if prompted, type the administrator's password and then click the OK button.

If you see a UAC warning when you're not expecting one, click the Cancel button. For example, when you're on the Internet and you see a UAC warning about installing software or changing your home page, click Cancel!

Part V
Your Digital Life

The 5th Wave   By Rich Tennant

"The funny thing is he's spent 9 hours organizing his computer desktop."

In this part . . .

Welcome to the digital future. Digital clocks began the revolution years ago, quietly at first and then noisily at about 6:30 a.m. every morning. Now, everything is digital. The pictures you take are digital. Movies are made with digital cameras and viewed on digital screens. Music is stored digitally. You use digital phones. The games you play are digital. It's a digital world.

At the center of your digital life is the computer, enabling you to manage your photos, watch or create movies, listen to music, and basically run your 21st-century life. Your 21st-century digital life.

Chapter 25

The Whole Digital Photography Thing

In This Chapter

▶ Using a digital camera

▶ Getting images from your digital camera

▶ Setting up a scanner

▶ Creating images with a scanner

▶ Working with images in Windows

▶ Converting picture file formats

▶ Understanding resolution

▶ Setting the right resolution

*B*ack up! Move left! Move right! Roger, you're not smiling! Okay, everyone say "Cheese!" Such is the ritual of taking the traditional photograph. Captured on film and developed using a chemical process, the picture would take a while to return to you from the "developer." Only then would you discover that, once more, Grandma had cut off the top of Uncle Ed's head in the picture. But never mind: It was a memory.

Today's images are captured digitally. After the shutter clicks, a quick check of the camera confirms whether the image looks okay. If not, you can delete that image and instantly snap another one. The outfit known as the "developer" has been replaced by the personal computer, which stores, organizes, and prints your photos and lets you fling them far and wide by using e-mail or a social networking website. Welcome to the 21st-century version of photography.

The Digital Camera

Snapping digital pictures is easy. A digital camera is as simple to operate as the Brownie cameras of a century ago. No, the problem with a digital camera is how to move those images from the camera into the PC. After they're in the computer, you can store the pictures, edit, print, or send them off hither and thither on the Internet. But before all that happens, the images must get inside the PC. This section explains how that's done.

Connecting a digital camera

The pictures you take with a digital camera are stored on a mass storage device in exactly the same confusing manner as information is stored on your computer. To move those images from the camera into the computer, you have to make both the camera and the computer talk with each other. You have a few ways to do that:

- Point a gun at the camera, demanding that it obey the PC.

- Connect the camera to the PC with a cable. The cable came with your digital camera.

- Remove the media card from the camera and insert it into the PC's console.

- Use an Eye-Fi media card, which can be accessed over a wireless network, in the camera.

Only two of these methods generate positive results, with the camera's storage media mounted into the PC's mass storage system. That makes it easy for you to copy the digital images from the camera's media to the PC's media.

- You don't have to use the PC to print digital images. Many printers can read memory cards from digital cameras and print the images directly. See Chapter 11 for more information on printers.

- Another non-PC option is to drop off the digital camera's memory card at the "developer." These days, the developer prints the pictures for you in "about an hour" and probably gives you an optical disc copy of the images to sweeten the deal.

- See Chapter 7 for more information on the media cards used by digital cameras. Chapter 20 covers wireless networking.

Importing images

When you connect a digital camera, or insert its media card into your PC console, Windows recognizes the intruder and sneers. That sneer appears as an AutoPlay pop-up, similar to what's shown in Figure 25-1. Use that pop-up to help import the images from the camera into the PC.

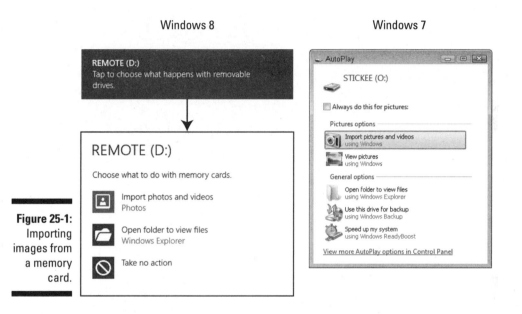

Windows 8   Windows 7

Figure 25-1:
Importing
images from
a memory
card.

If you don't see the AutoPlay dialog box, follow these steps:

1. **Open the Computer window.**

   Press the Win+E keyboard shortcut.

2. **Right-click the icon representing the digital camera's media card.**

3. **Choose the Open AutoPlay command from the pop-up menu.**

The AutoPlay dialog box lists several options for dealing with the digital camera's images. My advice is to choose the option Import Pictures and Videos (refer to Figure 25-1). In Windows 8, you need to touch the initial "choose what happens" pop-up to get to the Import Pictures and Videos option.

In Windows 8, the Photos app runs. All images from the camera's media card are selected for import. Type a name for the album in the box at the bottom of the screen, and click the Import button. The pictures are then available through the Photos app, which appears on the Start screen.

In Windows 7, after choosing the Import Pictures and Videos and option, a dialog box appears in the lower-right corner of the screen, monitoring the input progress. Type a *tag* to identify the images, such as *Volcanic eruption during grandpa's retirement party,* and then click the Import button. When the import is complete, a window appears and shows you the pictures, which are now saved on the PC's mass storage system. You can view, edit, print, or share the images.

For more ancient versions of Windows, choose the command Import Pictures Using Windows. The pictures are imported using the Windows Photo Gallery program.

✔ If you've installed a photo management program on your PC, choose that program's option from the AutoPlay dialog box rather than the Import Pictures and Videos option.

✔ The imported images are stored on the PC's main mass storage device, in the Pictures or My Pictures folder. See the later section "Storing pictures in Windows" for information.

✔ After you import the images, feel free to remove the originals from the digital camera's media. Erase or reformat the media card using the digital camera's control panel. That way, you have plenty of room to store a new batch of pictures.

The Scanner

Your prehistoric paper photographs, slides, and daguerreotypes aren't barred from entering the digital realm. You can use a gizmo called a *scanner* to take those flat pictures and transform them into digital images, stored right inside your PC.

Introducing the scanner

A scanner works like a combination photocopier and digital camera. You place something flat, like a photograph or transparency, in the scanner — just like it's a photocopier. Press a button or run a program and the image is scanned and then beamed into the computer, ready for you to save, edit, or print.

Figure 25-2 illustrates a typical, standalone computer scanner. Your printer may also function as a scanner, if it's an all-in-one model. In that case, it looks more like a printer or copy machine than the lovely illustration shown in Figure 25-2.

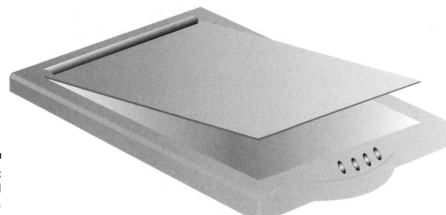

Figure 25-2:
A typical
scanner.

Most scanners are thin (like the model in the picture), use the USB interface, and have handy function buttons that let you immediately scan, copy, fax, e-mail, or read text from whatever item is placed on the scanner glass.

- ✔ The scanner must have something called a *transparency adapter* to be able to scan slides and film negatives.

- ✔ Those buttons on the scanner can be handy. For instance, I use the Copy button all the time to make quick copies. The only reservation I have about the buttons is that the tiny icons by the buttons are confusing; if need be, use a Sharpie and write down the button's function in English.

Scanning an image

Scanners come with special software that helps you scan an image and transfer it into the PC. The scanner might also come with some primitive form of image-editing software as well. My advice is to use the software that came with the scanner, which is often your best choice.

If you don't have any scanner software, you can use Windows to scan an image. Follow these steps:

1. **Turn the scanner on, if necessary.**

   Some USB scanners are on all the time, so there's no power switch.

2. **Summon the Devices and Printers window.**

   Open the Control Panel, and then click the link View Devices and Printers, found below the Hardware and Sound heading.

3. **Open the scanner's icon in the Devices and Printers window.**

Double-click the scanner's icon to open it. A New Scan dialog box appears, looking similar to the one shown in Figure 25-3.

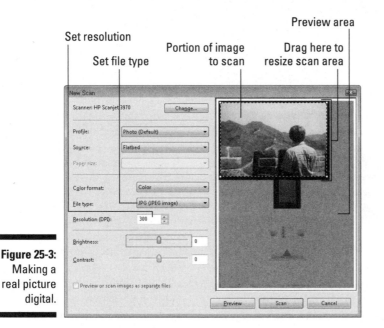

Set resolution

Set file type

Portion of image to scan

Preview area

Drag here to resize scan area

Figure 25-3:
Making a
real picture
digital.

4. **Place the material to be scanned into the scanner, just as though you were using a photocopier.**

5. **Click the Preview button.**

The scanner warms up and shows you a preview of the pictures in the scanner, as shown in Figure 25-3.

6. **Adjust the scanning rectangle so that it encloses only the part of the image you want scanned.**

Drag the corners of the rectangle by using the mouse to resize it. Only the portion of the preview inside the rectangle is scanned as an image and stored on the computer.

7. **Click the Scan button.**

The scanner reads the image, turning it into digital information to be stored in your PC.

8. **Type a tag for the images.**

The *tag* is a general description for all the images. Use short, descriptive text, such as *Summer 2010 Vacation, Meteorite Hit,* or *Chaim's Bris.*

Scanners that read documents

One of the software packages that probably came with the scanner is OCR (optical character recognition) software. This type of program scans a text document (printed material) and turns the scanned image into editable text.

The OCR scan procedure works just like scanning an image: You place the document in the scanner and then run the OCR software to start a new scan. The OCR software "reads" the document being scanned and saves the information as a text file. You can then edit the text file, print it, and so on. It's not perfect, but using OCR software is better than having to sit and type text.

---

9. **Click the Import button.**

   The image is saved to the PC's storage system and displayed in a folder window.

10. **Close the folder window.**

11. **Repeat Steps 4 through 10 to scan additional images.**

After you become comfortable with scanning, you can add some extra steps. For example, you can set the image resolution, brightness, and contrast options, and even choose another source for scanning, such as the scanner's transparency adapter.

✔ When you have lots of images to scan, such as a lifetime of vacation slides, consider sending the slides to a scanning service. No, this option isn't cheap, but consider what your time is worth and how badly you yearn to digitize your pictures.

✔ Information about graphics file types and image resolution is found elsewhere in this chapter. Bone up on that stuff to help you make the best scans possible.

Picture Files

After an image makes the journey from your digital camera to the computer, it becomes a *file* on your PC's mass storage system. Specifically, it becomes a *picture* file. Windows allows you to do quite a few things with picture files, and you should know a few picture-file concepts if you plan to get the most from your PC as the center of your digital photography universe.

✔ To work with picture files, you need an image editing program, something like Photoshop Elements or another program whose name I can't think of now. Those programs let you perform image editing — tasks such as cropping, resizing, rotating, and removing red-eye.

✔ A good photo management program to start with is Windows Photo Gallery. To download a free copy, visit `http://download.live.com/photogallery`.

✔ See Chapter 16 for more information on the fun topic of computer files.

Storing pictures in Windows

Windows organizes your pictures into the Pictures folder. Any images you import or scan into the PC using Windows eventually end up in that location.

To view the Pictures folder, summon a Windows Explorer window by pressing Win+E. From the list of categories on the left side of the window, choose Pictures.

You may find the Pictures item in the Libraries category. Click the triangle by that category to open it up and access Pictures.

The Pictures folder window looks similar to what's shown in Figure 25-4. You see icons there representing images stored on your PC, including folder icons that are used to organize the pictures by date.

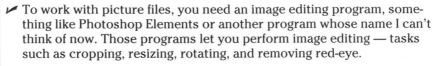

Windows 8   Windows 7

Quick link to
Pictures folder   Images (large icons)   Folders containing   Views button
                                                   more images   menu thing

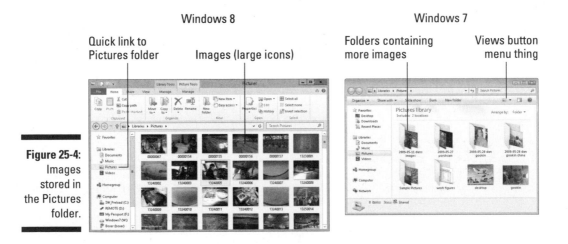

Figure 25-4: Images stored in the Pictures folder.

Picture file formats

Just as different flavors of ice cream are available to delight your tongue, different flavors of picture files are available to frustrate your brain. Not that you should care: Your computer can open, display, and even edit just about any odd picture file format. The problem comes when you deal with someone who isn't as graphically flexible. In that case, knowing a modicum of information about the PC picture file formats is unavoidable.

A file format is known by its filename extension, which is the very last part of a filename. The filename extension doesn't show up in Windows unless you recajigger Windows to make it show up. See Chapter 16.

Here are the popular picture file formats:

JPG: Pronounced "jay peg," this common image file format is used by just about every digital camera and all over the Internet. JPG is also written as JPEG.

PNG: Pronounced "ping," this picture format is also quite common, but not as popular as JPG.

TIFF: This picture file format is good for keeping detailed images, such as photos you want to edit or enlarge, or images you want to put in documents. It isn't a good format for e-mail or the Internet because, unlike JPG and PNG, TIFF picture files are very large. TIFF can also be written TIF.

BMP: The Windows Bitmap file format is used primarily in Windows — specifically, in the Paint program. BMP files are too large for e-mail or the Internet and, honestly, aren't good for storing digital photographs.

CRW: Camera Raw, or CRW, format is used in an uncompressed, unmodified image taken at high resolutions in certain high-end digital cameras. It's preferred by professional photographers and people who need the purest, rawest images possible. Unless you're doing professional work, you can avoid this format.

GIF: Pronounced "jif," this older, simple format is for storing simple color images. It was (and still is) popular on the Internet because the file size is small, but the files don't contain enough information to make them worthy of modern digital imaging.

Many, many other graphics file formats are out there, including those specific to various photo-editing programs. My bottom line bit of advice is to keep and save all your digital images in either the JPG or PNG file format.

See the next section for what you can do with pictures in the Pictures folder or any other folder window containing pictures both clean and dirty.

- ✔ The Pictures folder is also referred to as My Pictures in some versions of Windows.
- ✔ Also see Chapter 16 for more information on how folders are used to organize your stuff in Windows.

Viewing pictures in Windows

Images are viewed automatically in Windows simply by setting the proper icon size. The icon size is set using the folder's window.

In Windows 8, click the View tab. Use options in the Layout group to choose how icons are displayed. The Large Icons and Extra Large Icons settings are ideal for previewing pictures.

In Windows 7 and Windows Vista, use the View menu to choose Large Icons or Extra Large Icons. Refer to Figure 25-4 to see where to find the View menu for Windows 7. In that figure, icons are shown using Large Icons view.

You can also preview images simply by opening their icons. Unless you've installed specific image-editing software, Windows displays the image in a preview app or program.

Changing picture file formats

Occasionally, you need to convert an image from one picture file type to another. For example, you may have been silly and saved your digital camera images as TIFF files. Although that file format has its purposes, and TIFF images are by no means shoddy, they're just *too freakin' huge* to send as e-mail attachments. Instead, you're better off converting the TIFF image to PNG. Here's how I do it:

1. **Open the folder window containing the icon of the image file that you want to convert.**

   See Chapter 16 for information on folders.

2. **Right-click that icon.**

3. **Choose Open With⇨Paint from the shortcut menu.**

   The picture opens in the Paint program. If it won't open, you'll need to use another image-editing program to accomplish the same thing as Steps 4 through 7.

4. **Click the File tab.**

   The File tab is on the far left edge of the tabs, where the File menu would be in older versions of the Paint program.

5. **Choose Save As, and then choose the new file format from the Save As submenu.**

   For example, choose Save As⇨PNG Picture to save the image in the PNG file format.

Choosing the Other Formats option merely skips ahead, displaying the Save As dialog box. You can choose a format from the Save As Type drop-down list.

6. **If necessary, work the Save As dialog box to locate a folder in which to save the image, and optionally give the image a new filename.**

7. **Click the Save button to save the image in the new format.**

8. **Close the Paint program's window.**

If you have a more sophisticated graphics program, such as Photoshop Elements, you can use it, rather than Paint, to make the conversion. Or you can use any popular image conversion program.

In older versions of Windows Paint, choose the File➪Save As command to summon the Save As dialog box. Then use the Save as Type drop-down list to choose the picture file type.

Image Resolution

When you deal with digital images, the topic of resolution rears its hideous head. It isn't an area you need to know about, but by understanding it, you can better deal with issues such as big images on the screen or images that look dreadful when they're enlarged.

Resolution deals with dots — specifically, the number of *dots per inch,* or *dpi.* Each dot represents the smallest part of an image, a teeny splotch of color. Resolution comes into play in two areas: when an image is created and when an image is reproduced.

Setting resolution

An image's resolution is set when that image is created. You set resolution when you set up your digital camera, when you scan an image, or when you create an image from scratch using a painting program.

Resolution determines how much detail, or visual information, the image contains. So, an image set at 400 dpi has four times the detail of an image created at 100 dpi. More dots per inch means greater resolution, more information, more detail.

Although it might seem that setting the highest possible resolution is always best, that's not always the case. Keep reading in the next section.

Choosing the best resolution

To set the proper resolution, it helps to know where the image will end up. Images can end up on the computer monitor or on a printer or simply stored for future use.

For example, a PC monitor has a resolution of 96 dpi. If you scan a 4 x 6 photograph at 100 dpi and then display that image on the PC's monitor, it appears at nearly exactly its original size and detail. That's because the input and output resolutions are nearly identical.

If you were to scan the same photograph (4 x 6) at 200 dpi, it would contain twice the information and detail as the same image scanned at 100 dpi. When displayed on a computer monitor, the image would appear twice as large. That's because the image's 200 dpi is more than twice the 96 dpi of the monitor.

A printer's resolution can often be 300 dpi or 600 dpi. An image created at 100 dpi prints at one-third its original size when the printer uses 300 dpi output resolution. To properly render an image at its "real" size on a printer, create the image at the printer's output resolution, 300 dpi or 600 dpi — or even higher.

Bottom line: Low resolutions are fine for the Internet. For printing your digital photographs, choose a higher resolution. For enlarging photographs, choose the highest resolution possible.

✔ To produce the best results, you must set an image's *original* resolution based on its eventual output.

✔ Although you can resize an image to make its resolution higher, the result isn't as good as setting it when the image is created; the image becomes jagged and boxy looking. Bottom line: You cannot create more detail where none exists.

✔ The 100 dpi resolution is also known as *web resolution* in many graphics applications and as a setting on various digital cameras.

Chapter 26

Electronic Entertainment

In This Chapter

▶ Connecting a video camera

▶ Turning the PC into a DVR

▶ Viewing TV on the Internet

▶ Getting the Internet on your TV

▶ Enjoying music on the computer

▶ Borrowing music from a CD

▶ Sending music to a portable gizmo

O PC, entertain me! You don't really need to bark that order, because the PC — despite its disdain for all humans — is fully capable of providing you with electronic entertainment. It can sing. It can dance. It can put you in a trance. Well, maybe not a trance, but you can watch video, TV, movies, and listen to music by coercing the computer in the many subtle ways outlined in this chapter.

PC Movies

Are you old enough to remember watching home movies? The family would gather in a large room. The projector went clackity-clack as a silent, fuzzy, three-minute color film danced upon a sheet hung on the wall. Then you'd watch it run backwards and everyone would laugh. Many Hollywood producers owe their professional careers to that simple concept.

Today, home movies are shot using digital video cameras. Sound is recorded. The images are clear. And the movies last as long as you can tolerate sitting in the dark watching your family's vacation antics, forward or backwards.

Getting video into your PC

Video slithers into your PC from a digital video camera. It can come in live, such as from a *webcam,* or you can import images directly from a digital video camera's storage media.

The webcam: The simplest digital camera you can get for your PC is the desktop video camera, also referred to as a *webcam.* Most of these cameras are fist-sized, although some are smaller. They commonly cling to the top of the monitor, with a USB cable making the connection with the PC. Some webcams are embedded inside the monitor.

Video camera: For more traditional movie making, you'll probably use some type of digital video camera. That device stores video on internal or removable storage, usually in the form of a media card. To transfer the video from the camera into the PC, you either connect the camera directly or plug its media card into a slot on the computer console.

Generally speaking, the process of importing video works like this:

1. **Attach the camera to the PC or insert the camera's media card into a media slot on the computer console.**

   At this point in Windows 8, you're pretty much done. You can open the Computer window (press Win+E) to access the camera's media. You can then manually copy the video from the camera's storage to your PC's mass storage. Refer to Chapter 17 for file copying info.

   In older versions of Windows, you see an AutoPlay dialog box. If not, open the Computer window (press Win+E), right-click the camera's storage or media card, and choose the Open AutoPlay command.

2. **Type a tag for the video (optional).**

   The tag is a short, descriptive bit of text that helps you search for the videos later. Good tags are *Mary's birthday, Zoo trip,* and *I think this might be a UFO.*

3. **Click the Import button.**

After the videos are imported, you see them displayed in a folder window. You can then mess with them as you please: Create a movie, send them as e-mail attachments, or upload them to the Internet, for example.

✔ No, you cannot save or import video from a movie DVD. Those films are copyrighted, and copying them from the DVD is restricted.

✔ Webcams are normally used for video chat, though the software that comes with the camera lets you save snippets of video to the PC's mass storage system. It's not Hollywood, but it works.

✔ Video files are *huge!* They not only are the most complex type of files but also gobble up lotsa disk space.

Video file formats

Video is stored on your computer in the form of a file, just like all the other stuff stored on your computer. Like other media files (pictures and sound), the computer universe hosts a whole slate of video file formats, all depending on which camera recorded the video, which program edited it, which type of compression is being used, and other tedious details. Generally speaking, the following types of video files are popular in the computer world:

MOV: The MOV file, used by Apple's QuickTime player, can store not only videos but also audio information. MOV is quite popular on the Internet, although you need to obtain a free copy of QuickTime to view or hear MOV files on your PC: www.apple.com/quicktime.

MPEG: The Motion Pictures Experts Group is a general compression format for both video and audio.

WMV: The Windows Media Video format is the most popular video format used in Windows and pretty common on the Internet as well.

Other formats exist, but these are the most common. Also see Chapter 16 for information on the filename extension, which is how you identify file types in Windows.

Storing video in Windows

A special place exists in your PC's storage system for video. It's the My Videos or Videos folder. That's the location where any videos you add to the computer are saved. Here's how to display the contents of that folder:

1. **Press Win+E to summon the Computer folder window.**

2. **In the list of folders on the left side of the window, choose either My Videos or Videos.**

   The My Videos folder is found below the Libraries entry in Windows 8 and Windows 7. In Windows Vista, choose your account's folder and you'll find the Videos folder.

The folder lists video files available on your computer's storage system. The files are shown as icons, and even more video files may be available in folders within the main My Video or Video folder.

Windows may come with sample videos. If not, don't fret if the folder is empty; you can easily create your own videos.

Viewing a video

Have you been reading this book and wondering why I'm so harsh with Windows 8? Well, here's an answer: Windows 8 is the first release of that operating system that lacks a method for viewing videos. Short answer: You cannot view a video in Windows 8 unless you have special video-viewing software on your PC. Sorry.

Older versions of Windows use the Windows Media Player program to let you view videos. To see the video play on your PC, double-click the video's icon. The Windows Media Player program starts and shows you the video.

Double-click a video in Windows 8 and what happens? The computer laughs at you.

You can also view a video by inserting a movie DVD into your PC's optical drive. The DVD also plays in the Windows Media Player, appearing on the screen just as though you were watching it on TV. That's not gonna happen in Windows 8, though.

- ✔ Other video viewing programs are available, including Apple's popular QuickTime. I find it droll that Windows 8 users must obtain Apple software to watch videos on their PCs. Go to `http://quicktime.apple.com`.

- ✔ You can obtain a copy of Windows Media Player for Windows 8 PC, but only if you pay Microsoft for a copy.

Editing video

Armed with a video camera, a PC, and the right software, you can soon become a budding Steven Spielberg or perhaps your own Jack Horner. The software takes your video files — or just snatches the movies right from the video camera — and lets you weave them into a major motion picture using the power of the computer.

Well, maybe not *major* motion picture, but perhaps enough to impress your friends.

The Windows Movie Maker program is a good place to start your film career. It comes free with Windows Vista, or you can download it free from the Internet for other versions of Windows at `http://downloads.live.com/moviemaker`.

TECHNICAL STUFF

About that codec thing

When you deal with media on a computer, such as audio or video stored in a file, you often encounter the word *codec*. It's a combination of two words — *compressor* and *decompressor*. A codec works with compressed information stored in a media file so that you can be entertained or enlightened.

A variety of codecs are used to encode and decode media information. The problem with the variety is that your PC doesn't come with all the codecs needed for every type of media file. So, when you go to view a certain media file, you may see a message saying that a codec is unavailable or prompting you to visit a certain web page to download a codec. And that's where you can get into trouble.

My best advice is to be cautious about installing codecs. Often, the bad guys disguise a malevolent program as a codec required to view a media file — typically, pornography. Installing that false codec is detrimental to your PC.

I'm not saying that all codecs are evil. Many are good and are required to view certain media files. But ensure that you obtain codecs only from reliable sources, such as brand-name websites or from Microsoft directly.

Using Windows Movie Maker is a topic for an entire book. Still, it's not as complex as other video production software, so you should get used to using it quickly.

- Refer to Chapter 15 for information on installing programs you download from the Internet, such as Windows Movie Maker.

- When your films are ready for the world, refer to Chapter 27 for information on how to share your videos on the Internet.

Your PC Is a TV

Thanks to high-speed Internet, watching TV on your computer is no longer considered unholy. It used to be that to accomplish such a thing you needed a hardware TV tuner jammed inside your computer. That's still possible, though it's more common these days to use the Internet to keep track of your favorite programs.

Getting a TV tuner

If it's been on your bucket list to use your PC as a DVR, or Digital Video Recorder, you can gleefully cross off that item. Computers have been able to host television for quite some time. The procedure involves buying TV tuner hardware and then using DVR software to watch and even record your favorite TV shows.

Two types of TV tuners are available, internal and external. The internal cards are more sophisticated, but require that you endure the prospect of opening the computer's case to install them. A saner alternative is the USB TV tuner, which hangs out the back of your PC like a limp noodle. In both cases, you connect the tuner to a TV cable, just as you would connect the TV cable to a TV set.

For DVR software, you can use the Windows Media Player Center program to watch and record TV. That software comes with *most* versions of Windows, but not all. It especially doesn't come with Windows 8. Regardless, DVR software does come with the TV tuner hardware, which makes Windows Media Player no longer a requirement.

- ✔ Using the TV tuner with your PC doesn't add to the cost of your cable or satellite subscription any more than adding a second TV in the house would.

- ✔ Windows Media Player is not the same as Windows Media Center. Windows Media *Player* is an audio and music program. Windows Media *Center* does what Windows Media Player does but also works with TV, FM radio, pictures, and digital video.

- ✔ The DVR software that comes with the TV tuner may also allow you to burn DVDs of your favorite shows. The DVD storage option is better than keeping video long-term on your computer. That's because:

- ✔ Recording television consumes a *ton* of storage space. The more you record, the more you should review the video library (using the DVR software) and purge older programs. Otherwise, your PC runs out of mass storage space faster than a politician runs out of excuses.

Watching Internet TV

I predict that traditional television will be a thing of the past — probably by the time this book's next edition rolls out. That's because more and more people are relying on the Internet — not traditional television and cable networks — to deliver their video entertainment.

Here are three sources I offer as consideration for your PC TV entertainment:

- ✔ YouTube
- ✔ Netflix
- ✔ Hulu

More options exist, but these are the big three and are excellent places to get started.

YouTube is perhaps the largest video repository on the planet. The idea is to "broadcast yourself," so you'll find lots of homemade and amateur content on YouTube. Some of it is very good and quite entertaining. But true to Sturgeon's Law, 90 percent of it is crap. Visit YouTube at www.youtube.com.

Netflix is the premiere online video content delivery system. It's stocked full of TV shows, movies, documentaries, foreign films, and other professionally produced content. You need a subscription, which is presently under $10 a month, and then you can watch that content as much or as little as you like. Sign up for Netflix at http://signup.netflix.com.

Hulu is a fine example of a useful website where the name is completely unrelated to the content. In this case, the content consists of TV shows and some older movies, all of which are free to watch. Well, yes, they do have commercials, but so does regular TV and the point of this section is to watch TV on your PC. You can visit Hulu at www.hulu.com.

- ✔ See Chapter 27 for information on publishing your own videos on YouTube.

- ✔ Netflix is also available on many Internet-ready televisions. See the next section.

- ✔ Hulu offers a premium service called Hulu Plus. It has fewer commercials and more recent releases of popular TV shows. The cost for the service is under $10 a month.

- ✔ Other services similar to Netflix and Hulu exist. I'm certain of it. And until they start sending me large quantities of cash in plain, brown envelopes, I won't be writing about any of them in this book.

Your TV Is a PC

This section has nothing to do with computers. That is, unless you consider the plethora of modern digital devices to be computers. Common items such as your car, game consoles, portable music players, and the Space Shuttle all feature full-blown computers in their gizzards. One of the newest kids on the block is the high-definition television, or HDTV — specifically, an *Internet-ready* HDTV.

The Internet-ready HDTV is essentially a PC unimpaired by the burden of Microsoft Windows. In addition to receiving high-definition TV signals, an Internet-ready HDTV often comes with Internet access and a complete software suite. That list often includes Netflix, Hulu Plus, YouTube, a web browser, Skype (for online chat), Facebook, Twitter, and other popular Internet programs and digital content providers.

Like other network gizmos, Internet-ready HDTV connects to the computer network, either by wire or wirelessly. The purpose of the connection is to access the Internet and give you all that nifty downloaded content. As a bonus, the Internet-ready HDTV may also act as a media station, letting you view pictures and videos, as well as listen to music, stored on other network computers and devices.

Will the PC be jealous? No. Computers are still far more flexible than devices designed for a specific purpose, such as an HDTV. In fact, there's little you can do with an HDTV that you can't already do on your PC, as described elsewhere in this chapter.

✔ Unless you have a wired network connection everywhere there's an Internet-ready TV, you'll need to use wireless networking to connect them. See Chapter 20.

✔ If your HDTV doesn't offer an Internet connection or a software suite, you can purchase an Internet TV set top box that provides the same features. Apple manufactures Apple TV for that purpose. Google also provides a set-top Internet box called the Nexus Q.

✔ Refer to Chapter 27 for information on sharing media between the HDTV and your PC.

✔ The biggest problem with Internet-ready HDTV is in the human interface. A TV remote — even one with upwards of 60 buttons — is no substitute for a mouse or computer keyboard.

Your PC Is Your Stereo

If you're over a certain age, you may know what a stereo system is. You may actually have one! I do. My kids don't. They use portable music players or their cell phones as music repositories. They stare at my ancient turntable with nostalgic fascination. In the digital century, your source of musical entertainment is now your computer.

Running Windows Media Player

The musical capital of Europe is Vienna. The musical capital of a Windows computer is a program called Windows Media Player. In older versions of Windows, you start the Media Player by clicking the Start button, choosing All Programs, and then clicking Windows Media Player.

In Windows 8 (and all other versions of Windows), you can press Win+R and type **wmplayer** in the Open box. Click OK.

Perhaps the most enlightened way to start the Windows Media Player is to insert a musical CD into the PC's optical drive. The Media Player program starts instantly, playing the music on the CD.

Of course, just listening to music isn't the end goal of the Media Player. What you should yearn for is copying, or ripping, music from your CDs and storing those tunes on your PC. That way, the music is available whenever you use your computer. You can use Windows Media Player also to copy that music to a portable music-playing thingie or to your smartphone. The next two sections cover the details

Ripping music from a CD

The most common way to get music into Windows Media Player is to *rip* that music from a CD you own. The process is easy and surprisingly quick. Follow these steps:

1. **Insert a musical CD into the PC's optical drive.**

   Windows Media Player automatically begins playing the CD. If not, open the Computer window (Press Win+E), right-click the optical drive icon, and choose the Play command from the pop-up menu.

   If you don't want to listen to the CD now, simply click the big Play button, which pauses the CD. The Play button is found at the bottom center of the window.

2. **If necessary, click the Switch to Library button to display the Windows Media Player library view.**

   The library view is shown in Figure 26-1.

Rip CD button found here | Save music to a portable player

Music library | Create a music CD

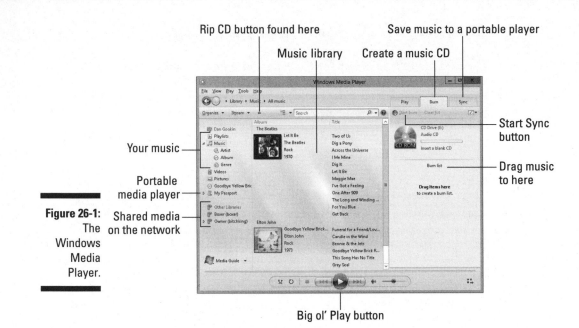

Your music

Portable media player

Start Sync button

Drag music to here

Figure 26-1:
The
Windows
Media
Player.

Shared media on the network

Big ol' Play button

3. **Click the Rip CD button on the toolbar.**

If you don't see the button, click the "show more" arrows to the right of the Stream button, and then choose the Rip CD command from the menu that's displayed.

Windows Media Player begins copying every track from the CD, storing it on the computer. You see the progress updated in the window.

4. **Eject the disc.**

You can repeat these steps with another disc to continue loading your musical library into the PC.

After the songs from the CD are ripped, they're available for your listening enjoyment at any time in the Windows Media Player library.

Copying music to a portable gizmo

Do you plan on hoisting your PC atop your shoulder and listening to music as if it were a 1970s boom box? I thought not. The best way to take your music with you is to copy it to a portable music-playing thing, also known as an MP3 player.

Copying your music to a portable music player works along these lines:

1. **Attach the portable MP3 player, cell phone, or other music gizmo to your PC.**

   Normally, you use a USB cable. I've not yet attempted the connection with string and lint.

   On cell phones, you may need to configure the USB connection. Set the device so that it's recognized as a portable media player.

2. **Open Windows Media Player, if necessary.**

   Directions for opening the Windows Media Player are found earlier in this chapter.

   The portable media player appears on the left side of the Windows Media Player window (refer to Figure 27-1).

3. **Click the MP3 player's icon on the left side of the Windows Media Player window.**

4. **Click the Sync tab.**

   The device should appear in the Sync tab panel on the right side of the window.

5. **From the left side of the Media Player window, choose the Music library item.**

6. **Drag music from the Music Library to the Sync tab.**

7. **Click the Start Sync button.**

   The music is copied to the portable music player.

8. **After the syncing is complete, disconnect the device.**

   Refer to directions that came with the device for proper disconnection instructions. With some devices, such as smartphones, you must disconnect the software before you unplug the USB cable.

Not every portable music player is capable of playing the music data files stored in Windows. Most players are, but a few may not recognize the music. Even after a successful file transfer you may discover that the tunes are unavailable. Bummer.

Listening to Internet radio

Another way to get music into your digital life is to take advantage of the many Internet radio stations out there. Although you can't get specific software to listen to the music, you can pop open your favorite web browser and tune into web pages abundant with songs and sounds from around the world.

Here is a sampling of websites you can browse for your listening enjoyment:

- ✔ Pandora Internet Radio: `www.pandora.com`
- ✔ Jango: `www.jango.com`
- ✔ Slacker Personal Radio: `www.slacker.com`
- ✔ iHeart Radio: `www.iheart.com`

Chapter 27

Sharing Your Life Online

● ●

In This Chapter

▶ Using Facebook

▶ Tweeting your thoughts

▶ Locating an image-hosting website

▶ Putting your pictures on the Internet

▶ Signing up for YouTube

▶ Publishing videos

▶ Sharing media on the network

● ●

*O*nce upon a computer time, the rage was to create your own web page. Doing so made you part of the high-tech in-crowd. You could use that web page to tell the Internet what was going on with your life and perhaps even share some pictures. It was a technical thing, but still many people decided that they couldn't live their lives without their personal web pages.

The days of needing your own web page are long gone. Sure, you can still have one, but most likely all the things you planned to do with that web page are now possible by sharing your digital life online.

The Scourge of Social Networking

Whither privacy? Why, privacy has taken leave of its senses and was last seen showering nude in the public square. In a culture where the phrase "none of your beeswax" is known by every 6-year-old, it seems odd that rational humans are eager to share their daily toil and each bodily episode with all the known universe. Odd, but true. And the electronic vehicle that takes humanity to that destination is a streetcar named Social Networking.

Sharing your life on Facebook

Facebook is the only social networking site worth your consideration. It's the only place online where you can connect with friends, share your thoughts, send messages, post photographs and videos, play games, take quizzes, waste time, and generally keep up-to-date. That's it. One-stop everything.

Of course, that's not true: social networking websites number in the kajillions, but Facebook is currently sitting atop the jungle gym, ruling the online playground.

Sign up

You start your extroverted cum voyeuristic Facebook journey by signing up at the main Facebook page, www.facebook.com. Enter the required information, which includes an e-mail address. You have to confirm your e-mail address, which completes the sign-up process.

Find some friends

The next step in your Facebook epoch is to look for people you know. Based on your e-mail address, some friends may already be waiting to be added. Having more friends on Facebook than all your friends have on Facebook is the goal of using Facebook, despite mathematicians' protestations that such a thing isn't possible.

Share your thoughts

You can lurk in Facebook, prowling into the private lives of your friends and associates, but to join the fray you share your thoughts. Look for the text box that says, "What's on your mind?" Type something pithy, personal, private, or preposterous into that box. Click the Post button and all your Facebook friends can see what's up.

You can also send your Facebook pals personal messages or write on their *walls*. Clicking a friend's name or picture allows you to do that.

Upload a picture or video

Besides text, which requires a modicum of brain horsepower to comprehend, other things you can share on Facebook are pictures and videos. The method for sharing pictures may change in the future, but for now you should follow these general steps:

1. **Click the mouse in the What's On Your Mind text box.**

   The text box expands, showing more options.

2. **Click the Add Photo/Video link.**

   The name of that link may be different, or the link could appear as an icon, or you might see some other change that can happen with web pages.

3. **Choose the Attach Photo/Video option.**

   On my screen, I also see a Use Webcam option, where I could use the PC monitor's built-in webcam to literally shoot myself and publish that video.

4. **Click the Choose File button.**

5. **Use the Browse dialog box to hunt down an image to post on Facebook.**

   Refer to Chapter 16 for information on using the Open dialog box, which operates in the same manner as the Browse dialog box.

6. **Choose the image or video, and then click the Open button.**

7. **(Optional) Write some text describing the photo or video.**

8. **Click the Post button.**

The image is made available instantly for your Facebook buddies to gawk at and add comments. Videos may take some time to process, but eventually they're made available for equivalent gawking and commenting.

✔ All of your friends will be able to see the picture or video. If you don't want them to, and you don't want the image or video hanging around the Internet universe until the end of time, don't post it!

✔ It's also possible to *tag* the image, identifying other Facebook friends who may appear: When viewing the image (click the image to view it in a larger format), choose Tag Photo. Then point the mouse at a human or object in the image and click. Type a friend's name or choose the person from the list that appears.

✔ You may have to install an ActiveX control in Internet Explorer to upload images. That's okay: Follow the directions on the screen.

Tweeting your thoughts

Another quite popular social networking website is Twitter. On Twitter, you share your thoughts with others and follow their thoughts as well, where a "thought" is composed of 140 or fewer characters of text. Those little bursts of text are *Tweets*.

Sign up for Twitter by visiting www.twitter.com. Configure your profile, and then I recommend using the e-mail scanning tool that Twitter provides to help you quickly locate some Twitter friends.

Twitter can be used to watch or follow others, to gather useful information on news or events, or just keep tabs on your buddies. In addition to being a harmless distraction, Twitter is relied on by many people for news because various news organizations Tweet as well. (I'm not much of a Twitter fan; otherwise I'd write more flowery and flattering prose about it.)

Share Your Photos Online

Even with Facebook and other social networking sites, dozens of better and more specific options exist for sharing your digital images on the Internet. Here's a small sampling:

- ✔ **Flickr:** www.flickr.com
- ✔ **Image Shack:** http://imageshack.us
- ✔ **Photobucket:** http://photobucket.com
- ✔ **Picasaweb:** http://picasaweb.google.com/home

Each of these services lets you set up an account, create an online gallery, and post images stored on your computer to that online gallery. There's no charge, though some of the services offer specials and discounts on related products. All the sites have advertising.

You might also be able to use an online hosting service with a traditional photo developer. For example, WalMart has an online photo service at photos.walmart.com.

Signing up for the site

You start with a photo-sharing website by setting up your account. I recommend doing this first, even though some of the services may let you upload an image without first creating an account. As an example, to create an account on Photobucket, follow these steps:

1. **Open your computer's web browser.**
2. **Type the online photo-sharing service's URL.**

   For Photobucket, it's www.photobucket.com.

3. **Click the link that says Join Now.**

   It might instead say Sign Up or Create Your Account. If you choose to use Flickr or Picasaweb, you can sign in using your Yahoo! or Google account, respectively.

4. **Fill in the blanks: Type a username and then choose a password.**

   Some sites may ask for more information, such as your e-mail address, gender, and birth year. If you feel uncomfortable answering those questions, write your congressperson. Better still, just use another photo-sharing service.

5. **Continue working through the steps as necessary, clicking the Next button as you go.**

   Be mindful that you don't accidentally sign up for a service you don't need: Many free hosting services offer special partner deals and options that aren't necessary to using the service. You can skip those offers if you don't want them.

6. **If prompted to create an initial album, do so.**

7. **After signing up, sign out or log out.**

   After you sign up, I recommend that you immediately log out and sign up again. That way, the web browser can more easily recall the photo-sharing website in the future, and maybe even remember your username and password.

8. **Immediately after logging out, go back to the main page of the image-hosting service.**

9. **Bookmark the image-hosting service's page: Press Ctrl+D in your web browser.**

   Click the Add button to add the hosting service to your browser's list of bookmarks.

10. **Log in to the hosting service.**

11. **If your web browser prompts you to remember your username and password for the site, do so. Then click Yes or OK.**

Now you're ready to add some images to the website. Keep reading in the next section.

Uploading images

The sending of an image from your computer to the Internet is known as an *upload.* Yes, it's the opposite of *download,* which is when your PC receives a file from the Internet. The steps to upload your digital pictures work similarly for most online image-hosting services:

1. **Log in to your account on the image-hosting service.**

2. **If necessary, click an Upload link.**

   Not every photo-hosting service features an Upload link. Some services let you upload directly from your account's home page.

3. **If necessary, choose or create an album in which the images will be saved.**

   Some online image-hosting services, such as Picasaweb, may want you to install an upload control. Do so when prompted.

4. **Click the Browse button to locate a digital photo on your computer.**

   Use the Choose File dialog box to locate the digital photo you want. At this point, you're merely choosing a file; the sending part happens later.

5. **Go to the folder that contains the digital image.**

   Remember that the My Pictures or Pictures folder is where those images are usually kept, though you can also use the dialog box to visit a removable storage device, such as your digital camera's media card.

   As with anything dealing with images, it helps if you know where the image is saved on your PC's storage system *and* the image's filename.

6. **Choose from the list the file you want to upload.**

7. **Click the Open button to select an image.**

8. **Repeat Steps 4 through 7 as necessary to choose additional images.**

   Most online image-hosting services allow you to batch upload images by selecting several at a time to upload.

9. **Choose an album, specify whether the images are public or private, and specify the image's size, if such choices are available.**

10. **Click the Upload or Start Upload button to send to the Internet the images you chose.**

    The procedure may take a few minutes as the images are sent and then processed by the hosting service.

11. **If prompted, add tags to your image or complete whichever additional steps might be presented.**

    Tags are merely text descriptions attached to the image. The tags help you search for images, identify who or what's in the images, and remember information about the images.

12. **You may need to click a Save button to save the options you set.**

13. **Enjoy your image on the Internet.**

In some cases, you can use companion software to the online photo-hosting service to help manage your uploads. For example, Google's Picasa application integrates seamlessly with the Picasaweb hosting service. To upload images using that program, choose Tools⇨Upload⇨Upload to Web Albums, and you're on your way.

Sharing your images

There's no point in having images floating around the Internet if you can't boast about them and share each one with your friends, family, coworkers, and anyone else on the planet who can use the web. The online image-hosting services are set up to meet those demands.

Most image-hosting services mentioned in this chapter sport buttons that let you quickly and easily share your images with popular social networking sites such as Facebook and MySpace, blog sites such as Blogger and WordPress, and any of a number of popular places that people frequent on the Internet. You also see buttons for adding links to e-mail messages.

The basic procedure involves viewing the image and then finding the web page address, or *link,* to that image. You then select the link and press Ctrl+C to copy it. After that, open your PC's e-mail program and start a new message. Press Ctrl+V to paste the link. The image doesn't appear in your message, but the recipients can click the link to see your image in their web browser.

Here are some specific tips for using the image-hosting sites mentioned in this chapter:

✔ If you're using Image Shack, after shooting an image, click the link Get Code for Email. Select the link text, copy it by pressing Ctrl+C, and then paste it into a new message in your e-mail program.

✔ For Photobucket, click the Share link, found directly above the image you want to share. Click the tab labeled Get Link Code, and then select the check box below the heading Direct Link for Layout Pages. Copy the link's text, and then paste it into an e-mail message.

✔ When you use the Flickr image-hosting site, double-click the image you want to share. Then from the right side of the window, click Share This. The second item down, Grab the Link, contains the text you should select, copy, and then paste into an e-mail message.

✔ In Picasaweb, click to select the image, and in the right side of the window, choose Link to This Photo. Click the mouse in the text box below the word *Link,* and then press Ctrl+C to copy the link. Paste the link into an e-mail message.

✔ These photo-hosting sites may change their web page layouts and methods from time to time. The information here is specific as this book goes to press, but may change subtly in the future.

Your Video Life

Unlike photos, videos are just too hulking huge to send in e-mail messages. Even when the videos aren't that large, it's just better to send a link to your video on the Internet than to send enormous files to your friends. Unlike sending enormous quantities of money, sending enormous files through e-mail is unwelcome because the process is slow and confusing.

The video-hosting service of choice is YouTube, www.youtube.com. Just about anyone and everyone uploads videos to YouTube, some of them professional but many of them amateur. You too can join their ranks, as long as you heed the advice found in this section.

Creating a YouTube account

You can't post a video to YouTube until you obtain a YouTube account. That account is the same as your Google or Gmail account. So if you already have a Google account, you're set up to use YouTube. Otherwise, visit YouTube and click the Sign Up link found near the top of the page.

After your Google (YouTube) account is set up, you can start putting videos on the Internet.

Uploading a video to YouTube

After signing in to your YouTube account, locate the large Upload button. Clicking that link takes you to a page that describes the upload process and offers some tips and suggestions.

Eventually, you click the Upload Video button, which lets you browse your PC's mass storage system for the video you prepared.

You need to supply a title, a description, tags, and other information about the video. Be mindful of what you type because the information there is used by others to search for videos on YouTube. Click the Save Changes button when you're done.

YouTube takes a few moments (or longer) to process your video. You might have to come back and visit your account's area on YouTube later so that you can share the link.

Sharing your videos

It's easy to share your videos with others using YouTube. Basically, you simply send your pals a web page link to your video. Because the link consists only of text, the e-mail message doesn't take an eternity to send and receive, nor is there any worry about malware-infected file attachments. The process works like this:

1. **Visit your account on YouTube, at** www.youtube.com/my_videos.

   You may have to log in first, but eventually you see a list of all your uploaded videos displayed on the web page.

2. **Right-click the title (link) of the video you want to share.**

3. **Choose the Copy Shortcut command from the pop-up menu.**

4. **Start a new e-mail message in your PC's e-mail program.**

5. **Press Ctrl+V to paste the YouTube video link into your e-mail message.**

YouTube videos all have a similar-looking link or URL. For example: http://www.youtube.com/watch?v=-QIQhoahbQ8

That's it! Clicking that link is how others can view your video on the Internet.

- ✔ When you view a video on YouTube, you see sharing options listed on the web page. You usually see two options: URL and Embed. Use the URL option as the direct link to the video's web page. The Embed option is used to stick the video into a blog or another web page.

- ✔ Right below the video, you'll see buttons for sharing. Use those buttons to instantly share the video on Facebook, Twitter, and other websites.

Network Media Sharing

Read this passage with your mother's voice in your head: "Sure, you can share your pictures, music, and video with utter strangers on the Internet. How about sharing in your own house?" Give yourself a bonus point if you added a little whine to her voice. Double points for a Long Island accent.

It's true: PCs on the local network can share their media with other devices connected to the network. Those devices include other computers, game consoles, smartphones, tablets, and even Internet-ready HDTVs or set-top boxes.

Setting up for media sharing

No computer willingly coughs up its media for sharing. You must command Windows to provide your PC's media as a resource, open and shared on the network. Heed these directions:

1. **Open the Control Panel.**

2. **Below the Network and Internet heading, click the link View Network Status and Tasks.**

   The Network and Sharing Center window appears.

3. **From the left side of the Networking and Sharing Center window, click the Change Advanced Sharing Settings link.**

   In Windows Vista, ensure that the Media Sharing item is on. If not, click the down-pointing arrow and turn that option on.

4. **Scroll down the list to locate the Media Streaming item.**

   You may need to click one of the down-arrow buttons to expand part of the sharing settings to find the Media Streaming item.

5. **Click the Choose Media Streaming Options link.**

   The Media Streaming Options window appears.

6. **Click the Turn On Media Streaming button.**

   If you don't see that button, media sharing is already configured. You're done. Otherwise:

   The screen that appears lists network computers and various sharing options. You can fiddle around here, but everything is pretty much set to share pictures, videos, and music from your PC to those network devices.

7. **Click the OK button, and close the various other windows you've opened.**

   You're all done.

Your PC is now sharing its media to other network devices. It's the digital equivalent of a Craigslist ad saying, "Come into my house and take my pictures, albums, and videos," but far less chaotic.

Rifling through a device's shared media

To access shared media on the local network, open the Network window. You can get to that window by choosing the Network item from the categories on the left side of any folder window. (Press Win+E to summon a folder window.)

When viewing the Network window, you'll see a list of media devices, similar to what's shown in Figure 27-1. Those icons could represent computers, game consoles, even HDTVs.

When you double-click a media device icon, the Windows Media Player window opens. (See the figure in Chapter 26.) Shared media devices appear at the bottom of the list on the left side of the Windows Media Player window. Choose a device to view which media are being shared. You can then look, listen, or watch the media using Windows Media Player right there on your computer.

✔ Other network devices access your PC's media in different ways. Obviously the HDTV is glad that it doesn't use Windows, so it probably has its own program, or app, which can be used to view media.

✔ Smartphones and tablets can access shared media provided that they are DLNA compliant. Devices that use the DLNA (Digital Living Network Alliance) standard can share media, and in many smartphones and tablets, the app that does the sharing is often called DLNA, though I assume other, equally cryptic app names are available.

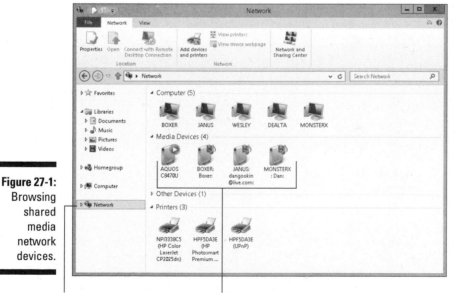

Figure 27-1: Browsing shared media network devices.

Network category   Devices with shared media

Chapter 28

Kid-Safe Computing

. . . .

In This Chapter

▶ Configuring computer accounts

▶ Limiting website access

▶ Limiting Junior's PC access

▶ Restricting games

▶ Preventing programs from running

▶ Seeing what your kids are up to

▶ Preventing online bullying

. . . .

Despite its attraction to kids, a computer can be a decidedly non-kid-friendly thing. Beyond malicious software, there are some places on the Internet that you definitely don't want your precious snowflake to discover. Games that you may enjoy playing could give a child nightmares. And, there's the issue of Too Much Computer Time. All these topics can be dealt with, first by being a responsible parent, and second by using the various kid-safe computing tools discussed in this chapter.

> ✔ The information in this chapter applies directly to Windows 8 and Windows 7. Some features are available in Windows Vista. The main difference comes from the innumerable User Account Control (UAC) warnings that pop up during the process in Windows Vista.
>
> ✔ Windows XP lacks parental controls as a feature.

An Account for Junior

To employ the parental controls in Windows, and to ensure your PC's security when Junior is online, give Junior his own account on the computer. Configure his account as a Standard User. Your account must be set up as an administrator. This section explains how to do that.

✔ The Administrator account has full control over the computer. An administrator can change computer settings, install new software, and control other accounts on the computer. These are the equivalent of PC superpowers, though wearing superhero tights is optional.

✔ The Standard User account can use the computer but cannot change computer settings, install new software, or access other accounts without an Administrator account's password.

✔ In Windows 8, you can specify a child's account when you first add the account. Use the PC Settings app to add the account.

✔ The Standard User account is also known as a *Limited* account.

✔ Those User Account Control (UAC) warnings exercise the administrator's privileges in Windows. See Chapter 24.

✔ When more than one kid is using the same computer, each should have his or her own Standard User account. Each account should have its own password.

Setting up your own account

You can't enable parental controls on the computer unless you have an Administrator-level account. For the family PC, you probably already have that type of account. Good, but follow the steps in this section anyway to confirm.

If your honey-bun has his or her own computer, you need to set up a new account for yourself on that system. Ensure that it's an Administrator-level account. Follow these steps:

1. **Log on to the computer using an existing account or the computer's only account, if it has only one.**

   If you don't have an account on your kid's computer, you need to add one: Have the kid log in, and then continue to create your own account after Step 4.

2. **Open the Control Panel.**

   Directions for getting to the Control Panel are found in Chapter 14.

3. **Choose User Accounts and Family Safety.**

4. **Choose User Accounts.**

   Information about your account appears on the right side of the window. You see your account picture, account name, and so on.

If you need to set up an account for yourself on your kid's computer, click the Manage Another Account link, and then click the Add a New User in PC Settings link (Windows 8) or the Create a New Account link (Windows 7). You'll have to run through these steps again after the account is created.

5. **Confirm that the word *Administrator* appears in the list of information about your account.**

   If it does, you're set. Keep reading in the next section. Otherwise:

6. **Click the Change Your Account Type link.**

7. **Choose Administrator.**

8. **Click the Change Account Type button.**

   You may be prompted at this point to enter the existing Administrator account password for the computer. You can get that from Junior if you're using his computer. Otherwise, your account type is Administrator, which is what you want.

After you ensure that you have an Administrator account on the computer, the next step is to check that Junior's account is the Standard or Limited type. Keep reading in the next section.

Limiting Junior's account

To apply the parental controls to Sunshine or Buster's computer account, first check to be sure that you have an Administrator account on the computer, as described in the preceding section. Then abide by these steps:

1. **Log in to the computer using your account.**

2. **Open the Control Panel.**

3. **Click the heading User Accounts and Family Safety.**

4. **Choose User Accounts.**

5. **Click the Manage Another Account link.**

   A list of all accounts on the computer appears. Sunshine's or Buster's account should be in that list.

6. **Choose your child's account from the list.**

7. **Click the Change the Account Type link.**

8. **Choose Standard User.**

9. **Click the Change Account Type button.**

10. **Close the window.**

After the account is configured, you're ready to apply the parental controls.

Parental Controls

To extend your parental love and discipline to the PC, and better regulate Junior's computer life, you must activate the parental controls in Windows. Here's how that's done:

1. **Log in to Windows using your account.**

2. **Open the Control Panel.**

3. **Below the User Accounts and Family Safety heading, choose the Set Up Family Safety for Any User link (in Windows 8) or the Set Up Parental Controls for Any User link (in Windows 7).**

   A window appears, listing all accounts on the computer.

4. **Choose the account to control; click its icon.**

5. **In the User Controls window, choose On, Enforce Current Settings.**

   The Windows 8 User Settings window is shown in Figure 28-1. In Windows 7, the window is titled User Controls and contains similar settings. It's where you apply the various parental controls mentioned in this chapter.

6. **Apply the parental controls; refer to the next few sections.**

7. **When you're done setting parental controls, click the OK button to close the window.**

Activate parental controls   Account being controlled

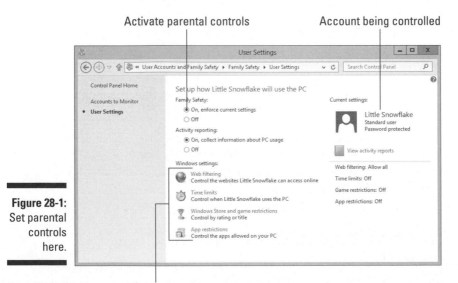

Figure 28-1: Set parental controls here.

Individual controls

Repeat the steps in this section for each kid's account on your PC.

Windows 7 lacks the Web Filtering control but otherwise features the same controls as shown in Figure 28-1 for Windows 8.

Filtering websites

Web filtering is perhaps the most complex setting you can make when limiting Junior's computer access. After applying parental controls, choose Web Filtering from the main control window (refer to Figure 28-1). The next screen has one big switch to throw: Choose the option Little Snowflake Can Only Use the Websites I Allow to activate website filtering.

Oh, and *Little Snowflake* is replaced with your kid's account name, unless your child is really named Little Snowflake.

Choose an option from the left side of the Web Filtering window, such as Web Restrictions or Allow or Block Websites. Web Restrictions is the more general option, although if you want to restrict access only to certain sites, as well as block specific sites, you need to use the Block Websites option.

I also recommend that you place a check mark by the Block File Downloads option in the Web Restrictions settings window. Children under a certain age have no business downloading anything.

Setting time limits

You can control when your kids can access the computer by placing time limits on their accounts. That way, they can log in and use the computer only during the hours you specify — and the computer logs them off when the time runs out.

To set time limits, open the User Settings or User Controls window (see Figure 28-1); refer to the earlier section, "Parental Controls." Choose the Time Limits link, and then use the gizmos on the screen that appears to restrict computer access to the times you specify.

Controlling access to games

Windows lets you combine the parental controls with the Entertainment Software Rating Board (ESRB) game rating system to control which computer games your kid can play on the PC. You can restrict access to games by the game name, its rating, or the contents of the game (violence or adult themes, for example).

To restrict access to certain games, open the User Settings or User Controls window (refer to Figure 28-1) by following Steps 1 through 4 in the earlier section "Parental Controls." In Windows 8, click the Windows Store and Game Restrictions link; in Windows 7, the link is titled Games.

Choose the option to apply game restrictions to your offspring's account. You can then choose to block the games by their ESRB ratings or block specific games by their titles.

✔ The ESRB defines and sets ratings for computer games in a way similar to how the MPAA rates movies.

✔ Visit the ESRB website www.esrb.org for more information on the ratings system.

Blocking programs

In addition to blocking computer games, you can restrict your kid's access to any program or app that runs on your computer. For example, you can prevent them from running your computer's home finance program or other programs you'd rather have them not playing with. Or, you might want to block them from using instant messaging tools that they might be abusing.

To activate the Applications Restrictions feature, follow Steps 1 through 4 in the earlier section, "Parental Controls." Choose the App Restrictions link (Windows 8) or the Allow or Block Specific Programs link (Windows 7). Use the screen that appears to choose which programs are allowed. Click the OK button when you're done.

✔ Yes, the program names are technical and mysterious! When you don't recognize a program name, don't put a check mark in its box.

✔ Beyond restricting program access, you don't need to worry about your sweetums getting into your account and looking at your stuff. First, your account has a password, right? Second, all accounts in Windows are separate from each other. When your child has a Standard User account, the little one cannot peek into your account's folders or access your own computer data, e-mail, or other private information without knowing your account's password.

Reviewing the activity log

The Family Safety feature in Windows 8 also sports an activity log. It lists the things that Petunia does while using the computer, which you can review during times of parental urgency. The log is activated automatically from the User Settings screen, shown earlier in Figure 28-1.

To view the activity log, click the View Activity Reports link, found on the User Settings screen (refer to Figure 28-1). The User Activities screen that appears describes when Petunia was last using the computer, for how long, which programs were run, whether she attempted to access blocked apps or websites, and a whole host of nosy things that parents would appreciate.

> ✔ How you deal with digital transgressions is up to you as a parent, though I believe the Family Safety feature offers plenty of settings that would allow you to get your point across.
>
> ✔ Apparently there is no way to print the activity log.

PC Parenting

Here are my parental rules for kids who use computers:

> ✔ Know your kids. Talk with them. Be their parent.
>
> ✔ Exercise your duty to drop in on them and see what they're doing on the computer.
>
> ✔ Use the parental controls provided in Windows, as covered in this chapter.

Spying on your kids

Before jumping into your James Bond suit and beginning the art of snooping around Junior's PC, talk with your children. Ask what's up or whether anything is bothering them. It may be nothing, but as a parent, you should know your own children, so use your best judgment when you suspect that something is amiss.

When mood swings and unusual behavior dictate, you can check up on your kid's account to see what they've been up to. In Windows 8, you can use the Activity Reports, as covered elsewhere in this chapter. Beyond that, you can log in under their account and review their recent web pages visited.

To review the web history, open your child's web browser and press Ctrl+H in Internet Explorer. Open the various dates and websites listed on the History tab (on the left side of the browser window). If the sites look suspicious, click their links to visit them. You'll know in a few minutes whether you have cause for concern.

✔ I don't recommend buying PC snooping software. If the situation with your child is so great that you feel this type of software is necessary, you already have a big problem on your hands. Sit down and discuss the situation with your child immediately.

✔ Your children can cover their tracks, especially when they're already computer savvy. In fact, if you notice that the web browser history seems surprisingly empty for the amount of time Buster spends on the PC, something is probably going on.

✔ Today's kids would probably be more apt to use cell phones for surreptitious activities than they would the family PC. If you allow your offspring to have their own cell phones, routinely examine the text-messaging history for questionable activity.

✔ Talk with your kids, not at them.

Dealing with a cyberbully

Count among the many downsides of glorious technology the anonymous, nasty, and persistent creep commonly called a *cyberbully*. Like his (or her) schoolyard namesake, he can make life online a living hell for you, your child, and your entire family.

Unlike the bully you might remember from childhood, a cyberbully has the sneaky advantage of stealthy anonymity on the Internet. This person is found in social networks, chat rooms, instant messaging programs, and even cell phone text messages — places your technically adept child probably clings to for social interaction.

Beyond intimidation, the cyberbully can use personal attacks, such as making private information public, creating false images using photo-editing techniques, faking messages from other friends, and generally misrepresenting your child's behavior. Such attacks have devastating emotional effects, especially on vulnerable children.

✔ The best way to avoid having personal or embarrassing information float around the Internet is not to put it on the Internet in the first place. Teaching your children about modesty and self-respect goes a long way.

✔ Many areas have laws against cyberbullying. Check with the police if you or your children become a victim.

✔ Cyberbullying may also violate the terms of the Internet service provider (ISP) contract. Contact your ISP if you feel victimized.

✔ It helps to document cyberbullying episodes: Print web pages, and note when the attacks occur.

✔ Adults can also be victims of cyberbullying, though the terms that are used are *cyberharassment* and *cyberstalking*.

Part VI
The Part of Tens

The 5th Wave   By Rich Tennant

In this part . . .

My grandmother told me that "things happen in threes." Maybe. I would counter Grandma with "Things *always* happen; it's just easier to name three things when given the chance." What's far more difficult is to move up from three to ten. Although anyone can name three state capitals, three famous bald guys, or three things not to step in, it's more difficult to repeat the task with ten items.

Rest easy: I'm not asking you to come up with lists full of ten items. Instead, I've done that job for you. I've created some handy lists of tens, helpful information for any computer user. And I've put those lists in this part of the book, the Part of Tens.

Chapter 29

Ten PC Commandments

In This Chapter

▶ Don't fear your computer

▶ Always save your work

▶ Back up your stuff

▶ Don't open or delete unknown files

▶ Don't fall prey to online predators

▶ Use antivirus and update software

▶ Be smart about upgrades

▶ Use the PC with proper posture

▶ Keep windows up-to-date

▶ Always properly quit Windows

*T*ake it from me: I've been there, I've done that. I've survived the worst of using a computer and have lived to write about it. Let me share my experiences with you by passing along a chunk of digital wisdom. I may not have descended from Mt. Sinai, and I certainly look nothing like Charlton Heston, but here are my Ten PC Commandments.

1. Thou Shalt Not Fear Thy PC

The computer isn't out to get you. It won't explode suddenly. It harbors no sinister intelligence. Honestly, it's really rather dumb.

Knowledge is the key to overcoming fear.

II. Thou Shalt Save Thy Work

Whenever you're creating something blazingly original, use the Save command at once! In fact, use the Save command even when you make something stupid that you don't even want to save. You're not going to run out of room on the PC's mass storage system by saving stuff you don't need, so why not save for the sake of it?

You never know when your computer will meander off to watch NASCAR or chat with the wireless router across the street while you're hoping to finish the last few paragraphs of that report. Save your work as often as possible. Save when you get up from your computer. Save when you answer the phone. Save! Save! Save!

III. Thou Shalt Back Up Thy Files

Nothing beats having that just-in-case copy of your stuff. The computer itself can run a backup program to make that safety copy, or you can duplicate your files yourself. Either way, that secondary backup copy can save your skin someday.

See Chapter 18 for information on backing up.

IV. That Shalt Not Open or Delete Things Unknownst

Here's the rule, written in modern English: Delete only those files or folders you created yourself.

Unlike computer hardware, where sticky labels with red letters read Do Not Open, unknown computer files have no warning labels. There should be! Windows is brimming with unusual and unknown files. Don't mess with 'em. Don't delete them. Don't move them. Don't rename them. And especially, don't open them to see what they are. Sometimes, opening an unknown icon can lead to trouble.

V. Thou Shalt Not Be a Sucker

The Bad Guys are successful in spreading their evil, malicious software on the Internet because people let down their guard. Don't be a sucker for human engineering. Basically, here's a list of don'ts to adhere to:

- ✔ Don't reply to any spam e-mail. Doing so brings you even more spam. A popular trick is for spammers to include some text that says "Reply to this message if you do not want to receive any further messages." Don't! Replying to spam signals the spammers that they have a "live one" and you then receive even more spam. Never, ever, reply to spam!

- ✔ Don't open unknown or unexpected e-mail attachments. Seriously, you're not missing anything if you don't open them. Yet that's how human engineering works: The e-mail fools you into believing that opening the attachment is important. It's not.

- ✔ Never open any program file attachment. These attachments end with the exe, com, or vbs filename extension. See Chapter 16 for more information on filename extensions and how to display them in Windows.

VI. Thou Shalt Use Antivirus Software, Yea Verily, and Keepeth It Up-to-Date

I highly recommend that you use antivirus software on your PC. Keep that software up-to-date. See Chapter 24 for more computer security advice.

VII. Thou Shalt Upgrade Wisely

New hardware and software come out all the time. The new stuff is generally better and faster, and it's important to some people to be the First on the Block to have a new hardware gizmo or software upgrade. You don't have to be that person.

- ✔ Upgrade the computer's software only if you truly need the new features it offers, you need to have that version to be compatible with your coworkers, or the new version fixes problems and bugs that you're experiencing.

- ✔ Buy hardware that's compatible with your PC. Especially when you have an older computer, confirm that the new hardware will work with your system.

VIII. Thou Shalt Compute at a Proper Posture

Using a computer can be a pain. Literally. You must observe proper posture and sitting position while you operate a PC. By doing so, you can avoid back strain and the risk of repetitive stress injury (RSI). Following are some suggestions.

Get an ergonomic keyboard: Even if your wrists are as limber as a politician's spine, you might consider an ergonomic keyboard. This type of keyboard is specially designed at an angle to relieve the stress of typing for long — or short — periods.

Use a wrist pad: Wrist pads elevate your wrists so that you type in a proper position, with your palms above the keyboard, not resting below the spacebar.

Adjust your chair: Sit at the computer with your elbows level with your wrists.

Adjust your monitor: Your head should not tilt down or up when you view the computer screen. It should be straight ahead, which doesn't help your wrists as much as it helps your neck.

IX. Thou Shalt Keepeth Windows Up-to-Date

Microsoft keeps Windows continually fresh and updated. The updates fix problems, but they also address vulnerabilities that the Bad Guys exploit. In my book (which you're reading now), that's a good thing, but it's effective only when you use the Windows Update service regularly. See Chapter 15.

There's a difference between updating Windows, which I recommend, and upgrading Windows, which I don't recommend.

X. Thou Shalt Properly Shut Down Windows

When you're done with Windows, shut it down. Choose the Shut Down command from the Start button menu. The PC automatically turns itself off.

Refer to Chapter 4 for detailed PC shutdown instructions.

Chapter 30

Ten Tips from a PC Guru

In This Chapter

▶ Remember that you're in charge

▶ Mind who "helps" you

▶ Give yourself time to learn

▶ Create separate accounts

▶ Use a UPS

▶ Consider some hardware upgrades

▶ Don't reinstall Windows

▶ Shun the hype

▶ Continue discovering the PC

▶ Don't take this computer stuff too seriously

I don't consider myself a computer expert or genius or guru, although many have called me those nasty names. I'm just a guy who understands how computers work. Or, better than that, I understand how computer people think and I can translate it into English for you. Given that, here are some tips and suggestions so that you and your PC can go on your merry way.

Remember That You're in Charge

You bought the computer. You clean up after its messes. You feed it optical discs when it asks for them. You press the Any key (which is the Enter key). You control the computer — simple as that.

Think of the computer as an infant. You must treat it the same way, with respect and caring attention. Don't feel that the computer is bossing you around any more than you feel that a baby is bossing you around during its 3 a.m. feedings. They're both helpless creatures, subject to your every whim. Be gentle, but be in charge.

Mind Who "Helps" You

Nothing beats getting computer help when you need it. Most computer nerds love to help beginners. Sometimes, they help you at no cost, though you shouldn't abuse a good relationship by becoming a pest.

When you can't find help, use the support you paid for: from your manufacturer, computer dealer, software developers, and Internet service provider.

Above all, keep in mind that not everyone who tries to help you truly knows what they're doing. My advice is to avoid friends or (especially) relatives who offer to "fix" your PC when you haven't asked them to. That leads to big trouble.

✔ Treat your PC like your wallet. You wouldn't hand it over to anyone, right?

✔ You may like your smart nephew Victor, but don't let him near your computer. Don't let the grandkids or out-of-town relatives "play" on the Internet while they come to visit. You'll thank me later.

Give Yourself Time to Learn

Things take time. No one sits down at a computer and instantly knows everything, especially with new software. True, the boss may have given you only a day to learn how to work some new program. Such a task is unrealistic and unfair (and you can literally point to this sentence for support).

It takes about a week to become comfortable with any software. It takes longer to really figure out how it works, even if you get a good book on the topic. Honestly, I don't think that anyone out there knows *everything* about a major software product. Don't set the bar so high that you can't leap over it.

Create Separate Accounts

If two people are using one computer, make two computer accounts. That way, you can each keep your stuff separate. The issue is not secrecy but organization. Having one account for each person who uses the computer is better than having two or more people share — and mess up — the only account.

The same guideline applies to e-mail: Get yourself separate e-mail accounts, one for you and one for your partner or one for each human who uses the computer. That way, you receive only your mail and you don't miss anything because someone else has read or deleted it.

Use a UPS

The uninterruptible power supply (UPS) is a boon to computing wherever the power is less than reliable. Plug your console into the UPS. Plug your monitor into the UPS. If the UPS has extra battery-backed-up sockets, plug your external hard drive into one.

Chapter 3 has information on using a UPS as well as using a power strip.

Consider Some Hardware Upgrades

Now that the computer is a consumer commodity, people don't take the time to research their purchases beforehand. Often, the result is that you buy less computer than you truly need. To remedy the situation, a hardware upgrade is in order.

The first consideration is upgrading computer memory. Unless your PC is already packed with RAM (and my guess is that it isn't), you could see a massive increase in performance by adding more memory at a relatively low cost.

The second consideration is getting a second hard drive, such as an external hard drive for making backups. You can add a second internal hard drive to most PCs, which gives you more storage. Or you can replace your PC's main hard drive with a higher-capacity, faster model.

A third consideration is getting a headset for online communications as well as for computer games. A *headset* resembles a pair of headphones but with the addition of a microphone. I recommend that you avoid the cheaper headsets; the more expensive versions are more comfortable and reproduce sound better.

✔ Your computer dealer can upgrade PC memory, or you can do it yourself. I recommend Crucial for online memory purchases: `www.crucial.com`. The website even scans your computer to determine which memory upgrades you need. But:

✔ Upgrading PC memory can be a scary thing! You might consider having someone else do it for you.

✔ See Chapter 10 for information on adding external storage to your PC.

- Replacing the PC's main hard drive adds years to your computer's life, but the process of copying over the original hard drive's contents — referred to as *cloning* — can be very technical. My advice: Have someone else do it.

- Try to get a headset with a built-in volume adjuster and mute button.

Don't Reinstall Windows

A myth floating around tech support sites says that the solution to all your ills is to reinstall Windows. Some tech support people even claim that it's common for most Windows users to reinstall at least once a year. That's rubbish.

You *never* need to reinstall Windows. All problems are fixable. It's just that the tech support people are urged by their bottom-line-watching overlords to get you off the line quickly. Therefore, they resort to a drastic solution rather than try to discover the true problem. If you press them, they *will* tell you what's wrong and how to fix it.

- In all my years of using a computer, I have never reinstalled Windows or had to reformat my hard drive. It's not even a good idea just to refresh the bits on the hard drive or whatever other nonsense they dish up. There just isn't a need to reinstall Windows, ever. Period.

- Refer to my book *Troubleshooting & Maintaining Your PC All-in-One For Dummies,* 2nd Edition (Wiley) for all the various solutions you can try instead of reformatting your hard drive or reinstalling Windows.

Shun the Hype

The computer industry is rife with hype. Magazines and websites tout this or that solution, crow about new trends, and preannounce standards that supposedly will make everything you have obsolete. Ignore all of it!

My gauge for hype is whether the thing that's hyped is shipping as a standard part of a PC. I check the ads. If they're shipping the item, I write about it. Otherwise, it's a myth and may not happen. Avoid being lured by the hype.

Keep on Going!

There's no reason to stop discovering new things about your PC. If you're into books (and you seem to be), consider getting another computer book on a topic that interests you. Bookstores, both physical and on the Internet, are brimming with titles covering just about every computer topic. Also peruse computer magazines and periodicals.

For example, perhaps you want to take up programming. I'm serious! If you enjoy solving puzzles, you'll probably enjoy programming. Or maybe you want to learn how to get the most from a graphics program. In a time when people try to glean knowledge from mediocre (but free) information on the Internet, why not take time to truly educate yourself?

Remember Not to Take This Computer Stuff Too Seriously

Hey, simmer down. Computers aren't part of life. They're nothing more than mineral deposits and petroleum products. Close your eyes and take a few deep breaths. Imagine that you're lying on a soft, sandy beach in the South Pacific. Having just dined on an exotic salad, you close your eyes as the sounds of the gentle surf lull you into a well-deserved afternoon nap.

Next, you're getting your feet rubbed as you sip champagne and feel the bubbles explode atop your tongue. Soothing music plays as everyone who's ever said a bad thing about you in your life tosses you $100 bills.

Now, slowly open your eyes. It's just a dumb computer. Really. Don't take it too seriously.

Index

• *Numerics* •

802.11 standards, 232

• *A* •

A drive, 88
Academy Standard aspect ratio, 94
access points, 233
accessibility features, 144
accounts
  Administrator, setting up, 310–311
  for children, 309–310, 311
  creating separate for users, 324–325
ACPI (Advanced Configuration and Power
    Interface), 150
Action Center, 265–266
activating parental controls, 312
activity log, 314–315
ad hoc networks, 227
adapters
  Bluetooth, 249
  digital-to-VGA, 33
  display, 89–93
  network, 229
  RJ-45, 229
  transparency, 277
  video, upgrading, 93
Administrator account, 310–311
Adobe Premier Pro, 70
Advanced Configuration and Power
    Interface (ACPI), 150
air vents, 21, 22, 24
alerts, 143–144
All Programs menu, 165
all-in-one PC, 20
all-in-one printers, 126, 128
alphanumeric keys, 103

Alt Graph key, 107
Alt key, 104
antispyware programs, 268
antivirus software, 265, 268–269, 321
app, defined, 170
applications
  antispyware, 268
  blocking, 314
  defined, 170
  image editing, 280
  installing from optical discs, 173
  from Internet, 174–175
  Nero, 215
  running from desktop, 171–172
  running manually, 172
  Sound Recorder, 145–146
  starting in Windows, 170–171
  uninstalling, 175–176
  updating, 176–177
  upgrading, 176–177
  video-editing, 70
  Windows, updating, 177–178
  Windows, upgrading, 178
Applications Restrictions feature, 314
Apps screen, 171
arrow keys, 103
aspect ratio, 94
audio
  alerts, 143–144
  connecting, 34
  hardware for, 137–138
  headphones, 140
  microphones, 140
  overview, 137
  recording, 145–146
  speaker options, 138–139
  speech recognition, 146–147
  Windows settings for, 141–143
audio (line in) connector, 26, 27

• B •

B drive, 88
back of console, items on, 23–25
backslash key, 107
backups, 207–208, 220, 264, 320
banks of memory, 67
Basic Input/Output System (BIOS), 63
battery, internal, 60, 62
battery-powered PCs, power options
      for, 152
BIOS (Basic Input/Output System), 63
blackouts, 37
blocking
   downloading, 313
   programs for children, 314
   websites, 313
Bluetooth
   adapters, adding, 249
   checking for, 248
   expansion with, 123
   general discussion, 247–248
   logo, 248
   pairing devices, 250–253
   unpairing devices, 253
   Windows settings for, 249–250
Blu-ray Disc logo, on optical drive, 82
Blu-ray discs, 80
BMP files, 281
bookmarking web pages, 259
boot disk, 78
boxes, keeping in case of returns, 30
Break key, 107
broadband modems, 233–234
brownouts, 37
Burn button, on window toolbars, 219
burning discs, 80, 215–219
buying PCs, 14–15
bytes, 68–70

• C •

C drive, 88
cable modems, 233

cables
   networking, 229
   overview, 32
   USB, 117–120
cameras
   connecting, 274
   importing images from, 275–276
   overview, 274
canceling printing jobs, 136
Caps Lock key, 105, 106
cartridges, ink, 128–129
Cat 5 networking cable, 229
cathode ray tube (CRT) monitors, 91
CD drive. *See* optical drives
CD/DVD Player format for optical
      discs, 217, 218–219
CD-R, 214
CD-RW, 214, 219–220
CDs
   booting from, 78
   burning, 215–219
   CD/DVD Player format, 217, 218–219
   degradation over time, 218
   disposing of, 221
   ejecting from drives, 84
   erasing RW discs, 219–220
   general discussion, 80, 212–215
   inserting in drives, 83
   installing software from, 173
   labeling, 220
   live file system format, 216, 217–218
   mastered format, 217, 218–219
   ripping music from, 293–294
   USB flash drive format, 216, 217–218
cell phones, copying music to, 294–295
center speaker connector, 25, 27
central processing unit (CPU), 19, 57.
      See also processors
charms bar, 162–163
chipset, 62–63
click action, mouse, 112
client-server networks, 227
clock, PC
   Internet, setting with, 61–62
   overview, 60

setting, 60–61
viewing date and time, 60
cloning, 326
closing console, 56
cloud-based storage, 85–86
codecs, 289
color printers, 126
colors for PC connectors, 27–28
COM port, 123
compressed folders
    compressing files, 208–209
    extracting contents of, 210
    installing software from, 211
    overview, 208
    viewing contents of, 209–210
computer cables, 32
Computer folder, 187
Computer window
    drive letters, 87–88
    shortcut for opening, 84
    viewing storage devices in, 86–87
computers. *See also* hardware
    advantages over mobile devices, 11
    buying, 14–15
    function of, 12–13
    general discussion, 10–11
    leaving on, 50
    plugging in to power supply, 35–40
    software, 13
    turning off, 44–49
    turning on, 41–42
    unpacking, 29–30
condenser microphones, 140
connecting
    keyboards, 102
    monitors to PC, 95
    mouse, 109–110
    to networks, 235–238
    printers, 131–132
    USB devices, 120
connectors
    digital video, 27
    DVI video, 95
    HDMI video, 26, 27, 95
    I/O, 57
    on I/O panel, 25–28

keyboard, 25, 27, 102
mouse, 26, 28
SPDIF in/out, 26
symbols and colors for, 27–28
USB, 26, 28
VGA video, 26, 28, 95
video, 26, 28
consoles
    back of, items on, 23–25
    battery, 62
    chipset, 62–63
    clock, 60–62
    closing, 56
    connectors, symbols and
        colors for, 27–28
    front of, items on, 21–23
    hardware inside of, 54–55
    I/O panel, 25–26
    motherboard, 57
    opening, 55–56
    overview, 18, 19
    peripherals, connecting to, 31–35
    power button, 46, 47
    power supply, 63
    processor, 57–59
    setting up, 30
    turning on, 42
    types of, 19–21
    working inside, 56
contacts, Facebook, 298
Contacts folder, 188
Context key, 107
Control Panel, 167–168
control panels on printers, 128
copying
    files, 197–198
    music to MP3 players, 294–295
copyrights on web images, 260
cordless 3D mice, 111
CPU (central processing unit), 19, 57.
        See also processors
CRT (cathode ray tube) monitors, 91
Crucial website, 71
CRW files, 281
Ctrl key, 104
Ctrl-drag action, mouse, 112

Cursor-control keys, 103
cursors, 103
custom keys, 108
cyberbullying, dealing with, 316
cyberharassment, 315
cyberstalking, 315

• *D* •

D drive, 88
date, viewing, 60
default printers, setting, 133
defragmenting SSDs, 79
Delete key, 105
deleting files, 200, 320
desktop, 163–164, 171–172
desktop console, 20
Desktop folder, 186–187, 188
Devices and Printers window, 132–133
dial-up modems
  adding, 153
  configuring connections, 154–155
  connecting, 35
  connecting to Internet with, 257–258
  overview, 153
  speed of, 154
dictating to PC, 146–147
digital cameras
  connecting, 274
  importing images from, 275–276
  overview, 274
digital desert, 218
Digital Living Network Alliance (DLNA), 307
digital video connectors, 27
Digital Video Recorder (DVR), 290
digital-to-VGA adapters, 33
DIMM (dual inline memory module), 66–67
dips, 37
directories, 185
Disc logo, on optical drive, 82
disconnecting from networks, 239
disk drive cage, 55
disk drives, 76
display
  adjusting, 96
  defined, 92

display adapter expansion card, 72
display adapters
  general discussion, 92
  GPU, 92–93
  graphics memory, 92
  overview, 89–90
  types of monitors, 91
  understanding graphics, 90–91
Display Pointer Trails option, Mouse
    Properties dialog box, 113
disposing of optical discs, 221
DL (dual-layer) discs, 80
DL label, on optical drive, 82
DLNA (Digital Living Network Alliance), 307
dots per inch (dpi), 283
double-click action, mouse, 112
double-click rate, 114
double-tap operation, for touchscreens, 115
downloading
  blocking, for children, 313
  screen savers, 100
  software, 174–175
Downloads folder, 188
dpi (dots per inch), 283
drag action, mouse, 112
Dragon Naturally Speaking, 147
DRAM (dynamic random access
    memory), 68
drivers, 120, 170
drives
  defined, 77
  letters for, 87–88
  for removable storage, 81–82
Dropbox, 86
DSL modems, 233
dual inline memory module (DIMM), 66–67
dual monitor features, 98
dual-layer (DL) discs, 80
DVD drive. *See* optical drives
DVD logo, on optical drive, 82
DVD R DL, 214
DVD RAM, 214
DVD+R, 214
DVD+RW, 214, 219–220
DVD-R, 214, 215
DVD-RW, 214, 219–220

DVDs
  booting from, 78
  burning, 215–219
  CD/DVD Player format, 217, 218–219
  copying movies from, 286
  degradation over time, 218
  disposing of, 221
  ejecting from drives, 84
  erasing RW discs, 219–220
  general discussion, 80, 212–215
  inserting in drives, 83
  installing software from, 173
  labeling, 220
  live file system format, 216, 217–218
  mastered format, 217, 218–219
  USB flash drive format, 216, 217–218
DVI video connectors, 95
DVR (Digital Video Recorder), 290
dynamic microphones, 140
dynamic random access memory
     (DRAM), 68

● E ●

editing video, 288–289
802.11 standards, 232
ejecting removable storage, 84
electrical problems, 37, 63
e-mail, security precautions for, 321
Enter keys, 106
Entertainment Software Rating Board
     (ESRB) game rating system, 313
erasing RW discs, 219–220
ergonomic keyboards, 322
eSATA port, 27, 121
Escape key, 106
ESRB (Entertainment Software Rating
     Board) game rating system, 313
Ethernet, 227
Ethernet card, 229
expansion
  of audio capabilities, 137–138
  legacy ports, 123–124
  of networks, 230
  opening and working inside console, 55–56
  overview, 117

ports, 117–118
  slots for, 21, 22, 24, 124
  USB devices, 118–122
expansion cards, 124
explosions of computers, 11
extensions, filename, 184–185, 281
external hard drives, 18, 85, 207
external media card readers, 81
external modems, 153
external storage
  adding, 85
  on Internet, 85–86
  overview, 77, 84
extracting contents of Zip files, 210

● F ●

F1 key, 106
Facebook, 298–299
Family Safety feature
  accounts for children, configuring,
     309–310, 311
  activating, 312
  activity log, 314–315
  Administrator-level account,
     setting up, 310–311
  blocking programs, 314
  cyberbullying, dealing with, 316
  gaming controls, 313–314
  overview, 309
  reviewing activity of children, 315–316
  time limits, 313
  web filtering, 313
fans, 24
Favorites folder, 188
File and Printer Sharing option, 242
file attachments, 321
file formats
  photos, 281
  video, 287
File History feature, 204–205
file management
  copying files, 197–198
  deleting files, 200
  moving files, 198
  overview, 193–194

file management *(continued)*
recovering deleted files, 200–201
renaming files, 199–200
searching for files, 201–202
selecting files, 194–196
shortcuts, creating, 198–199
unselecting files, 197
File Sharing Connections option, 242, 243
filename extensions, 184–185, 281
filenames, 180, 181, 183–184
files. *See also* file management
backups, 207–208
characteristics of, 180–181
compression, 208–211
creating, 181–183
deleting, 320
filename extensions, 184–185
naming, 183–184
overview, 179–180
recovering with File History, 204–205
restoring previous versions, 206–207
saving on cloud, 86
filtering websites, 313
firewalls, 266–267
FireWire connector, 25, 27, 119
flash memory, 67
flick operation, for touchscreens, 115
Flickr, 300–304
Folder Options dialog box, 184
folders. *See also* compressed folders
common to Windows, 186–187
Computer, 187
Contacts, 188
creating, 189–190
deleting, 320
Desktop, 186–187, 188
Downloads, 188
Favorites, 188
libraries, 190–191
Links, 188
My Documents, 188
My Music, 188
My Pictures, 188
My Videos, 188, 287
Network, 187

in Open dialog box, 191–192
overview, 179, 185
parent, 185–186
Pictures, 280–281
Public, 243
root, 187
Saved Games, 188
Searches, 188
sharing over networks, 243–244
subfolders, 185–186
User Profile, 187–189
footprints, 21
force shutdown, 47
front of console, items on, 21–23
Function keys, 103

• G •

gadgets, Windows sidebar, 164
games, parental controls for, 313–314
gateways, 230, 233
GIF files, 281
gigabytes (GBs), 68, 69
gigahertz (GHz), 58
Google Drive, 86
GPU, 92–93
graphical user interface
Charms bar, 162–163
desktop, 163–164
notification area, 166–167
overview, 160–161
Start menu, 165–166
Start screen, 161–162
taskbar, 164–165
graphics, overview, 90–91
graphics memory, 92
graphics system
display adapter, 92
GPU, 92–93
graphics memory, 92
overview, 89–90
types of monitors, 91
understanding graphics, 90–91

• H •

hard copies, 18
hard drives
    external, 18, 85
    general discussion, 78
    light on console for, 23
    overview, 76
    reformatting, 326
    upgrading, 325–326
hardware. *See also* consoles
    audio, 137–138
    overview, 13, 17
    PC purchases based on desired, 15
    plugging in to power supply, 35–40
    typical computer systems, 17–19
    unpacking PC, 29–30
    upgrading, 321, 325–326
HDMI video connectors, 26, 27, 95
HDTV, 91, 95, 291–292
headphone connector, 25, 28
headphones
    connecting, 34–35
    general discussion, 140
headsets, 140, 325
Hibernate command, 49, 151–152
history, viewing in web browsers, 315
HomeGroup Connections option, 242, 243
hubs, USB, 121–122
Hulu, 291
humidity, effect on consoles, 30

• I •

IBM, 10, 11
icons
    desktop, 164
    for files, 180, 181
    for storage devices, 87
    used in book, 4–5
IEEE 1394 (FireWire) connector, 25, 27, 119
iHeart Radio, 296
image editing programs, 280
image resolution, 283–284
Image Shack, 300–304

images
    digital cameras, 274
    file formats, 281, 282–283
    image resolution, 283–284
    importing, 275–276
    overview, 273
    photo-sharing websites, 300–304
    picture files, 279–283
    saving from Internet, 260
    scanning, 276–279
    storing in Windows, 280–281
    uploading to Facebook, 298–299
    viewing in Windows, 282
importing
    photos, from camera, 275–276
    video, 286
infrared connector, 27
ink cartridges, 128–129
ink for printers, 127, 128–129
inkjet printers, 125–126
input, 12
input devices. *See also* keyboards; mouse
    stylus, 21
    touchscreen monitors, 114–115
Insert key, 105
inserting removable storage, 83
insertion pointers, 103
installing software
    from optical discs, 173
    from Zip files, 211
integrated video, 91
Intel Core processors, 58
interface, 77
internal modems, 153
internal storage, 77
international keyboards, 107
Internet
    backup services, 207
    clock, setting with, 61–62
    connecting to, 155, 256–258
    copying text from, 261
    downloading screen savers from, 100
    external storage on, 85–86
    general discussion, 255
    image resolution for, 284
    ISPs, 256–257

Internet *(continued)*
  printing web pages, 259
  radio, 295–296
  saving images from, 260
  searches, 259–260
  sharing on networks, 226
  sharing pages, 261
  software from, 174–175
  sound files on, 144
  web-browsing tips, 258–259
Internet Explorer, 263
Internet Service Provider (ISP),
    256–257, 265
Internet Time Settings dialog box, 61–62
Internet-ready HDTV, 292
I/O, 12
I/O connectors, 57
I/O panel, 22, 24, 25–26
ISP (Internet Service Provider),
    256–257, 265

● *J* ●

Jango, 296
joystick connector, 27
JPG files, 281

● *K* ●

Kbps (kilobits per second), 154
KBs (kilobytes), 68, 69
Kensington SmartSockets-brand power
    strips, 37
Keyboard port, 123
Keyboard Properties dialog box, 108–109
keyboard shortcuts, 104
keyboards
  connecting, 31–32, 102
  connectors, on I/O panel, 25, 27, 102
  ergonomic, 322
  lock keys, 105–106
  math, keys used for, 107–108
  modifier keys, 103–105
  other keys, 107
  overview, 18, 101–102

parts of, 102–103
  useful, 106
  Windows settings for, 108–109
  wireless, 102
kilobits per second (Kbps), 154
kilobytes (KBs), 68, 69

● *L* ●

labeling optical discs, 220
LANs (local area networks), 227
laptops
  overview, 21
  power management options for, 152
  SSDs in, 79
laser printers, 37, 125–126
LCD (liquid crystal display) monitor, 91
left button, mouse, 111
left-handed settings for mouse, 114
legacy ports, 123–124
libraries, 187, 190–191
light, hard drive, 23
line conditioning, 36
line in (audio) connector, 26, 27
line noise, 37
line noise filtering, 36
links, to YouTube videos, 305
Links folder, 188
liquid crystal display (LCD) monitor, 91
live file system format for optical
    discs, 216, 217–218
local area networks (LANs), 227
Lock keys, 105–106
locking computer, 48, 49
Log Off option, 48
logging in to Windows, 42–44
long-press operation, for touchscreens, 115
long-term storage, 13

● *M* ●

Macs, 10
main button, mouse, 111
malware, 170, 264, 321

mass storage
  external storage, 84–86
  general discussion, 75–76
  hard drives, 78
  overview, 75
  primary storage media, 78–79
  removable storage, 79–84
  SSD, 79
  terminology, 77
  types of, 76–77
  viewing in Windows, 86–88
mastered format for optical discs,
      217, 218–219
math, keys used for, 107–108
Mavis Beacon Teaches Typing
      software, 104
MBs (megabytes), 68, 69
measuring monitors, 93–94
media, defined, 77
media card readers
  ejecting cards, 84
  external, 81, 85
  inserting cards, 83
  interface, 81–82
  on printers, 127
media cards
  ejecting from drives, 84
  general discussion, 80, 81
  inserting in drives, 83
  slots on console for, 21, 22
media sharing on networks, 226, 305–307
Media Streaming/Media Sharing
      option, 242, 243
megabytes (MBs), 68, 69
memory
  adding, 71
  amount needed, 70–71
  bytes, 68–70
  finding information about in Windows, 70
  flash, 67
  general discussion, 65–66
  limit of, 72
  memory chips, 66–68
  overview, 13, 65
  shared video, 73
  sizes of, 69

testing amount of, 71
  upgrading, 325
  video, 72–73, 92
  virtual, 72
memory chips, 66–68
messages on monitor, 95
mice
  connecting, 31–32, 109–110
  connectors, on I/O panel, 26, 28
  overview, 18
  parts of, 110–111
  types of, 111
  using, 112
  Windows settings for, 113–114
  wireless, 110
microcomputers, 10
microphone connector, 26, 27
microphones
  connecting, 35
  general discussion, 140
  setting up in Windows, 142
  switching between speakers and, 143
microprocessors, 10
Microsoft Live e-mail address, signing
      in using, 43
Mini 1394 connector, 26, 27
mini-desktop console, 20
mini-DIN connector, 34, 35
mini-tower, 20
mobile devices, 11
modem connector, 27
modems. *See also* dial-up modems
  broadband, 233–234
  connecting, 35
  overview, 153
modifier keys, 103–105
monitors
  adding second, 97–98
  adjusting display, 96
  connecting, 33
  connecting to PC, 95
  CRT, 91
  display adapter, 89–93
  LCD, 91
  measuring, 93–94
  messages on, 95

monitors *(continued)*
  overview, 18, 89
  position of, 322
  resolution, setting, 99
  screen savers, 100
  touchscreen, 91, 93, 94, 114–115
  turning on, 42
  types of, 91
  widescreen, 94
  Windows settings for, 96–100
monochrome printers, 126
motherboard
  battery, 62
  chipset, 62–63
  components of, 57
  expansion slots, 124
  overview, 55
  processor, 57–59
mouse
  connecting, 31–32, 109–110
  connectors, on I/O panel, 26, 28
  overview, 18
  parts of, 110–111
  types of, 111
  using, 112
  Windows settings for, 113–114
  wireless, 110
mouse pointer, 164
Mouse port, 123
Mouse Properties dialog box, 113
MOV files, 287
moving files, 198
MP3 players, copying music to, 294–295
MPEG files, 287
multiple monitors, setting up, 97
multitouch monitors, 91
music
  copying to MP3 players, 294–295
  Internet radio, 295–296
  overview, 292
  ripping music from CDs, 293–294
  Windows Media Player, 293
My Documents folder, 188
My Music folder, 188
My Pictures folder, 188
My Videos folder, 188, 287

• N •

names of processors, 58
naming files, 183–184
Narrator, 144
Nero program, 215
Netflix, 291
network adapter, 229
Network and Sharing Center, 154–155,
    239–240, 306
network cables, 31
network connector, 26, 28
Network Discovery option, 242
Network folder, 187
network folders, accessing, 244
network information card (NIC), 229, 232
Network window, 240, 241
networks. *See also* social networks
  ad hoc, 227
  broadband modems, 233–234
  client-server, 227
  confirming connections, 239
  connecting to, 33, 235–238
  disconnecting from, 239
  folders, sharing, 243–244
  general discussion, 225–226
  LANs, 227
  media sharing on, 305–307
  network folders, accessing, 244
  peer-to-peer, 227
  printers, sharing, 34, 245–246
  public, 237–238
  sharing, enabling, 241–243
  in Windows, 239–241
  wired, 226, 227–230
  wireless, 226, 230–233
NIC (network information card), 229, 232
nonremovable storage, 76
notebooks
  overview, 21
  power management options for, 152
  SSDs in, 79
notification area, 165, 166–167
notifications, setting sounds for, 144
Num Lock key, 105
Numeric keypad, 103

• *O* •

OCR (optical character recognition) software, 279
onscreen menu, monitor, 96
Open command, 76
Open dialog box, 191–192
opening console, 55–56
operating system, 13, 160. *See also* Windows
optical character recognition (OCR) software, 279
optical discs
  booting from, 78
  burning, 215–219
  CD/DVD Player format, 217, 218–219
  degradation over time, 218
  disposing of, 221
  ejecting from drives, 84
  erasing RW discs, 219–220
  general discussion, 212–215
  inserting in drives, 83
  installing software from, 173
  labeling, 220
  live file system format, 216, 217–218
  mastered format, 217, 218–219
  overview, 80
  USB flash drive format, 216, 217–218
optical drives
  on console, 21, 22
  ejecting discs, 84
  emergency eject button, 82
  external, 85
  general discussion, 80
  inserting discs, 83
  interface, 81
  labels on, 82
  overview, 76
output, 12

• *P* •

Page Up/Down key, 105
pairing Bluetooth devices, 250–253
Pandora Internet Radio, 296
paper feed on printer, 126
paper for printers, 129–131
parent folders, 185–186
parental controls
  accounts for children, configuring, 309–310, 311
  activating, 312
  activity log, 314–315
  Administrator-level account, setting up, 310–311
  blocking programs, 314
  cyberbullying, dealing with, 316
  gaming controls, 313–314
  overview, 309
  time limits, 313
  viewing activity of children, 315–316
  web filtering, 313
Password Protected Sharing option, 242, 243
passwords, Windows login, 43–44
patches, software, 176
Pause key, 107
PCI (Peripheral Component Interconnect), 124
PCs. *See also* hardware
  advantages over mobile devices, 11
  buying, 14–15
  function of, 12–13
  general discussion, 10–11
  leaving on, 50
  plugging in to power supply, 35–40
  software, 13
  turning off, 44–49
  turning on, 41–42
  unpacking, 29–30
peer-to-peer network, 227
Pentium processors, 58
Peripheral Component Interconnect (PCI), 124
peripherals, connecting to console, 31–35
phishing, 264
photo printers, 126
Photobucket, 300–304
photos
  digital cameras, 274
  file formats, 281, 282–283

photos *(continued)*
image resolution, 283–284
importing, 275–276
overview, 273
photo-sharing websites, 300–304
picture files, 279–283
saving from Internet, 260
scanning, 276–279
storing in Windows, 280–281
uploading to Facebook, 298–299
viewing in Windows, 282
photo-sharing websites, 300–304
Picasaweb, 300–304
picture files
changing formats, 282–283
overview, 279–280
storing in Windows, 280–281
viewing in Windows, 282
pictures. *See* photos
Pictures folder, 280–281
Pin area, 165
pinch operation, for touchscreens, 115
pinning icons
to Start menu, 172
to taskbar, 172
pixels, 99
PNG files, 281
point action, mouse, 112
Pointer Options tab, Mouse Properties
dialog box, 113
pop-ups, 264
ports
I/O panel, 25–28
legacy, 123–124
overview, 117–118
USB, 117
posting to Facebook, 298
posture, 322
power button, on console, 22, 23, 46, 47
power connector, 23, 24, 28
power management
battery-powered PCs, 152
hibernation command, assigning to
console power button, 151–152
overview, 149–150
power plans, choosing, 150–151

Power Options window, 150–151
power outages, 37
power plans, choosing, 150–151
power strips
plugging hardware into, 35–37
turning on, 42
power supply
in console, 54, 63
power strips, using, 35–37
UPS, 38–40, 63, 152, 325
press operation, for touchscreens, 114
previous versions, restoring, 206–207
primary storage media, 78–79
Print dialog box, 134–135
Print Screen key, 105, 107
Printer port, 123
printers
canceling printing, 136
connecting, 34, 131–132
control panels on, 128
default, setting, 133
ink, 128–129
laser, plugging in, 37
overview, 18, 125
paper for, 129–131
parts of, 126–127
photos, printing, 274
printing on, 133–135
sharing over networks, 226, 245–246
types of, 125–126
Windows settings for, 132–133
printer's Properties dialog box, 135
printing, 133–135
processing, 12–13
processors
finding information about in Windows, 59
function of, 12–13
GPU, 92–93
names of, 58
overview, 57
role of, 58
speed of, 58–59, 66
programs
antispyware, 268
blocking, 314
defined, 170

image editing, 280
installing from optical discs, 173
from Internet, 174–175
Nero, 215
running from desktop, 171–172
running manually, 172
Sound Recorder, 145–146
starting in Windows, 170–171
uninstalling, 175–176
updating, 176–177
upgrading, 176–177
video-editing, 70
Windows, updating, 177–178
Windows, upgrading, 178
Programs and Features window, 175–176
Public folder, 243
Public Folder Sharing option, 242
public networks, 237–238

• Q •

quarantined files, 269
QuickTime player, 288

• R •

R label, on optical drive, 82
radio, Internet, 295–296
RAM (random access memory)
adding, 71
amount needed, 70–71
bytes, 68–70
flash memory, 67
general discussion, 65–66
limit of, 72
memory chips, 66–68
overview, 13, 65, 67
shared video memory, 73
sizes of, 69
testing amount of, 71
video memory, 72–73
viewing in System window, 59, 70
virtual memory, 72
RAM label, on optical drive, 82
read-only memory (ROM), 67

recording
audio, 145–146
TV, 290
recovering files
with File History, 204–205
overview, 200–201
restoring previous versions, 206–207
Recycle Bin, 187, 201
recycling computer parts, 150
reformatting hard drives, 326
refreshing web pages, 258
reinstalling Windows, 326
Remember icon, 5
removable storage
drives for, 81–82
ejecting, 84
inserting, 83
overview, 79
types of, 76, 79–81
renaming files, 199–200
reset button, on console, 23
resolution, 99, 283
Restart command, 49
restoring previous versions, 206–207
reverse printing, 135
reviewing activity of children, 315–316
right button, mouse, 111
right-click action, mouse, 112
right-drag action, mouse, 112
ripping music from CDs, 293–294
RJ-45 adapter, 229
ROM (read-only memory), 67
root folder, 187
rotate operation, for touchscreens, 115
routers, 230, 233
Run dialog box, 172
RW discs, erasing, 219–220
RW label, on optical drive, 82

• S •

SATA (Serial Advanced Technology
    Attachment), 77
satellite modems, 234
Save As dialog box, 181–182
Save command, 76, 320

Save screen, 182
Saved Games folder, 188
scanners
  general discussion, 276–277
  images, scanning, 277–279
screen, defined, 92
Screen Resolution dialog box, 97, 98, 99
Screen Saver Settings dialog box, 100
screen savers, 100
screen snapshots, 107
Scroll Lock key, 105
SCSI port, 123
search engines, 259–260
Searches folder, 188
searching for files, 201–202
second monitors, adding, 97–98
security
  Action Center, 265–266
  antivirus software, 265, 268–269, 321
  avoiding malware, 321
  Bluetooth, 248
  cyberbullying, dealing with, 316
  e-mail, 321
  tools, 263–265
  UAC warnings, 269–270
  Windows Defender, 268
  Windows Firewall, 266–267
selecting files, 194–196
Serial Advanced Technology
    Attachment (SATA), 77
servers, 227
service, PC, 15
shared video memory, 73
sharing over networks
  enabling, 241–243
  folders, 243–244
  printers, 245–246
ShieldsUP!, 267
Shift key, 104
Shift+drag action, mouse, 112
shortcuts, creating, 198–199
Show Location/Ctrl Key option, Mouse
    Properties dialog box, 113
Shutdown command, 46–47
Shutdown menu, 44–46

shutdown options
  finding, 44–46
  other options, 48–49
  overview, 322
  Shutdown command, 46–47
  Sleep mode, 50
signing in, to Windows, 42–44
signing up
  Facebook, 298
  photo-sharing websites, 300–301
SkyDrive, 85, 86
Slacker Personal Radio, 296
Sleep mode, 48, 49, 50
slide operation, for touchscreens, 115
slots, expansion, 124
small footprint PCs, 21
smartphones, 11
SmartSockets-brand power strips,
    Kensington, 37
Snap To option, Mouse Properties
    dialog box, 113
social networks
  Facebook, 298–299
  overview, 297
  Twitter, 299–300
software
  antispyware, 268
  antivirus, 265, 268–269, 321
  blocking, 314
  image editing, 280
  installing from optical discs, 173
  installing from Zip files, 211
  from Internet, 174–175
  learning about, 324, 327
  Mavis Beacon Teaches Typing
      software, 104
  memory requirements, 70
  Nero, 215
  OCR, 279
  overview, 13, 169
  PC purchases based on desired, 14
  printer, installing before connecting, 131
  running from desktop, 171–172
  running manually, 172
  Sound Recorder, 145–146

starting in Windows, 170–171
terms for, 169–170
uninstalling, 175–176
updating, 176–177
upgrading, 176–177, 321
video-editing, 70
Windows, updating, 177–178
Windows, upgrading, 178
solid-state drive (SSD), 76, 79
sound
  alerts, 143–144
  hardware for, 137–138
  headphones, 140
  microphones, 140
  overview, 137
  recording, 145–146
  speaker options, 138–139
  speech recognition, 146–147
  Windows settings for, 141–143
Sound Blaster Audigy system, 138
Sound dialog box, 141, 142, 144
Sound Recorder program, 145–146
spam e-mail, 321
SPDIF in/out connectors, 26
speaker connector, 25, 28
speakers
  connecting, 34–35
  overview, 18
  surround sound, 138–139
  switching between microphones and, 143
  Windows setting for, 142
speech recognition, 146–147
speed
  of modems, 154
  of processors, 58–59, 66
spike protection, 37
spikes, 37, 63
spread operation, for touchscreens, 115
spyware, 264
SSD (solid-state drive), 76, 79
Standard User accounts, 309–310
Start button, 164
Start menu, 165–166
Start screen, 161–162, 170–171
static electricity, 56

storage, 13. *See also* mass storage;
    temporary storage
stylus, 21, 111
subfolders, 185–186
subwoofers, 25, 27, 138
support, PC, 15
surge protection, 37, 63
surges, 37, 63
surround sound, 26, 28, 138–139
S-video connector, 28
swipe operation, for touchscreens, 115
Switch User command, 48
switches, 230
symbols for PC connectors, 27–28
System Request key, 105, 107
System window, 59, 70

• *T* •

Tab key, 106
tablets, 11, 21
tagging photos, Facebook, 299
tap operation, for touchscreens, 114
taskbar, 164–165, 172
TBs (terabytes), 68, 69
Technical Stuff icon, 4
technical support, PC, 15, 324
temperature, effect on consoles, 30
temporary storage, 13, 73.
    See also memory
terabytes (TBs), 68, 69
testing amount of memory, 71
thumb drives
  ejecting, 84
  general discussion, 76, 80
  inserting, 83
TIFF files, 281
time, viewing, 60
time limits for children, 313
time server, 61
timeline of PC, 10
Tip icon, 5
toner, 128–129
tool, defined, 170
touch and hold operation, for
    touchscreens, 115

touch operation, for touchscreens, 114
touchscreen monitors, 91, 93, 94, 114–115
tower console, 20
trackballs, 111
transparency adapters, 277
Trojans, 264
turning off PCs, 44–49
turning on PCs, 41–42
TV, watching on PC, 289–291
TV tuners, 290
tweets, 299
Twitter, 299–300
typewriter keys, 103
typing, learning how to, 104

• *U* •

(UAC) User Account Control warnings,
   269–270
uninstalling software, 175–176
uninterruptible power supply (UPS),
   38–40, 63, 152, 325
unpacking PC, 29–30
unpairing Bluetooth devices, 253
unselecting files, 197
updating
   software, 176–177
   Windows, 177–178, 322
upgrading
   external storage, 85
   hardware, 321, 325–326
   memory, 71
   software, 176–177, 321
   video adapters, 93
   video memory, 72
   Windows, 178
uploading
   to Facebook, 298–299
   to photo-sharing websites, 301–302
   to YouTube, 304
UPS (uninterruptible power supply), 38–40,
   63, 152, 325
USB devices. *See also* USB ports
   Bluetooth adapters, 249
   cables, 117–120
   connecting, 120

removing, 121
sound devices, 138
TV tuners, 290
USB-powered devices, 120
USB flash drive format for optical discs,
   216, 217–218
USB hubs, 121–122
USB ports
   expanding storage with, 84–85
   general discussion, 118
   on I/O panel, 26, 28
   keyboards, connecting, 102
   mouse, connecting, 109
   thumb drives, ejecting, 84
   thumb drives, inserting, 83
USB-powered devices, 120
User Profile folder, 187–189
utility, defined, 170

• *V* •

VGA video connectors, 26, 28, 95
video
   connectors, on I/O panel, 26, 28
   editing, 288–289
   file formats, 287
   HDTV, 291–292
   importing, 286
   overview, 285
   TV, watching on PC, 289–291
   uploading to Facebook, 298–299
   Videos folder, 287
   viewing, 288
   YouTube, 304–305
video cameras, 286
video card
   general discussion, 92
   GPU, 92–93
   graphics memory, 92
   overview, 89–90
   types of monitors, 91
   understanding graphics, 90–91
video driver, 97
video memory, 72–73
video RAM (VRAM), 92
video-editing programs, 70

Videos folder, 287
virtual memory, 72
viruses, 264, 269
voltage switch, 24
volume, adjusting, 142–143
VRAM (video RAM), 92

• *W* •

wallpapers, setting web images as, 260
Warning! icon, 5
warranty cards, 30
watts, power supply measured in, 63
WDS (wireless distribution system), 233
web browsers, 263, 315
web filtering, 313
web pages
  copying text from, 261
  printing, 259
  saving images from, 260
  searches for, 259–260
  sharing, 261
web resolution, 284
webcams, 286
websites
  blocking, 313
  Crucial, 71
  Facebook, 298–299
  filtering, 313
  photo-sharing, 300–304
  Twitter, 299–300
wheel button, mouse, 111
widescreen monitors, 94
Wi-Fi
  connecting to, 236
  connecting to unknown networks, 238
  hardware connections, 230–233
  overview, 226
WiMAX, 234
window buttons, on taskbar, 165
Windows
  Bluetooth settings, 249–250
  charms bar, 162–163
  Control Panel, 167–168
  date and time, setting, 60–61
  desktop, 163–164

folders in, 186–187
hibernation command, assigning to
    console power button, 151–152
keyboard settings, 108–109
logging in, 42–44
mass storage, viewing in, 86–88
memory, finding information about in, 70
monitor settings, 96–100
mouse settings, 113–114
network settings, 239–241
network sharing, setting up, 241–243
notification area, 166–167
operating system, function of, 160
overview, 159, 160–161
picture files, 279–283
power plans, choosing, 150–151
printer settings, 132–133
processors, finding information
    about in, 59
reinstalling, 326
scanning images with, 277–279
sound settings, 141–143
Start menu, 165–166
Start screen, 161–162
starting programs in, 170–171
System window, 70
taskbar, 164–165
updating, 177–178
upgrading, 178
Windows 7
  Control Panel, 167
  disconnecting from networks, 239
  dual monitor features, 98
  libraries, 188, 190–191
  previous versions of files,
      restoring, 206–207
  shutdown options, 45–46, 48–49
  starting programs in, 171
  wireless networks, connecting to, 236–237
Windows 8
  charms bar, 162–163
  Control Panel, 167
  desktop, 163
  dual monitor features, 98
  File History feature, 204–205
  libraries, 188, 190–191

Windows 8 *(continued)*
  memory requirements, 69
  Search command, 202
  Shutdown command, 46
  shutdown options, 44–45, 48–49
  signing in using Microsoft Live e-mail
    address, 43
  Start screen, 161–162
  starting programs in, 170–171
  time and date information, 60
  videos, viewing in, 288
  volume, adjusting, 143
  wireless networks, connecting to, 236
Windows Defender, 264, 268
Windows Firewall, 264, 266–267
Windows key, 104
Windows Media Center, 290
Windows Media Player, 288, 293, 295, 307
Windows Movie Maker, 288, 289
Windows Photo Gallery, 280
Windows Security Center, 266
Windows Update, 177–178, 264, 322
Windows Vista
  disconnecting from networks, 239
  dual monitor features, 98
  previous versions of files,
    restoring, 206–207
  shutdown options, 45–46, 47, 48–49
  starting programs in, 171
  wireless networks, connecting to, 236–237
Windows XP
  shutdown options, 46, 47, 48–49
  wireless networks, connecting to, 236–237

wired networks
  connecting to, 235
  hardware connections, 227–230
  overview, 226
wireless distribution system (WDS), 233
wireless keyboards, 102
wireless mice, 110
wireless networks
  connecting to, 236
  connecting to unknown, 238
  hardware connections, 230–233
  overview, 226
wireless NICs, 232
WMV files, 287
worms, 264
wrist pads, 322

• Y •

YouTube, 291, 304–305

• Z •

Zip files
  compressing files, 208–209
  extracting contents of, 210
  installing software from, 211
  overview, 208
  viewing contents of, 209–210
zooming, on web pages, 258